Supervising the School Counselor Trainee

Guidelines for Practice

Jeannine R. Studer

AMERICAN COUNSELING ASSOCIATION
5999 Stevenson Avenue
Alexandria, VA 22304
www.counseling.org

Supervising the School Counselor Trainee
Guidelines for Practice

10 9 8 7 6 5 4 3 2 1

American Counseling Association
  5999 Stevenson Avenue
  Alexandria, VA 22304

Director of Publications
  Carolyn C. Baker

Production Manager
  Bonny E. Gaston

Editorial Assistant
  Natasha Yetman

Copy Editor
  Elaine Dunn

Cover and text design by Bonny E. Gaston.

Library of Congress Cataloging-in-Publication Data
Studer, Jeannine R.
   Supervising the school counselor trainee : guidelines for practice / Jeannine R. Studer.
      p. cm.
   ISBN 1-55620-268-7 (alk. paper)
1. Educational counseling.   2. Student counselors—In-service training.   I. Title.

LB1027.5.S85323 2006
371.4–dc22   2006002176

This book is dedicated to the many committed supervisors who have worked diligently to train students for the school counseling profession.

Table of Contents

Part IV

Evaluation

Appendixes

Acknowledgments

IN MY OPINION, there is no profession that makes more of a difference in the lives of children and adolescents than that of the school counselor. I am encouraged and pleased when I see talented, motivated individuals entering our profession and carrying out the responsibilities for which they have been trained. The dedication and passion to the profession are evident when these individuals put their training to use as practicing school counselors and work diligently to assist school-age children and adolescents with academic, career, and personal/social issues. Their enthusiasm and competence are due, to some degree, to the many inspirational supervisors who have offered their own talents, expertise, and knowledge to train these students. It is to these professionals that this book is dedicated.

Writing this book has been educational for me. Throughout the years I have developed many useful strategies that I have used to train students for the profession of school counseling. Reading the literature and attending various seminars on this topic have given me even greater insight into how I can teach and supervise even better. Supervisors with whom I have worked have also been instructional. However, nothing has been more satisfying than to work with the individuals who have offered their expertise for the creation of this book. My thanks to Dr. Joel Diambra, Dr. Tricia McClam, Dr. Marla Peterson, and Dr. Marianne Woodside and students Daniel Fudge and Valerie Fulbright, the University of Tennessee; Dr. Carol Dahir, New York Institute of Technology; Dr. Susan Norris Huss, Bowling Green State University; and Shamshad Ahmed and Song Lee, doctoral students, North Carolina State University.

Preface

TODAY'S SCHOOL-AGE youths are experiencing greater stressors and concerns than the youths of yesterday. Divorce, suicide, depression, pregnancy, drug and alcohol abuse, and bullying are just a few of the issues that children and adolescents are encountering in greater numbers and intensity. The professional school counselor plays a significant role in equipping youths with the skills they will need to manage these issues and others.

Practicing school counselors have an ethical obligation to mentor and instruct school counselors-in-training so that these future school counselors are able to apply classroom knowledge to the real-world setting. Unfortunately, many school counselors are uncertain of the "how to," of supervision, unaware of the various developmental stages, uninformed of the various supervisory roles, and unsure of the legal and ethical issues surrounding the supervisory process. Professional school counselors who have been practicing for many years and have achieved numerous achievements are sometimes embarrassed to admit that they do not have training in supervision, and they are often reluctant to work with college and university school counseling programs because of this lack of knowledge. However, supervisory training is not usually part of a master's degree program and curriculum and is generally not acquired until after the counselor credential is received, and only if this type of training is available. Because supervisory training has only been given cursory attention in the past, more thought is being given to the significance of this preparation today.

When I first entered the school counseling profession, my counselor education training only required a practicum; an internship class was not part of the curriculum. At the time, a certificate and experience as a teacher were required in the state where I was working. Although I felt somewhat comfortable with my clinical skills and knowledge of a school system, I soon learned that there was much more to the school counseling profession, and even the skills and knowledge I learned in my teacher training were not enough. Fortunately, there was another high school counselor in the school who patiently mentored me through the process, but this counselor was unable to help me work through a number of situations for which I felt totally unprepared. I can remember thinking, "If this is what school counseling is all about, I need out!" At the end of the school year I decided to see what it would be like as a school counselor in a neighboring high school, and if I was still unhappy with this position, I knew that I could apply for a job as a teacher when an opening was available. This change turned out to be a good decision, and I stayed in this role for many years before I decided to make a professional change as a counselor educator.

One of my responsibilities as a novice counselor educator at a small liberal arts college was to coordinate the school counselor program, including the clinical experiences. Because it had been years since I had taken my own clinical courses, I was unsure what was expected of school site supervisors, and I was even less certain of my own role. In addition, it was frustrating that school counselors who agreed to serve as supervisors were performing this task differently at each school site, and in some sites the principal delegated supervisory functions that were not consistent with the training of the school counselor.

As more states were eliminating the teacher credential requirement, it became evident that counselor trainees without this background were struggling with issues such as classroom management, lesson plans, and teacher collaboration, among others. In addition, teachers and administrators were noticing that some trainees lacked the ability to work collaboratively with educational personnel and groups of students. Furthermore, when the American School Counseling Association (ASCA) adopted the National Standards and later the National Model, supervisors who were trained in a traditional school counseling program were now asked to revise their program into a model that was comprehensive and developmental and to provide activities for trainees that reflected this transformation. These issues presented a challenge for supervisors who were satisfied with their program as it was and for counselor educators who wanted their students to perform in a program that was a reflection of the model endorsed by ASCA.

These concerns were difficult enough for supervisors, but the paucity of supervisory materials made this task even more complicated. Although several books and other resources are available that were written for psychologists, social workers, and others in the helping professions, little was available specifically for practicing professional school counselors who were serving as supervisors of school counselor trainees. This omission served as the catalyst for writing this book. Information on the supervisory process, self-check activities, case studies, creative ideas for supervision, resources, and forms that can be used in supervision are found in this manual.

Practicing professional school counselors who serve as supervisors of school counselors, counselor educators who instruct the clinical experiences, and school counselor trainees can all benefit from the materials in this book.

FOR THE SCHOOL COUNSELOR SUPERVISOR

Your contributions as a supervisor are vital to the professional growth of the school counselor trainee, and it is my hope that the materials in this book will give you a better understanding of supervision so that your role as a supervisor will be more satisfying. Under your mentorship, trainees will have opportunities to reflect on their compatibility with the profession, practice various school counselor activities, implement counseling skills, collaborate with teachers, and consult with parents with the aim of developing into a skillful practitioner. You are an indispensable vehicle for preparing school counselors of the future.

FOR THE SCHOOL COUNSELOR TRAINEE

When you first enter your clinical experiences with the expectation of putting knowledge into practice in an actual setting, it is not uncommon to feel anxiety mixed with anticipation and excitement. As in any new experience, the more you know about the process the better able you will be to understand your feelings, thoughts, and personal and developmental growth that naturally accompany this process. This book has several experiential activities, case studies, resources, and materials that will help you as you negotiate your way through the practicum and internship courses. In all likelihood, your own school counseling program will have similar forms for you to complete, so keep in mind that these materials are not intended to replace them but rather to supplement these materials.

FOR THE PROGRAM SUPERVISOR

It is my hope that this book will assist you in training school counselors for the school counseling profession and in educating school counselors for their role as site supervisors. Too often we assume that school counselors know how to supervise, yet in reality, supervisors have not always received this training because they work or live in remote geographical locations, because of time constraints, or because they have not had workshops or classes on supervision. The materials in this manual may be useful resources for any workshop that you may conduct on supervision and as a training guide for instructing school counselors about the art of supervision.

OVERVIEW OF CHAPTERS

This book is divided into four sections, with each section containing chapters relevant to the various aspects of the supervisory relationship. Although the information in each of these chapters is relevant to the program and site supervisors as well as the school counselor trainee, some information is more applicable for different individuals based on their role in the supervision relationship. Each chapter is labeled for those individuals for whom the information is specifically relevant.

Part I: Introduction to Supervision

The first two chapters are written for the site and program supervisors as well as the trainee entering the profession of school counseling. Chapter 1, Fundamentals of Supervision in the Schools, includes a historical overview of school counselor supervision along with definitions, standards for supervisors, general expectations, and development activities for supervisors and trainees. Chapter 2, Getting Started: Setting Up the Supervisory Relationship, provides a more detailed discussion of how the supervisory process can be initiated, considerations for forming a supervisory partnership, materials that can facilitate the experience, and essential resources to understand supervision better.

Part II: Supervision Paradigms

The next three chapters are for site and program supervisors and trainees who desire more comprehensive knowledge on specific supervisory models and strategies that integrate with these models. Chapter 3, Models of Supervision, summarizes a few of the more common supervisory models, including developmental, theory-specific, and integrated approaches. Additional resources are provided for more specific information on each of these models. Chapter 4, The Supervisory Process From a Developmental Perspective, expands on developmental supervisory models, in particular the integrated developmental model by Stoltenberg and Delworth. Various strategies and activities for supervisor and trainee personal growth are included as they work and grow through the various stages. Chapter 5, Supervision Integrated to the ASCA National Model, combines the ASCA National Model Standards with supervision. Dr. Carol Dahir, one of the authors of the ASCA National Standards, includes suggestions and activities for supervisors to access to help trainees learn about the school counselor's role.

Part III: Current and Emerging Supervisory Issues and Techniques

The next five chapters provide current information on various areas of interest and concern that many supervisors and trainees encounter. Chapter 6, Critical Issues in Multicultural Supervision, includes information on how the supervisory process can be influenced through differences between the supervisor and trainee, such as culture, gender, and sexual orientation. Sensitivity to the differences in the supervisory relationship and how these differences may impact an effective experience are discussed. Chapter 7, Working With the Difficult Trainee, provides important information for supervisors who are uncertain about the procedures that need to be taken when a school counseling trainee is professionally or personally impaired and displaying problematic behaviors. When a trainee is able to handle the academic aspects of the program but has personal issues such as communication difficulties that could jeopardize counseling relationships, then supervisors, who serve as gatekeepers to the profession, have an obligation to offer remedial alternatives to assist the trainee.

Chapter 8, Supervision and Technology, gives a new perspective in supervision through technological advances. As technology continually changes, current supervisory methods are challenged with various implications for training individuals for the profession of school counseling.

Chapter 9, Creative Approaches to Supervision, presents new ideas for supervisors to "think outside of the training box." Because of their different developmental needs, not all trainees learn best through discussion or reading. Creative strategies can be used to help make issues more concrete, to increase understanding, or to emphasize a particular point. This is where creative approaches such as those found in this chapter can be implemented as alternative methods for enhancing the trainee's professional identity. Chapter 10, Ethical and Legal Considerations in Supervision: A Well-Planned Supervision Journey, contains a wealth of information and checklists surrounding the legal and ethical issues in supervision. Just as counselors need to have an understanding of these subjects when working with counselees and others, effective supervisors are also cognizant of the legal and ethical issues surrounding supervision.

Part IV: Evaluation

Evaluation is one of the crucial supervisory tasks supervisors must apply with trainees. It is also one of the most disliked tasks. Assessment serves as a professional gatekeeping mechanism so that trainee strengths are noted and areas to improve are identified. Furthermore, evaluation of practicing professional school counselors' clinical skills is an area that is often not part of their regular assessment procedure yet is desired by many practicing school counselors. Information on strategies practicing professional school counselors can implement for gaining feedback on clinical skills is included in the final chapter.

Chapter 11, The Evaluation Process and Supervision, outlines the various types of evaluation that are commonly used, assessment focal points, significant supervisory components, and the valuable role assessment plays in supervision. Supervisors are charged with the task of providing feedback and evaluating the individuals they are training, a task that is often considered as onerous and undesirable. The materials in this chapter are intended to make this responsibility easier, placing more emphasis on skill benchmarks as a measure of growth. Chapter 12, Supervision of Practicing School Counselors, is written for practicing professional school counselors. For the most part, when the coursework ends and the credential is conferred, school counselors do not receive evaluative feedback on counseling skills. Strategies for school counselors who would like to improve their clinical skills and suggestions for viewing critical counseling cases through consultation are included.

About the Authors

CAROL A. DAHIR, EdD, is an assistant professor and coordinator of the Counselor Education programs at the New York Institute of Technology. She recently served as the American School Counselor Association (ASCA) *National Standards* project director and coauthor, has published numerous articles, and coauthored *School Counselor Accountability: A Measure of Student Success*, published by Merrill Prentice Hall, and *The Transformed School Counselor*, published by Houghton Mifflin.

JOEL F. DIAMBRA, EdD, is an associate professor and clinical supervisor in the Counselor Education, Educational Psychology and Counseling Department at the University of Tennessee. He is also a licensed professional counselor, mental health service provider, and nationally certified counselor.

DANIEL L. FUDGE is a 4th-year doctoral candidate in school psychology specializing in counseling at the University of Tennessee. His research interests include reducing undesired classroom behavior, increasing desired classroom behavior, and increasing academic performance in elementary school students.

VALERIE A. FULBRIGHT is the administrative assistant for the Great Schools Partnership and is finishing her BA degree in psychology at the University of Tennessee. She plans to pursue her master's degree in school counseling. She has an avid interest in using technology.

SUSAN NORRIS HUSS, PhD, LPC, is an associate professor in the Mental Health and School Counseling Program, School of Intervention Service, Bowling Green State University. She was a former school counselor and was the ethics chairperson on the Ohio School Counselor Association board.

TRICIA MCCLAM, PhD, is a professor in the Department of Educational Psychology and Counseling at the University of Tennessee. She has been a counselor educator since 1978 and is active in local and national human services and counseling organizations. She is a coauthor of three textbooks: *Introduction to Human Services* (5th edition), *Introduction to Human Services: Cases and Applications*, and *Generalist Case Management* (3rd edition), all published by Brooks/Cole/Thomson.

MARLA PETERSON, PhD, received her doctorate in counselor education from Ohio State University, where she also served as director of the ERIC Clearinghouse on Adult, Career and Vocational Education. She has been a counselor educator at the University of Tennessee for the past 25 years and, for 5 years, was the campuswide dean for research at Tennessee. She was a public school teacher and counselor for 8 years. Her teaching, research, and scholarly contributions have been focused on career development and use of technology to enhance career planning.

JEANNINE R. STUDER, EdD, is an associate professor and school counseling coordinator at the University of Tennessee, Knoxville. Dr. Studer was a former high school counselor, developed the first school counselor program at Heidelberg College in Tiffin, Ohio, and was co-coordinator of the school counseling program at California State University, Stanislaus. She has many articles published and is the author of the book *The Professional School Counselor: An Advocate for Students*, published by Brooks/Cole/Thomson.

MARIANNE WOODSIDE, EdD, is a professor in the Department of Educational Psychology and Counseling, University of Tennessee. She has been a counselor educator since 1978 and is active in local and national human services and counseling organizations. She is a coauthor of three textbooks: *Introduction to Human Services* (5th edition), *Introduction to Human Services: Cases and Applications, and Generalist Case Management* (3rd edition), all published by Brooks/Cole/Thomson.

PART I

Introduction to Supervision

CHAPTER 1

Fundamentals of Supervision in the Schools

THE PURPOSE of this chapter is to

- provide the school supervisor with an overview of the process of supervision
- facilitate readiness for supervision through a self-assessment of the knowledge and competencies that are considered essential for an effective supervisory partnership
- assist school counselor trainees to prepare for the supervision process by being familiar with supervisory expectations, and for appraising personal attitudes, values, behaviors, skills, knowledge, and professional orientation
- aid program supervisors in the selection of placements

Recently, one of my practicum students was having difficulty getting her direct hours in individual and group counseling. Her site supervisor told her to "just sit in the guidance office until someone comes in with a problem." Apparently her supervisor regarded her own role as a member of the administrative team. Even though the supervisor was hired as a school counselor, her tasks consisted of discipline when the assistant principal was unavailable, checking attendance in classes, and constructing the master schedule. In my visit with this supervisor, she remarked that she "wanted the trainee to see what the job would really be like, not what is taught in the ivory tower." Although we were able to work out a plan for the student to receive her practicum hours, this incident reminded me of the importance of forming a supervisory partnership between higher education and school counselors who share the same vision and philosophy of school counseling.

Appropriate supervision is one of the most essential training components for students training for the profession of school counseling. Practicing school counselors play a vital role by making certain that students training for the profession of school counseling are prepared for the myriad concerns children and adolescents encounter. Yet, the question many school counselors ask is, "What is my role as a supervisor?" Every supervisor takes on this role differently. Some are with the trainee every minute he or she is in the school, even to the extreme of sitting in on every counseling session the trainee conducts. Others take a more independent approach to the point where the trainee is never certain where to locate his or her supervisor. Neither of these positions is in the best interest of the trainee or supervisor. However, the reality is that most school counselors have not been trained in the process of supervision because it is rarely a requirement in most master's-level classes.

Milly Malone is a professional school counselor in a suburban middle school. She has been in this position for 9 years and taught seventh-grade math before she became a school counselor. Milly has presented at national conferences and received recognition for her professional work by the state counselor's association. Because Milly is active in the American School Counselor

Association (ASCA) and her state school counselor association, she has remained current with the trends in the school counseling profession. Recently, a counselor educator at a local university asked her if she would be willing to serve as a site supervisor for a school counselor student enrolled in the practicum course. Milly thought about this request and declined, stating that she "did not really have the time to spend on yet another duty that she felt would take her away from her time with her middle school students."

An urban high school with a diverse population of students has five professional school counselors, each with different assignments. One counselor is strictly a career counselor for all of the students enrolled in Grades 9 through 12. The other counselors are assigned to a specific grade level. Although the counselors share a collaborative relationship, each handles his or her tasks with little understanding of what the other counselors do. Mr. Langley, the 9th-grade counselor, agreed to be the site supervisor for a school counselor internship trainee. He decided to give the intern all the duties that he disliked such as cafeteria monitor, detention teacher, clerical duties, and hall guard to get relief from doing these assignments.

The university counselor educator was adamant that the school counseling students receive clinical experiences that reflect the duties school counselors perform in a developmental school counselor program. The problem was in identifying not only practicing professional school counselors who applied this model in the schools but also those who had training in supervision. Many practicing counselors in the area worked in a traditional school counselor program with little knowledge of a transformed school counselor program, and even fewer had received any instruction in supervision. The counselor educator's dilemma was how to train experienced school counselors in a supervision model that reflected the developmental approach that was taught in the counselor education program.

Each of these situations exemplifies common concerns surrounding the issues of supervision and the professional school counselor. Social, economic, and political pressures have been instrumental in the transformation of school counseling programs (Akos & Galassi, 2004). Guidance workers, as they were known when they first entered the schools in the early 1900s, were charged with the task of providing guidance to students who needed career direction. Today's school counselors continue this task in addition to assisting students with academic concerns and personal/social issues that often leave school-age youths overwhelmed and incapacitated.

School counselors are often asked to serve as mentors of school counselor trainees. The unfortunate truth is that most professional school counselors are the first to admit that they are not trained in supervision knowledge for several reasons: (a) Supervision is generally not a component of master's degree programs due to the breadth of coursework that is required and is generally taught only in specialist and doctoral programs, (b) there are few opportunities to receive training (Nelson & Johnson, 1999), and (c) little literature is available on the supervisory process (Sutton & Page, 1994, as cited in Nelson & Johnson, 1999) of school counselors-in-training. As stated by one practicing professional high school counselor:

> Our secondary counselor supervisor has never been a counselor before and is not familiar with the profession or standards, nor does she seem interested in learning about them. Hopefully, as we get newly educated counselors into the system, things will start to change.

As is evident in the quotation above, many practicing school counselors operate under a traditional school counselor approach with few supervisory experiences that reflect a comprehensive, developmental school counseling program as advocated by ASCA. Even the most seasoned, effective school counselor supervisors ask the questions, "What am I supposed to do?" "What are the expectations?" and "How am I supposed to find the time to add one more task to my already overburdened schedule?"

WHAT IS SUPERVISION?

The word *supervision* comes from Latin roots meaning "to look over" or "to oversee" (Garthwait, 2005). Although supervision does encompass guiding a less experienced member of the profession (Bernard & Goodyear, 2004), it is much more than this. It is also a contractual, formal process in which a relationship is formed between the supervisor and the trainee (Herlihy, Gray, & McCollum, 2002) for the purpose of facilitating the trainee's personal and professional development (Boyd, 1978). The supervisor is also responsible for the welfare of the individuals the trainee assists, as well as for the assessment of the trainee's performance and aptitude for professional competence (Association for Counselor Education and Supervision [ACES], n.d.).

HISTORY OF SCHOOL COUNSELOR SUPERVISION

Supervision of the school counselor has received little attention. Historically, guidance workers in the schools were teachers who provided career direction without any training in guidance (Ginn, 1924). As societal needs changed, recognition for trained guidance workers in the schools increased. In the 1920s Harvard University took the lead in establishing the first school counselor certification program that included the requirements of teaching and vocational experience (Schmidt, 1993). At this time inconsistency in training and role performance was the norm, with variations in credit hours and curricula (Nugent, 1994). When psychoanalytic practice emerged between 1925 and 1930, the issue of supervision was introduced and discussed. Many believed that counseling and supervision were parallel processes with similar strategies used for both (Williams, 1995). What little supervision school counselors received was usually conducted using a psychodynamic focus. In the latter part of the 1920s, four or five courses were required by a few states to be qualified to perform guidance services. Yet, credit hours and curricula continued to vary from state to state and among counselor education programs, with vast discrepancies in role performance and supervision.

The 1950s have been described as the decade that "had the most profound impact on counselors" (Aubrey, 1977, p. 292). The number of school counselors increased dramatically owing to the passage of the National Defense Education Act. In addition, the American Personnel and Guidance Association, the forerunner to the American Counseling Association (ACA), was formed through the merger of four like-minded counseling groups. One of these groups was the National Association of Guidance Supervisors and Counselor Trainers, now known as the Association of Counselor Education and Supervision (ACES) (Aubrey, 1983).

As the need for counselors in the schools increased, the U.S. Office of Education created standards for counselor education training that increased coursework and training (Stripling, 1978). During the 1960s, supervision was still in its infancy, and there were myriad opinions on how it should occur. Some believed that this process should be a democratic process with little structure, whereas others showed preference for an instructional, structured environment that provided feedback (Lister, 1966). In 1964 ACES issued standards for the preparation of secondary school counselors. In 1967 these standards were revised to include courses in human behavior, educational practices, and professional studies in school counseling and guidance, with a *supervised experience* that included laboratory, practicum, and an optional internship (American Personnel and Guidance Association, 1967).

Despite these guidelines, supervision continued to be ill defined, with trainees engaging in a wide variety of tasks often with little relationship to their training by supervisors who were uncertain of their responsibilities. For the most part, the clinical skills of counselor trainees were evaluated on the basis of how they described and recalled their counseling sessions. Carl Rogers, who believed that listening to sessions provided greater insight and understanding, was the first to use audiotapes and transcripts as a supervisory tool (Bernard & Goodyear, 2004). Others eventually followed his lead.

It is interesting that even at this time, there was discussion that the supervisory role was one that required special preparation and training (Appleton & Hansen, 1968). In 1969 ACES defined a supervisor as one who (a) is experienced and trained in supervision, (b) facilitates the trainees' personal and professional growth, and (c) purposefully oversees the work of counselor trainees' (Boyd, 1978). Although efforts were made to standardize the role and function of supervisors, many school counselor training programs continued to be dissimilar, with differences in purposes and mission.

The Council for Accreditation of Counseling and Related Educational Programs (CACREP) was established in 1981 as an independent accrediting agency that provided guidelines for counselor education coursework, including supervision. Today, school counselor training programs following CACREP standards require a minimum of 48 semester hours, and this recognized organization accredits over 159 school counselor education programs nationwide (CACREP, 2001). Although not all school counselor education programs are CACREP accredited, the standards do offer a compass for school counseling programs to follow. Yet, despite the guidelines, there is a lack of consistency as to how the standards are to be addressed (Pérusse, Goodnough, & Nöel, 2001) within the programs. Some individuals even predict that the counseling profession is evolving to the point that supervisors will need to be credentialed not only as school counselors but also as supervisors (Dye & Borders, 1990). Some states already require that supervisors hold a supervisor credential.

WHAT ARE THE CLINICAL EXPERIENCES?

The clinical experiences, often referred to as the *practicum* and *internship*, are usually the first opportunities for trainees to put basic counseling skills into reality through experience in the school setting. The practicum is taken prior to the internship with the purpose of enhancing counseling skills. The internship experience provides the opportunity for students to perform activities that a practicing professional counselor implements within the school setting.

WHAT ARE THE QUALIFICATIONS FOR BEING A SUPERVISOR?

A *site supervisor, program supervisor,* and *trainee* (also known as a supervisee or school counselor-in-training) form a cooperative relationship for the clinical experiences with a set of explicit guidelines. The site supervisor should have "a minimum of two (2) years of pertinent professional experience in the program area in which the student is completing clinical instruction; and knowledge of the program's expectations, requirements, and evaluation procedures for students" (CACREP, 2001, Section III). ACES supplements these requirements by stating that supervisors must have "training in supervision prior to initiating their role as supervisors" (Association for Counselor Education and Supervision, n.d.). This requirement is supported by the *ACA Code of Ethics* that maintains supervisors must be adequately prepared in supervision (American Counseling Association, 2005). The remainder of this chapter includes a definition of terms according to CACREP standards, guidelines for conducting supervision, an explanation of clinical experiences of school counselor trainees, and self-reflection exercises.

DEFINITIONS

Because various institutions use different supervisor terminology, it is important to understand the various terms that are used, the individuals who are responsible for the clinical experiences, and the guidelines of the training institution. For instance, a school counselor student is generally supervised during his or her *clinical experiences*, generally referred to as the *practicum* and *internship*. Some institutions combine the practicum and internship into one clinical experience known as *fieldwork*. This type of fieldwork is distinct from those experiences found in some counselor education programs (also called fieldwork) in which counselors-in-training without an educational background are required to fulfill a number of activities (such as teacher observation, tutoring, interviewing various educators, team-teaching a class, and so on) in the school setting, for the purpose of learning about the school milieu. Supervisors and trainees are to be clear of the purpose of the fieldwork if such an experience is required.

Program supervisor: The individual employed by the college or university who is responsible for the clinical course in which the trainee is enrolled.

Practicum or internship school counselor student: The student who is working on a credential as a school counselor. This individual is sometimes referred to as a *trainee, supervisee,* or a *counselor-in-training.*

Site supervisor: A practicing school counselor who holds a credential in school counseling with a minimum of 2 years of experience as a school counselor, with the expectation that this individual has received training in supervision. Although ASCA does not have supervisor guidelines in place at the present time and is presently working on a role statement for supervisors, the organization does endorse the ethical guidelines adapted by ACES (J. Cook, personal communication, September 24, 2004).

Counselee: An individual receiving counseling services. Although this term seems awkward, school counselors work with *students,* not *clients.* The term *counselee* is used in this book instead of client to distinguish between the two.

Practicum: The purpose of this clinical experience is to practice, improve, and strengthen counseling skills under supervision. Students are to complete a minimum of 100 clock hours, with 40 hours of direct service that includes both individual counseling and group experiences.

Practicum site supervisor: A supervisor who provides opportunities for the trainee to understand the school environment; introduces the trainee to the students, faculty, and staff; and serves as a mentor by facilitating the understanding of the professional school counselor's purpose and role. The practicum site supervisor makes arrangements for the supervisee to acquire practice in individual and group counseling, provides opportunities for self-reflection, and is responsible for performance feedback.

Practicum requirements: While the student is enrolled in practicum, the student will engage in weekly individual or triadic supervision for an average of 1 hour per week. In addition, the student will meet for group supervision for an average of 1½ hours per week. *Triadic supervision* involves two practicum students meeting with supervisor for feedback on their counseling skills.

Internship: This clinical experience follows successful completion of the practicum. During the internship the trainee will complete a minimum of 600 hours of which a minimum of 240 hours will be in direct contact with students.

Internship site supervisor: The internship site supervisor provides the trainee with opportunities to become familiar with the various resources within the school, to engage in activities commonly provided by professional school counselors, and to provide feedback and assessment of the trainee's performance.

Internship requirements: The intern will receive either individual or triadic supervision usually by the on-site supervisor, for a minimum of 1 hour each week, in addition to group supervision that is generally provided by a program supervisor for an average of 1½ hours each week.

Supervisors and trainees can benefit from being aware of specific qualities each brings to the supervisory partnership. Exercise 1.1 is designed to assist supervisors in identifying the areas in which they feel more supervision training is needed.

Because trainees are so actively involved with their own personal and professional lives, it is rare to take the time to analyze personal attitudes and values, behavior, skills, knowledge, and readiness for the profession. The intent of Exercise 1.2 is to assist the trainee in understanding his or her abilities and knowledge as they relate to the profession.

WHAT CHARACTERISTICS ARE NEEDED BY AN EFFECTIVE SUPERVISOR?

The Supervision Interest Network (1993), a committee of the Association for Counselor Education and Supervision, established 11 standards for counseling supervisors. Read and complete the standards checklist in Exercise 1.1.

Exercise 1.1

Standards for Counseling Supervisors

As a supervisor, read over these standards and indicate your level of knowledge by placing an "X" in the appropriate column using the following scale: 1 = *not at all* and 5 = *very much*.

		1	2	3	4	5
1.	**Knowledge and Competencies** I am able to . . .					
1.1	demonstrate knowledge of various counseling theories, systems, and their related methods					
1.2.	demonstrate knowledge of personal philosophical, theoretical, and methodological approach to counseling					
1.3	demonstrate knowledge of assumptions about human behavior					
1.4	demonstrate skill in the application of counseling theory and methods that are appropriate for the school setting					
2.	**Personal Traits and Characteristics** I . . .					
2.1	am committed to updating my counseling and supervisory skills					
2.2	am sensitive to individual differences					
2.3	recognize my own limits through self-evaluation and feedback from others					
2.4	am encouraging, optimistic, and motivational					
2.5	possess a sense of humor					
2.6	am comfortable with the authority inherent in the role of supervisor					
2.7	can demonstrate a commitment to the role of supervisor					
2.8	can identify my own strengths and weaknesses as a supervisor					
2.9	can describe my own pattern in interpersonal relationships					
3.	**Knowledge of Ethical, Legal, and Regulatory Aspects of the Profession** I am able to . . .					
3.1	communicate to the trainee a knowledge of the professional codes of ethics (ASCA, ACA)					
3.2	demonstrate and enforce ethical and professional standards					
3.3	communicate to the trainee an understanding of legal and regulatory documents and their impact on the profession					
3.4	provide current information regarding professional standards and licensure					
3.5	communicate a knowledge of trainee rights and appeal procedures specific to the school setting					
3.6	communicate to the counselor a knowledge of ethical considerations					
4.	**Conceptual Knowledge of the Personal and Professional Nature of the Supervisory Relationship** I . . .					
4.1	demonstrate knowledge of individual differences with respect to gender, race, ethnicity, culture and age and understand the importance of these characteristics in a supervisory relationship					
4.2	am sensitive to the trainee's personal and professional needs					

(Continued)

Exercise 1.1 *(Continued)*

Standards for Counseling Supervisors

As a supervisor, read over these standards and indicate your level of knowledge by placing an "X" in the appropriate column using the following scale: 1 = *not at all* and 5 = *very much*.

		1	2	3	4	5
4.3	expect trainees to own the consequences of their actions					
4.4	am sensitive to the evaluative nature of supervision and effectively respond to the trainee's anxiety relative to performance evaluation					
4.5	conduct self-evaluations, as appropriate, as a means of modeling professional growth					
4.6	provide facilitative conditions (empathy, concreteness, respect, congruence, genuineness, and immediacy)					
4.7	establish a mutually trusting relationship with the trainee					
4.8	provide an appropriate balance of challenge and support					
4.9	elicit trainee thoughts and feelings during counseling or consultation sessions, and respond in a manner that enhances the supervision process					
5.	**Conceptual Knowledge of Supervision Methods and Techniques** I am able to . . .					
5.1	state the purposes of supervision and explain the procedures being used					
5.2	negotiate mutual decisions regarding the needed direction of learning experiences for the counselor					
5.3	engage in appropriate supervisory interventions, including role-play, role-reversal, live supervision, etc.					
5.4	perform the supervisor's functions in the role of teacher, counselor, or consultant as appropriate					
5.5	elicit new alternatives from trainees for identifying solutions, techniques, and responses to counselees					
5.6	integrate knowledge of supervision with personal style of interpersonal relations					
5.7	clarify own role in supervision					
5.8	use media aids to enhance learning					
5.9	interact with the trainee in a manner that facilitates his/her self-exploration and problem solving					
6.	**Conceptual Knowledge of the Counselor Developmental Process** I am able to . . .					
6.1	understand the developmental nature of supervision					
6.2	demonstrate knowledge of various theoretical models of supervision					
6.3	understand the trainee's roles and functions in the school setting					
6.4	understand the supervisor's roles and functions in the school setting					

(Continued)

Exercise 1.1 *(Continued)*

Standards for Counseling Supervisors

As a supervisor, read over these standards and indicate your level of knowledge by placing an "X" in the appropriate column using the following scale: 1 = *not at all* and 5 = *very much.*

		1	2	3	4	5
6.5	identify the learning needs of the counselor					
6.6	adjust supervision session content based on the trainee's personal traits, conceptual development, training, and experience					
6.7	use supervisory methods appropriate to the trainee's level of conceptual development, training, and experience					
7.	**Knowledge and Competency in Case Conceptualization and Management** I am able to . . .					
7.1	recognize that a primary goal of supervision is helping the counselee (student) of the counselor					
7.2	understand the role of other professionals (school psychologist, nurse) and assist with a referral process, when appropriate					
7.3	elicit trainee perceptions of counseling dynamics					
7.4	assist the trainee in selecting and executing data collection procedures					
7.5	assist the trainee in analyzing and interpreting data objectively					
7.6	assist the trainee in planning effective student goals and objectives					
7.7	assist the trainee in using observation and assessment in preparation of counselee goals and objectives					
7.8	assist the trainee in synthesizing counselee psychological and behavioral characteristics into an integrated conceptualization					
7.9	assist the trainee in assigning priorities to counseling goals and objectives					
7.10	assist the trainee in providing rationale for counseling procedures					
7.11	assist the trainee in adjusting steps in the progression toward a goal based on ongoing assessment and evaluation					
8.	**Knowledge and Competency in Student Assessment and Evaluation** I am able to . . .					
8.1	monitor the use of tests and test interpretations					
8.2	assist the trainee in providing rationale for assessment procedures					
8.3	assist the trainee in communicating assessment procedures and rationales					
8.4	assist the trainee in the description, measurement, and documentation of counselee and trainee change					
8.5	assist the trainee in integrating findings and observations to make appropriate recommendations					
9.	**Knowledge and Competency in Oral and Written Reporting and Recording** I am able to . . .					
9.1	understand the meaning of accountability and the supervisor's responsibility in promoting it					

(Continued)

Exercise 1.1 *(Continued)*

Standards for Counseling Supervisors

As a supervisor, read over these standards and indicate your level of knowledge by placing an "X" in the appropriate column using the following scale: 1 = *not at all* and 5 = *very much*.

	1	2	3	4	5
9.2 assist the counselor in effectively documenting supervisory and counseling-related interactions					
9.3 assist the trainee in establishing and following policies and procedures to protect the confidentiality of counselee and supervisory records					
9.4 assist the trainee in identifying appropriate information to be included in a verbal or written report					
9.5 assist the trainee in presenting information in a logical, concise, and sequential manner					
9.6 assist the trainee in adapting verbal and written reports to the work environment and communication situation					
10. Knowledge and Competency in the Evaluation of Counseling Performance I am able to . . .					
10.1 interact with the trainee from the perspective of an evaluator					
10.2 identify the trainee's professional and personal strengths, as well as weaknesses					
10.3 provide specific feedback about such performance as conceptualization, use of methods and techniques, relationship skills, and assessment					
10.4 determine the extent to which the trainee has developed and applied his or her own personal theory of counseling					
10.5 develop evaluation procedures and instruments to determine program and trainee goal attainment					
10.6 assist the trainee in the description and measurement of his or her progress and achievement					
10.7 evaluate trainee skills for purposes of grade assignment, completion of internship requirements, professional advancement, and so on					
11. Knowledgeable Regarding Research in Counseling and Counselor Supervision and Consistently Incorporate This Knowledge Into the Supervision Process I am able to . . .					
11.1 facilitate and monitor research to determine the effectiveness of programs, services, and techniques					
11.2 read, interpret, and apply counseling and supervisory research					
11.3 formulate counseling or supervisory research questions					
11.4 report results of counseling or supervisory research and disseminate as appropriate (e.g., in-service, conferences, publications, etc.)					
11.5 facilitate an integration of research findings in individual case management					

(Continued)

Exercise 1.1 *(Continued)*

Standards for Counseling Supervisors

Based on your responses to the checklist, complete the following:

What are your goals as a supervisor?
1. _____
2. _____
3. _____

List the strategies you will use to reach these goals:
1. _____
2. _____
3. _____

How will you evaluate your progress on these goals?
1. _____
2. _____
3. _____

Note. From "Ethical Guidelines for Counseling Supervisors," by the Supervision Interest Network, Association for Counselor Education and Supervision, 1993 (Summer), *ACES Spectrum, 53*(4), pp. 5–8. Copyright 1993 by the Association for Counselor Education and Supervision. Adapted with permission.

WHAT CHARACTERISTICS ARE NEEDED FOR A SCHOOL COUNSELING SUPERVISEE?

As an individual entering the school counseling profession, the trainee must be supervised by an individual within the school counseling profession with experience as a school counselor, training in supervision, and the ability to provide opportunities for the supervisee to understand the school counselor's role. Too often, a building principal, school psychologist, or others outside of the profession provide supervision, often resulting in a trainee emerging without a thorough understanding of the integral role a school counselor plays in a developmental, comprehensive program. As a school counselor trainee ready to enter the clinical experiences, you must apply self-reflection to assist you in recognizing values, attitudes, behaviors, skills, and knowledge. On the list provided in Exercise 1.2, check each of the items that apply to you. There are no right or wrong answers, but it is hoped that the exercise will give you an opportunity to identify the areas in which you would like to improve.

Exercise 1.2

Supervisee Readiness for Supervision Checklist

Attitudes and Values
I have the ability to:
____ relate to others both personally and in professional relationships
____ develop a caring, empathic relationship with others
____ recognize my personal philosophy and beliefs
____ respect the thoughts, feelings, and beliefs of others
____ commit to advocating for others
____ be sensitive to individuals from diverse backgrounds
____ provide counseling to individuals who are different from me
____ engage in new activities

Behaviors
I have the ability to:
____ respond to a situation in an ethical manner
____ recognize personal biases and prejudices
____ understand the consultation process
____ be effective in consultation skills
____ be competent in group work
____ select appropriate assessment instruments
____ organize effective time management
____ identify a theoretical model appropriate for the counselee
____ select an appropriate intervention strategy
____ devote time to the clinical experience
____ develop my counselee's view of life
____ accept constructive feedback

(Continued)

Exercise 1.2 *(Continued)*

Supervisee Readiness for Supervision Checklist

Skills

I have the ability to:

____ apply technology and am competent in computer literacy

____ use developmentally appropriate intervention strategies

____ use career development theories to assist counselee decision making

____ administer and interpret assessment instruments

____ use appropriate counseling skills

____ effectively express myself through written communication

____ effectively express myself through interpersonal communication

____ effectively use listening skills

____ follow directions

____ effectively collaborate with others

____ educate stakeholders about the school counseling program

____ provide leadership in a comprehensive, developmental school counseling program

Knowledge

I am knowledgeable of:

____ children of alcoholics

____ the role of the school counselor in relationship to others in the school setting

____ resources available through the professional organizations such as ASCA and ACA

____ the credentialing process for school counselors

____ developmental issues across the life span

____ assessment and evaluation

____ research methods and evaluation techniques

____ a comprehensive, developmental school counseling program

____ the school rules and policies

____ chemically dependent youths

____ individuals with different lifestyles

____ individuals from culturally diverse backgrounds

____ self-mutilation

____ depression and suicide

____ students with special needs

____ educational nomenclature

____ effective classroom management strategies

____ the ACA counseling divisions, regions, and branches

____ crisis intervention strategies

____ research methods and program evaluation techniques

Professional Orientation

I am knowledgeable of and able to work with:

____ ethical and legal codes

____ school policies and procedures

____ school rules

____ legislation concerning human rights

____ seek guidance from my supervisor when needed

Based on the checklist, what are some of the strengths you bring to the clinical experience?

1. _____
2. _____
3. _____
4. _____

Based on the checklist, in what areas would you like to receive more training during the clinical experience?

1. _____
2. _____
3. _____
4. _____

What strategies can you implement to improve the targeted areas of improvement?

1. _____
2. _____
3. _____
4. _____

How will you evaluate your efforts?

1. _____
2. _____
3. _____
4. _____

SUMMARY

Understanding the professional school counselor's role during the clinical experiences is one of the most valuable educational opportunities provided to students training for the profession of school counseling. School counselors are vital links in the educational process, and when trainees are supervised inappropriately by individuals outside of the field or by practicing school counselors who have not received supervision training, not only is the counselee's learning jeopardized, but the individuals with whom he or she works may also be affected negatively.

Because supervision is a relatively new process that has evolved subsequent to the emergence of the school counseling profession, guidelines for the clinical experiences, known as the practicum and internship, have been introduced and revised to reflect our societal and professional needs. The CACREP was established in 1981 as an accrediting agency to monitor and regulate the counseling profession and the supervisory experiences. Supervisors are expected to receive supervision training and to develop an awareness of this role.

ACES established a committee to identify supervisory knowledge and competencies for an effective training and mentoring relationship with the school counseling program and students preparing for the profession. However, an effective supervisor is only part of the equation in producing talented, knowledgeable school counselors. It is also essential for trainees to have appropriate attitudes and values, behaviors, skills, and knowledge to work productively as a school counselor. Self-reflecting and determining readiness for the profession during program training provide a clearer lens for self-evaluation and identification of areas to improve.

REFERENCES

Akos, P., & Galassi, J. P. (2004). Training school counselors as developmental advocates. *Counselor Education and Supervision, 43,* 192–206.

American Counseling Association. (2005). *ACA Code of Ethics.* Alexandria, VA: Author.

American Personnel and Guidance Association. (1967). Standards for the preparation of secondary school counselors. *Personnel and Guidance Journal, 46,* 97–106.

Appleton, G. M., & Hansen, J. C. (1968). Continuing supervision in the school. *Counselor Education and Supervision, VII,* 273–281.

Association for Counselor Education and Supervision. (n.d.). *Ethical guidelines for counseling supervisors.* Retrieved December 21, 2005, from http://www.acesonline.net/index.asp

Aubrey, R. F. (1977). Historical development of guidance and counseling and implications for the future. *Personnel and Guidance Journal, 55,* 288–295.

Aubrey, R. F. (1983). The odyssey of counseling and images of the future. *Personnel and Guidance Journal, 62,* 78–82.

Bernard, J. M., & Goodyear, R. K. (2004). *Fundamentals of clinical supervision* (3rd ed.). Boston: Pearson.

Boyd, J. D. (1978). *Counselor supervision: Approaches, preparation, practices.* Muncie, IN: Accelerated Development.

Council for Accreditation of Counseling and Related Educational Programs. (2001). *CACREP standards.* Alexandria, VA: Author.

Dye, H. A., & Borders, L. D. (1990). Counseling supervisors: Standards for preparation and practice. *Journal of Counseling & Development, 69,* 27–29.

Garthwait, C. L. (2005). *The social work practicum: A guide and workbook for students.* Boston: Pearson.

Ginn, S. J. (1924). Duties of a vocational counselor in Boston public schools. *The Vocational Guidance Magazine, 3,* 3–7.

Herlihy, B., Gray, N., & McCollum, V. (2002). Legal and ethical issues in school counselor supervision. *Professional School Counseling, 6,* 55–60.

Lister, J. L. (1966). Supervised counseling experiences: Some comments. *Counselor Education and Supervision, VI,* 69–72.

Nelson, M. D., & Johnson, P. (1999). School counselors as supervisors: An integrated approach for supervising school counseling interns. *Counselor Education and Supervision, 39,* 89–100.

Nugent, F. A. (1994). *An introduction to the profession of counseling* (2nd ed.). Upper Saddle River, NJ: Prentice-Hall.

Pérusse, R., Goodnough, G. E., & Nöel, C. J. (2001). A national survey of school counselor preparation programs: Screening methods, faculty experiences, curricular content and fieldwork requirements. *Counselor Education and Supervision, 40,* 252–262

Schmidt, J. J. (1993). *Counseling in schools: Essential services and comprehensive programs.* Boston: Allyn & Bacon.

Stripling, R. O. (1978). Standards and accreditation in counselor education: A proposal. *Personnel and Guidance Journal, 56,* 608–611.

Supervision Interest Network, Association for Counselor Education and Supervision. (1993, Summer). Ethical guidelines for counseling supervisors. *ACES Spectrum, 53*(4), 5–8.

Williams, A. (1995). *Visual and active supervision: Roles, focus, technique.* New York: Norton.

CHAPTER 2

Getting Started: Setting Up the Supervisory Relationship

THE PURPOSE of this chapter is to

- make sample forms available that may be used to fulfill various requirements
- provide specific information for the program and site supervisors
- introduce essential resources for school counselor trainees

When I started as a practicum student, I thought I would have a chance to watch and observe my supervisor in action. Instead, I was not allowed in any of my supervisor's sessions because she felt that my presence in a counseling session would compromise confidentiality.

Watching my supervisor helped us build a relationship. It also helped in being able to get parents' permission to tape the student because they knew that I was working closely with the counselor they trusted. After I was first on my own, I would think about what my supervisor would do in this situation and I would try to do it. Later on, I felt comfortable in developing my own style.

As the statements of school counselor trainees above indicate, learning the role of a school counselor is complex and often overwhelming. One essential component of counselor training is helping trainees develop a coherent philosophical understanding of the profession (Spruill & Benshoff, 2000), yet too often, it is not until the clinical experiences that *knowing* becomes *doing* (Williams, 1995).

Because site supervisors assist trainees in developing skills necessary to be capable school counselors, it is incumbent on the training institution to select supervisors who are competent, appropriately credentialed, and experienced members of the profession (McCordy, 2003; Pehrsson & Ingram, n.d.). Historically, the selection of an appropriate supervisory site was seen as one that occurred through chance, yet today's counselor educators recognize that supervision takes time, must be nurtured, and in some cases must even be subsidized (Lister, 1966). Some institutions allow the trainee to choose his or her placement from an approved list of sites and supervisors. Other training programs select sites on the basis of the trainee's needs, the site supervisor's qualifications, and the educational setting.

GUIDELINES FOR CHOOSING A SITE SUPERVISOR

For the Supervisee and Program Supervisor

Although it is sometimes difficult to find a site supervisor who has experience, training in supervision, and time available to nurture a supervisory relationship, there are factors that may be considered in making this placement.

1. *Seek a supervisor who has experience as a professional school counselor.* When trainees are supervised by individuals who do not have a school counseling background, training may be interrupted, altered, and not reflective of the legitimate role of the school counselor.
2. *Determine the experienced professional school counselor's knowledge of supervision.* Practicing school counselors do not always receive training in supervision and instead base this role on how they had been supervised when they were school counselor trainees. This approach to supervision may not always be compatible with the philosophy of the counselor education program.
3. *Identify a professional school counselor who has an awareness of the counselor education program.* Potential supervisors are often not aware of program requirements of the training institutions in their area. Too often supervisors accept trainees for practicum supervision but provide experiences that are more reflective of an internship experience. When clinical requirements are not fully understood, the experience for all individuals involved may not be as positive or productive as it could be.
4. *Determine the supervisor's awareness and interest in cultural sensitivity.* The demographic makeup of the United States is rapidly changing, and the face of America is beginning to look quite different from the past. In the next few decades, classrooms will be even more diverse. As a result, multicultural counseling skills are becoming increasingly important for individuals who work in a school setting. Supervisors who value open-mindedness and who work to minimize personal bias facilitate trainee growth by challenging the trainees' biases and how these influences may negatively affect counseling relationships (Ellis & Robbins, 1993). Constantine and Gloria (1999, as cited in Boylan, Malley, & Reilly, 2001) suggested that exposure to diverse populations through work and being in contact with males and females with different gender orientations increase counseling sensitivity and effectiveness. The Association for Multicultural Counseling and Development, a division of the American Counseling Association (ACA), established multicultural competencies for individuals in the helping profession. These standards are in Appendix A.
5. *Connect with a supervisor who provides a comfortable, trusting atmosphere.* Because personal insight is as essential to trainee growth as is professional development, a trusting, respectful environment in which personal issues may be explored facilitates growth. It is not uncommon for a supervisee to feel inadequacy, inferiority, and anxiety, which are sometimes intensified when learning new skills under the evaluative eye of a supervisor (Williams, 1995).
6. *Identify a supervisor with compatible goals.* As a trainee enters a school system, one of his or her goals may be to become more experienced in providing classroom guidance. A supervisor who has an established classroom guidance plan will be more willing to provide the trainee with the opportunity to conduct these sessions. Other supervisors may not have classroom guidance identified as a part of the school counseling program. A site supervisor who is able to accommodate the goals of the trainee and the goals of the counseling program plays a significant role in the development of the trainee.
7. *Understand the supervisor's style and technique.* Different supervisors have various ideas for how supervision is to be conducted. Some supervisors may wish to be present while the supervisee performs all identified activities; other supervisors may meet with the trainee each day or at the end of each week. The Council for Accreditation of Counseling and Related Educational Programs (CACREP) requires an internship to be performed in a school counseling setting under the supervision of a site supervisor, with an average of 1 hour per week of individual or triadic supervision that is usually performed by the on-site supervisor (CACREP, 2001).
8. *Discuss practical matters.* When the trainee first enters the school building, simply taking the time to introduce the trainee to the various school personnel, K–12 students, and other constituents helps relieve some of the initial anxiety felt by the trainee, leading to a more productive experience. If the supervisee's role and training are not understood,

administrators and teachers may be reluctant to excuse students from class. In addition, parents or guardians may be unwilling to sign permission forms for their son or daughter to meet with the trainee, and students may be reluctant to meet with an individual they do not know.

9. *Identify a supervisor willing to provide an honest appraisal of the trainee's performance.* Talking about the evaluative process makes the topic one that can be openly discussed rather than one that is avoided (Williams, 1995). Unfortunately, supervisors reveal that this is one aspect of their role that creates the most discomfort and anxiety, and they tend to deal with this issue by providing the trainee with high marks in all areas. This practice prevents trainee growth, particularly when target areas for improvement are not identified (Michaelson, Estrada-Hernández, & Wadsworth, 2003).

10. *Provide adequate facilities for the trainee.* Too often, satisfactory facilities are not available to practicing professional school counselors. School counselors are often forced to relinquish or share space with other educational personnel, such as the school psychologist or speech pathologist, or constantly search for any available space to conduct activities owing to overcrowding in schools. In such situations, it is probable that the trainee will also not have a private area to conduct activities. Furthermore, the lack of taping equipment can make a difference in a quality training experience (Boylan et al., 2001). Students generally have access to audio recorders but do not always have videotaping equipment.

11. *Find a supervisor with an eclectic theoretical approach.* Some school counselors favor one theoretical approach over others and may promote that particular counseling theory. If a supervisor adheres to a particular style (e.g., solution-focused), the trainee may be limited in learning other approaches that may more accurately reflect his or her belief system or alternative methods that may be a better approach for counselees (Boylan et al., 2001).

Matching an appropriate supervisor and trainee in a school setting is crucial for a successful experience for the site supervisor as well as the trainee. As stated in chapter 1, the training program may use different terminology for the clinical experiences. Programs that are CACREP approved require the clinical experiences of practicum and internship with specific required hours and responsibilities. The practicum experience is often the first time students are able to practice their newly acquired skills. During the internship, students refine these skills in addition to engaging in other activities commonly performed by the professional school counselor. Other training programs may identify the clinical experiences as fieldwork or some other designated term. It is important that the expectations and roles are clearly understood by all.

CRITICAL CONSIDERATIONS IN SUPERVISION

The information in this section explains the various forms and procedures that may be required for successful supervisory experiences. Examples of the contract for the practicum and internship experiences, liability insurance, skills checklist, release form for parental permission, progress log, and case study forms are provided. In addition, a summary of the stages of counseling with samples of the various procedures and resources that may be useful to the trainee and supervisor at each stage is included. Also provided in this chapter are examples of forms that can be used to aid the counseling process, time logs, journaling techniques, evaluation materials, and a professional disclosure form.

For the Site and Program Supervisors

Checklist to Determine Supervisee Readiness

Trainees are occasionally unprepared for clinical experiences that entail working with a variety of individuals, such as students, teachers, administrators, and parents. In some cases, supervisees are only focused on working with students and are unaware of the other constituents with whom the school counselor collaborates. For example, in one situation a young, inexperienced trainee "told off" the parents of a student she was counseling, believing that this type of confrontation was the best way of handling the counselee's problem. This encounter only accelerated the parents' distrust of the school and the counselor. Exercise 2.1 provides a checklist of qualities for site supervisors to determine supervisee readiness.

The Learning Contract for the Practicum

The contract defines and provides the direction for the trainee's learning activities during his or her clinical experiences. Each trainee determines what will be included in the contract on the basis of his or her personal needs, and the contract is negotiated among the trainee, clinical program supervisor, and site supervisor. A contract revision may be necessary to allow for additional unexpected opportunities that may occur. This learning contract should be realistic, attainable, measurable, and based on the trainee's needs, abilities, prior experience, and available time (Garthwait, 2005).

An example of a practicum contract that is divided into the areas of administrative, clinical, and developmental goals is found in Figure 2.1.

The Learning Contract for the Internship Experience

The internship begins after the practicum has been successfully completed. During the internship experience, the trainee is to have opportunities to use a variety of professional resources and to participate in a formal evaluation. In a comprehensive, developmental school counseling program, the American School Counselor Association (ASCA) National Standards serve as a template for the attitudes, values, and skills of K–12 students. The school counselor designs interventions to meet these needs. An example of various opportunities that can be provided to the trainee to experience the counselor's role in a developmental program is found in Figure 2.2.

Liability Insurance

The trainee will be involved in activities that require contacts with numerous individuals. Counseling professionals, including trainees, are held liable when they are in a *special relationship* that assumes responsibility for another. These individuals have a *duty to care* for those with whom they have established a relationship (Boylan et al., 2001). Because the trainee

---

Exercise 2.1

Evaluating Supervisee Readiness

Directions: Check the competencies your trainee has demonstrated. The areas that are not identified may assist in determining the trainee goals.

Knowledge

The trainee has knowledge of
_____ legal/ethical issues
_____ school policies and procedures
_____ diversity issues
_____ developmental issues of the students in the school population
_____ classroom management strategies
_____ counseling theories and techniques

Skills

The trainee has the ability to
_____ follow directions
_____ accept feedback
_____ carry out activities independently
_____ manage time appropriately
_____ meet teachers/parents appropriately

_____ take on a leadership role
_____ design an effective guidance lesson
_____ structure time effectively
_____ ask for help when needed
_____ be on time for appointments and other activities
_____ identify personal strengths and weaknesses
_____ handle frustration
_____ demonstrate resiliency

Attitudes and Values

The trainee has the ability to
_____ be sensitive to individuals from diverse backgrounds
_____ be flexible when unexpected events occur
_____ advocate for others
_____ assist students with special needs

Trainee: _____ Date _____

School: _____

Site Supervisor: _____

The practicum trainee will:

Administrative Goals: Administrative assessment includes such things as work habits, attendance, time management, compliance with ethical and legal issues, ability to communicate effectively, and the ability to follow school rules and policies (Schmidt, 1990).
1. Contact the site supervisor prior to the beginning of the academic term
2. Obtain and maintain liability coverage
3. Obtain student's signature and parent/guardian's signature for permission to tape counseling sessions
4. Prepare tapes for presentation and complete "Report of Counseling Sessions Form" as required by the program supervisor
5. Log a minimum of 100 on-site hours (including a minimum of 40 direct contact hours; a minimum of 10 hours will be in group work)
6. Maintain practicum time log
7. Obtain evaluation form from site supervisor
8. Complete and submit placement evaluation
9. Complete all the requirements specified in the class syllabus

Clinical Goals: Clinical skills are the skills that are associated with the counseling profession such as consultation, collaboration, counseling dynamics, and assessment knowledge and application (Schmidt, 1990).
1. Work with a minimum of 3 students for individual counseling sessions
2. Lead a small group for the purpose of improving self-concept for a minimum of 7 sessions
3. Conduct group guidance classes on study skills 1 time per week in Grades 2 and 3
4. Observe counselor–parent conference and participate as needed
5. Observe site supervisor conduct counseling sessions
6. Perform follow-up evaluations with individual students

Developmental Goals: Developmental goals include gaining greater competence, awareness of feelings, respect for individuals from diverse backgrounds, and increased professional identity (Henderson, Newsome, & Veach, 2005).
1. Meet with site supervisor at least 1 time per week to discuss progress and receive feedback
2. Maintain a journal of activities that includes thoughts/feelings/actions
3. Implement a minimum of three new intervention strategies
4. Attend a professional counseling conference
5. Self-reflect on personal counseling sessions

The goals stated above are to be completed by the trainee during the practicum experience. Throughout the academic term, if other opportunities are available to the trainee that would provide a valuable learning experience, the contract may be amended if the supervisors and trainee are in agreement.

I verify that the goals stated in the contract meet my approval.

_____   _____
Counselor Trainee   Date

_____   _____
Site Supervisor   Date

_____   _____
Program Supervisor   Date

Figure 2.1

Practicum Contract

Trainee: _____ Date _____

School: _____

Site Supervisor: _____

The intern student will:

Administrative Goals

1. Obtain and maintain liability coverage
2. Log 600 hours of which 240 will be direct contact hours
3. Complete all activities in an ethical manner
4. Maintain the internship time log
5. Obtain student's signature and parent/guardian's signature for permission to tape counseling sessions
6. Maintain log of conferences
7. Obtain evaluation form
8. Complete site evaluation form
9. Complete all assignments indicated on the course syllabus

Clinical Goals Using the ASCA National Model

Delivery Component	ASCA Domain	ASCA Standard	ASCA Indicator	Intern Activity
School Guidance Curriculum	Academic	Standard B: Students will complete school with the academic preparation essential to choose from a wide range of substantial postsecondary options, including college	Use knowledge of learning styles to positively influence school performance	Administer and interpret a learning style inventory
Individual Student Planning	Career	Standard B: Students will employ strategies to achieve future career success and satisfaction	Apply decision-making skills to career planning, course selection, and career transitions	Provide personal counseling on course selection
Responsive Services	Personal/Social	Standard C: Students will make decisions, set goals, and take necessary action to achieve goals	Know when peer pressure is influencing a decision	Describe a decision-making model, present a dilemma, and have counselee apply the model to the situation
System Support	Career	Standard C: Students will understand the relationship among personal qualities, education and training, and the world of work	Explain how work can help to achieve personal success and satisfaction	Design a brochure for teachers to use in relating career and subject matter

Figure 2.2

Internship Contract

(Continued)

Developmental Goals
1. Develop an evaluation form for assessing counseling effectiveness
2. Demonstrate effective classroom management skills

The goals stated above are to be completed by the trainee during the practicum experience. Throughout the academic term, if other opportunities are available to the trainee that would provide a valuable learning experience, the contract may be amended if the supervisors and trainee are in agreement.

I verify that the goals stated in the contract meet my approval.

Counselor Trainee   Date

Site Supervisor   Date

Program Supervisor   Date

Figure 2.2 *(Continued)*

Internship Contract

provides services under the supervision of a credentialed, professional school counselor, professional liability insurance is necessary not only for the trainee but also for the supervisor. This insurance may be obtained through ACA, ASCA, or the college or university with which the school counseling program is associated.

Checklist of Skills

Counseling skills involve structuring the session according to the trainee's style and counseling approach. Common learning strategies include listening to or receiving counseling tapes and analyzing case studies in which an evaluation is given. Too many trainees get overanxious about the evaluation and are afraid of how their grade will be affected. Trainees need to remember that this feedback is not directed at them as a person; it is about improving the skills or procedures observed and provides a benchmark for growth (Russell-Chapin & Ivey, 2004).

Release Form for Permission to Tape

During the clinical experiences the trainee will be required to do individual and group counseling and will receive feedback on the counseling dynamics and the skills exhibited. Because the trainee will be working with school-age youths, it is an ethical/legal obligation to obtain permission from the student as well as the parent or guardian. Because there may be on-site supervision by the program supervisor, and/or portions of the tapes may be used in the class for instructional purposes, the counselee and parent/guardian need to be informed that confidentiality cannot be completely guaranteed. If there is some reluctance to grant permission for taping, uneasiness may be alleviated if the camera is set to focus on the back of the student's head or just on the trainee. A sample parent/guardian release form is shown in Figure 2.3.

Trainees often complain about the difficulty in obtaining parent/guardian permission. Not only are parents/guardians reluctant to give permission for their son or daughter to see an individual they do not know, but school-age counselees also have difficulty remembering to take the permission slips home and returning it. The following suggestions have been helpful in managing these concerns:

1. Put the permission on brightly colored paper that is easily identifiable.
2. Call parents/guardians and explain how their son or daughter can help the trainee improve counseling skills.
3. Introduce the trainee to parent meetings such as the Parent Teacher Association (PTA).

Student's Name _____

Parent/Guardian Name _____

The school counseling program in the Department of Educational Psychology and Counseling at _____ conducts a practicum course each semester. The purpose of this class is to help the graduate student who will be serving as a school counselor trainee at _____ improve his or her counseling skills. The trainees are required to videotape and/or audiotape counseling sessions to be used for evaluation and/or supervision purposes only.

The counselor trainee _____ would like to work with your child _____ .
The professional school counselor _____ will be supervising the trainee in conjunction with the college/university supervisor _____
_____ .

- Precautions will be taken to protect the identity of your son or daughter
- The taping will be used for supervision only
- After the student trainee and supervisor have met to critique the trainee's counseling skills, the tape will be erased
- The tape or video recorder will be turned off at any time, and/or any portion of the tape will be erased if requested.

If you are interested in giving your son or daughter permission to help the counselor trainee, please sign below.

_____   _____
Parent/Guardian Signature   Date

I agree to assist the counselor trainee

_____   _____
Student (Counselee) Signature   Date

Figure 2.3

Parent/Guardian Release Form

4. Introduce the trainee to students so that they will know the procedures for contacting him or her.
5. Introduce the trainee to the teachers and other educational personnel with information on how the trainee may be contacted.
6. Ask counselees who are able to sign the forms to indicate their commitment and understanding of the purposes of the sessions.

After the tapes have been reviewed and are discussed with the trainee, the tapes are erased.

Individual Student Progress Log and Case Studies
The counseling relationship is an interactive process with a focus on helping the counselee identify goals to facilitate change (Faiver, Eisengart, & Colonna, 2004). Progress notes document the counselee's progress in working toward these goals. The trainee is cautioned to be careful in documenting only what is important and to check with the supervisor as to the amount of information that is necessary (Danowski, 2005). Trainees often voice concerns in writing a counseling session summary because the counselee's concern is typically unfocused

and vague and may not coincide with the counselor's assessment of the counseling concerns (Boylan et al., 2001). A structured form in Figure 2.4 may aid the trainee is describing the counseling session.

For the Supervisee

When the counseling relationship begins, it is not unusual for the novice counselor to feel anxiety and to think about the next thing to say or do. This distraction prevents the counselor from focusing on the counselee. The following section gives an overview of the stages of counseling and various resources that could be used to assist the counselee.

Stages of Counseling

The counseling process goes through four stages; these are not discrete stages as there is overlapping between the various stages. Various techniques and strategies are appropriate for each of these four stages, and several examples are included in this section.

Stage 1: Relationship building—establishing trust and rapport. For a trainee without much experience, it is sometimes helpful to have a structure that can alleviate the awkwardness that is

In writing notes, describe the counselee's presentation of his or her concern, and your impression of what you believe should be considered in working with this counselee. Keep in mind that the counselee's concerns may not always coincide with your assessment of what is occurring in his or her life. It is important to remember that some counselees may not be fully aware of what is really their issue, may have difficulty expressing themselves, or may present a problem they feel is more socially acceptable (e.g., grades) as a way of receiving help for more serious concerns such as abuse, depression, and so on.

The following examples can be helpful in writing case notes
The counselee seemed . . .
The counselee discussed . . .
The counselee appeared . . .
The counselee stated . . .

Additional items to consider in writing the progress notes include:

What is the nature of the concern(s)?

What are the precipitating factors in discussing this concern now? (e.g., divorce, loss, grades, etc.)

What are the physical symptoms that are reported?

What support system does the counselee have? (e.g., parents, friends, teachers, etc.)

What are the coping skills used by the counselee in past situations?

How has this concern impacted other aspects of the counselee's life? (e.g., school, work, relationships, eating, sleeping, etc.)

What are the counselee's interests/hobbies?

What are the counselee's living conditions?

What are the counselee's values and beliefs?

What stressors are influencing the counselee at this time or in the immediate past?

Figure 2.4

Individual Student Progress Log and Case Study

sometimes apparent during the initial sessions. Exercise 2.2 is a useful Stage 1 resource for trainees working in an elementary setting in the initial stage.

Stage 2: Assessment—gathering information that helps in understanding the counselee. Information is available from student records, teacher feedback, and parent information. Exercise 2.3 is designed to assist the trainee with suggestions for observation.

Stage 3: Intervention—choosing strategies that will assist the counselee in reaching his or her goal(s). After goals have been determined and interventions from various theoretical models chosen and implemented (Boylan et al., 2001), it is incumbent on the trainee to design an effective outcome assessment. A counselor can use an assessment form for elementary-age students to determine how the student is feeling when he or she enters the counseling session and again at the end of the session. To gain a better understanding of how the problem influences others in the counselee's life, the bottom of the worksheet in Exercise 2.4 may provide useful information.

Stage 4: Termination—ending each individual counseling session and the end of counseling. Termination occurs at the end of each individual session and then again when the counseling relationship ends. This process can be thought of as a bridge in which the counselee takes and applies the skills learned in counseling to the real-world setting. The last 5 minutes of a session can be spent asking the counselee to summarize what was discussed and learned in the time together as well as what behaviors the counselee will apply between sessions. The acronym WRAP (source unknown) is useful for trainees to remember when terminating sessions:

W—Warm feedback. Provide a statement that reflects the strengths of the counselee by emphasizing his or her positive characteristics and behaviors.
Counselor: "I am impressed with your ability to follow through on some of the homework assignments we discussed last time we met. I know that this took a lot of courage on your part."
R—Recall. Ask the counselee to summarize what he or she has learned in the session(s).
Counselor: "Now that our time together is ending, I would like you to summarize what we discussed and what you learned today."
A—Application. Ask the counselee to share how he or she will apply what was learned in the counseling session.
Counselor: "I was wondering what you will be doing when you leave this office to practice and continue the behaviors we discussed today."
P—Progress. Ask the counselee to evaluate the session.
Counselor: "On a scale of 1 to 10, with 10 being the best you have ever felt and 1 being the worst you have ever felt, where are you on the scale right now? What specifically happened to make you feel this way?"

Exercise 2.2

All About Me

My name is_____

My age is_____

My favorite color is _____

I feel sad when _____

I feel happy when _____

I am good at _____

One thing I would like to change about myself is _____

I live with _____

I like to be at school because _____

One thing I like to do at home is _____

My favorite things to do are_____

I am special because _____

Exercise 2.3

Behavioral Observations

Observing a counselee's behaviors provides a significant source of information in making a hypothesis about the individual who is the source of the observation.

Observation	Notes
What is your general impression of the counselee's physical appearance?	
Are the counselee's clothes appropriate for the season? Fit? Style?	
Does the counselee appear clean and neat or sloppy and dirty?	
Are the nonverbal messages and verbal communications congruent?	
Is there anything unusual about the counselee's body type? (e.g., short, heavy)	
What are the counselee's interactions with others? Are they appropriate?	
Do the counselee's behaviors seem developmentally appropriate?	
Is the counselee's affect appropriate?	
Is the counselee able to focus and concentrate?	
What is the counselee's attitude toward others?	
Does the counselee appear to be in good health?	
What are the counselee's grades? Is he or she working to ability?	

Practicum/Internship Time Log

Keeping track of how time was spent during the clinical experiences ensures that the trainee has engaged in appropriate activities and the strategies that were implemented to meet the identified contract goals. An example of a practicum time log is found in Figure 2.5. An example of an internship time log that encompasses the ASCA National Model components and activities for supervisees to gain experience as a professional school counselor in a developmental program is in Figure 2.6.

Journals

Some trainees note that journals provide a great opportunity to record thoughts, feelings, and behaviors and to learn from past mistakes. Various subjects that can be included in journals are found in Figure 2.7.

For the Site Supervisor and Supervisee

An evaluation from the site supervisor for the purposes of identifying the trainee's strengths and areas in which improvement is needed assists the trainee as well as the program supervisor who

Exercise 2.4

Counselee (Student) Assessment Worksheet

Choose the face that best describes how you are feeling

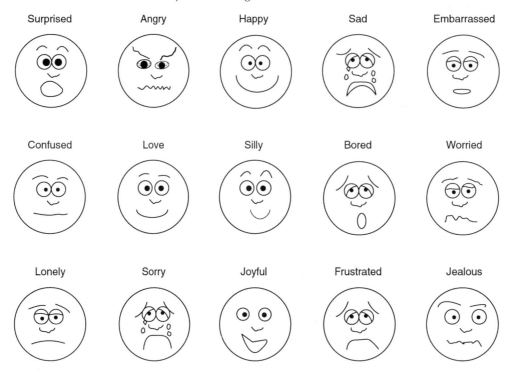

Now draw the face that shows your usual feelings when you are with different people. Draw their faces too.

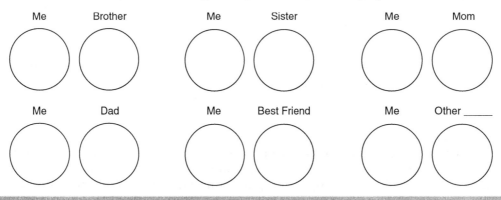

is required to assign a grade and credit. A procedure that is less known is the evaluation from the supervisee, who provides feedback to the program supervisor on the quality of the clinical site, the skills of the supervisor, and the school facilities. This section includes information about the evaluative process and the important role the professional school counselor plays when providing an assessment. Sample forms are included.

Evaluation From Site Supervisor

A site supervisor has a responsibility to evaluate the trainee's quality of services. This assessment will also be a factor in the trainee's final evaluation. An example of a skills checklist that can be used for assessment is found in chapter 11.

Trainee _____Term _____ 20_____

Supervisor _____

Date	Direct Contact Hours	Group/ Individual Supervision	Indirect Hours	Class Seminar	Consultation	Meetings With Site Supervisor	Other

Make copies as needed and return at the end of the term with total hours documented.

Total Hours							

Grand Total Hours _____

Signatures to Verify Hours

_____
Student   Date

_____
Site Supervisor   Date

_____
Program Supervisor   Date

Figure 2.5

Practicum Time Log

Date	Delivery Services	Foundation Components	Management	Accountability	Indirect Hours
	Guidance Curriculum (GC) Individual Planning (IP) Responsive Services (RS) Support Services (SS)	Philosophy and Mission (PM) Competencies (C)	Use of Data (D) Student Action Plan (AP) Calendars (C)	Results Report (RR) Evaluation (E)	Clerical (C) Scheduling (S) Duties (D)
7:00–7:30					
7:30–8:00					
8:00–8:30					
8:30–9:00					
9:00–9:30					
9:30–10:00					
10:00–10:30					
10:30–11:00					
11:00–11:30					
11:30–12:00					
12:00–12:30					
12:30–1:00					
1:00–1:30					
1:30–2:00					
2:00–2:30					
2:30–3:00					
3:00–3:30					
3:30–4:00					
4:00–4:30					
Total					

Total Accumulated Hours _____

Total Indirect Hours_____

Total Direct Hours _____

Trainee's Signature _____   Date _____

Site Supervisor's Signature _____   Date _____

Figure 2.6

Internship Time Log

Trainee Placement Evaluation

The trainee also has an opportunity to evaluate the quality of his or her clinical setting and supervisor efficacy. This feedback helps the program supervisor make decisions about future placements and whether or not the supervisor and site are appropriate. For instance, if the trainee was unable to meet with students in a private room because of limited space, this would probably not be the best placement for future trainees unless the situation can be improved. The site supervisor would also benefit from knowing things such as the trainee's feeling that not enough time was provided to meet on a regular basis, as well as any other concerns that

The following items may assist you in organizing your journal and items to include in the entries.

Activities
Summarize the activities and tasks you performed

Learning experiences	What have you learned from these activities?
Professional school counselor activities	What did you learn about the school counselor's duties?
Application of learning	How were classroom concepts applied to these activities?
Assessment of personal skills	What skills were needed to perform the activities?
Assessment of personal feelings	How did you feel about each of the activities?
Assessment of behaviors	What did you do in these activities?
Interpersonal communication	What communication skills helped or hindered the activity?
Legal/ethical issues	What ethical/legal issues did you encounter? How did you determine the course of action?
Miscellaneous	Summarize other issues not mentioned above

Meeting Personal Goals
How did the activities contribute to personal goal achievement?

Plan of Action
Make a list of the activities you will be involved in when you return to the setting

Application
How will you apply what you learned to a school counseling position?

Figure 2.7

Journal Entries

can be addressed. A sample trainee evaluation that was adopted from *The New Handbook of Counseling Supervision* by Borders and Leddick (1987) is provided in Figure 2.8.

A Professional Disclosure Statement
A statement that outlines the professional school counselor's education, experiences, the counseling relationship, the role of the counselor, and limits on confidentiality is known as a *professional disclosure statement*. Just as this statement is considered "best practices" for professional school counselors, it is also useful for school counselor trainees (Shaw, 2004). This type of record outlines the relationship among the supervisor, the trainee, and the individuals with whom the school counselor trainee will be interacting. In a school setting, teachers, administrators, and parents concerned about the presence of an unfamiliar person who will be working with children and adolescents will appreciate the information in this document. The professional disclosure statement contains the following information:

- Name and contact information
- Education and degrees earned, including present level of education

	Strongly disagree		Somewhat agree		Strongly agree		N/A
1. Provides me with useful feedback regarding skills	1	2	3	4	5	6	7
2. Helps me understand the school setting	1	2	3	4	5	6	7
3. Provides me with specific advice in areas I need to work on	1	2	3	4	5	6	7
4. Addresses my personal concerns as a counselor	1	2	3	4	5	6	7
5. Teaches me new alternative counseling strategies that I can use with my counselees	1	2	3	4	5	6	7
6. Helps me realize how counseling behavior influences relationships	1	2	3	4	5	6	7
7. Uses time for appropriate supervision	1	2	3	4	5	6	7
8. Discusses my strengths and capabilities	1	2	3	4	5	6	7
9. Enables me to brainstorm solutions, responses, and techniques that would be helpful in future counseling situations	1	2	3	4	5	6	7
10. Provides time for me to explain the reasons I chose particular counseling techniques	1	2	3	4	5	6	7
11. Makes me feel accepted and respected as a person	1	2	3	4	5	6	7
12. Deals appropriately with my feelings/thoughts in counseling sessions	1	2	3	4	5	6	7
13. Helps me to assess my own counseling behavior	1	2	3	4	5	6	7
14. Is competent and understands the supervision process	1	2	3	4	5	6	7
15. Is helpful with test administration and interpretation	1	2	3	4	5	6	7
16. Enables me to express opinions, questions, and concerns about my counseling	1	2	3	4	5	6	7
17. Makes certain students and teachers know who I am	1	2	3	4	5	6	7
18. Helps me clarify my counseling goals	1	2	3	4	5	6	7
19. Provides me with the opportunity to discuss the major problems I am facing with my counselees	1	2	3	4	5	6	7
20. Encourages me to conceptualize the counseling process differently	1	2	3	4	5	6	7
21. Motivates and encourages me	1	2	3	4	5	6	7
22. Gives me the chance to discuss personal issues related to my counseling	1	2	3	4	5	6	7
23. Is flexible enough for me to be spontaneous and creative	1	2	3	4	5	6	7
24. Provides suggestions for developing my counseling skills	1	2	3	4	5	6	7
25. Applies appropriate criteria for evaluating me	1	2	3	4	5	6	7
26. Helps me with classroom management concerns	1	2	3	4	5	6	7

Figure 2.8

Trainee Evaluation of Site Supervisor

Note. From "Evaluation of the Supervisor," by J. M. Bernard, 1987. In L. D. Borders and G. R. Leddick, *Handbook of Counseling Supervision* (Figure 7). Copyright 1987 by the American Counseling Association. Adapted with permission of the author.

- Names and numbers of all pertinent credentials (certificates, licenses)
- Names of supervisors
- Statement that a credential as a school counselor is being sought
- Description of the duties the trainee will be involved in
- An explanation of confidentiality including permission to tape and consultation with supervisors

Figure 2.9 is an example of a professional disclosure statement.

SUMMARY

Choosing a supervisor with the ability to provide a quality experience to the trainee is sometimes difficult. Not only does the supervisor need to have experience as a professional school counselor, training in supervision, and awareness of cultural issues in counseling, but he or she also needs to provide a trusting atmosphere in which concerns may be openly discussed. The site supervisor establishes a close partnership with the counselor education faculty in which each is aware of the expectations of the other. Sample forms that have been developed to assist in the training process of an effective supervisory process are included in this chapter.

The School Counseling Program in the Department of Educational Psychology and Counseling at the **University or College here** _____ conducts a school counseling experience each semester. During the _____ semester, **Trainee's Name**_____ will be working at _____ School under the supervision of a credentialed school counselor, **Supervisor's Name here** _____, and the university supervisor, Dr. _____.

Services Offered
Counselor practicum students may work with students, teachers, parents, and others in the school setting. These activities might include individual or small-group counseling for academic, career, and personal/social concerns. Large-group guidance, training of peer facilitators, or consulting with teachers and parents/guardians may also be required in an effort to gain experience and skills.

Practicum students are required to audiotape and/or videotape counseling sessions for the purpose of counseling supervision. All tapes made by the school counseling student will be erased at the end of the current semester.

Education and Experience
Before participating in practicum, students must possess a minimum of a bachelor's degree and be accepted into the school counseling program at the **Name of University or College here** _____. In addition, students must complete required coursework and demonstrate competency in and knowledge of counseling theories and techniques. The student has graduated from **Name of College or University here** _____.

Other educational experiences and training include being a **licensed teacher**, working for one year as a career counselor, and currently being educated and trained as a **Master's Degree School Counseling Student** at the **University or College Here** _____.

Professional Organizations
Member of the American School Counselor Association (ASCA)
Member of the State School Counselor Association
Member of the American Counseling Association (ACA)

Figure 2.9

Professional Disclosure Statement

REFERENCES

Bernard, J. M. (1987). Evaluation of the supervisor. In L. D. Borders & G. R. Leddick, *Handbook of counseling supervision* (pp. 62–70). Alexandria, VA: American Counseling Association.

Boylan, J. C., Malley, P. A., & Reilly, E. P. (2001). *Practicum and internship: Textbook and resource guide for counseling and psychotherapy.* New York: Brunner-Routledge.

Council for Accreditation of Counseling and Related Educational Programs. (2001). *CACREP standards.* Alexandria, VA: Author.

Danowski, W. A. (2005). *In the field: A real-life survival guide for the social work internship.* Boston: Pearson.

Ellis, M. V., & Robbins, E. S. (1993). Voices of care and justice in clinical supervision: Issues and interventions. *Counselor Education and Supervision, 32,* 203–212.

Faiver, C., Eisengart, S., & Colonna, R. (2004). *The counselor intern's handbook.* Belmont, CA: Brooks/Cole.

Garthwait, C. L. (2005). *The social work practicum: A guide and workbook for students* (3rd ed.). Boston: Pearson.

Henderson, D., Newsome, D., & Veach, L. (2005, April). *Using expressive arts in group supervision.* Paper presented at the American Counseling Association Annual Convention, Atlanta, GA.

Lister, J. L. (1966). Supervised counseling experiences: Some comments. *Counselor Education and Supervision, VI,* 69–72.

McCordy, K. G. (2003, Winter). Supervising counselor profile. *ACES Spectrum, 54,* 8–11.

Michaelson, S. D., Estrada-Hernández, N., & Wadsworth, J. S. (2003). A competency-based evaluation model for supervising novice counselors-in-training. *Rehabilitation Education, 17,* 215–223.

Pehrsson, D. E., & Ingram, M. A. (n.d.). *Supervision: A guide for beginning counselors.* Retrieved October 17, 2004, from http://www.shsu.edu/~piic/summer2001/pehrssoningram.htm

Russell-Chapin, L. A., & Ivey, A. E. (2004). *Your supervised practicum and internship: Field resources for turning theory into action.* Belmont, CA: Thomson.

Schmidt, J. J. (1990). Critical issues for school counselor performance appraisal and supervision. *School Counselor, 38,* 86–94.

Shaw, L. R. (2004, Summer). Professional disclosure practices: Supervisors have key responsibility with practicum students, interns. *ACES Spectrum, 64,* 1–4.

Spruill, D. A., & Benshoff, J. M. (2000). Helping beginning counselors develop a personal theory of counseling. *Counselor Education and Supervision, 40,* 70–80.

Williams, A. (1995). *Visual and active supervision.* New York: Norton.

PART II

Supervision Paradigms

CHAPTER 3

Models of Supervision

THE PURPOSE of this chapter is to

- assist trainees and supervisors to self-assess personal attitudes and values toward supervision
- present a discussion of the developmental, theory-specific, and integrated supervisory models
- provide additional resources for obtaining additional information on each model

I don't know what to do with my intern. She seems to do well with individual and group counseling, but when it comes to understanding classroom management, she just can't seem to get it. When we sit down for our session of supervision, she seems defensive, and at times I get the impression that she has personal problems that are interfering with her ability to be an effective counselor. Am I supposed to be a mentor to her, or am I supposed to be her personal counselor to help her sort out her issues?

The statement above is from a school counselor supervisor who was unsure of her role as a supervisor. Unless practicing school counselors receive training in supervision, they can only make assumptions as to how it is to be conducted. Many even use their own supervisory experience as a model for how it is to be conducted without regard to the trainee's personality, experiences, or educational background. Some supervisors presume that trainees should be responsible for directing their own training, whereas others believe that supervisees need constant, direct contact the entire time they are in the school setting.

There are various considerations surrounding the supervision process regardless of the structure. Numerous supervision models are cited in the counseling literature, and entire books have been written devoted to each theory and, as do counseling theories, each has similarities and differences. However, all of these models stress the importance of the supervisor–trainee relationship, the value of feedback, and the evaluative aspects of both the trainee and the supervisor. This chapter provides a summary of some of the more common supervisory models. Readers interested in learning more about a specific supervisory approach are encouraged to locate books that will describe each in more detail. Numerous resources are included in Appendix B for additional information on supervising concepts. Before a model is chosen, it is important for supervisors and trainees to determine their expectations from the supervisory experience.

FOR SUPERVISORS

As a supervisor, it is essential to reflect on yourself, your view of the world, past professional and personal experiences, and the education, values, and expectations of the individuals you will be supervising. Exercise 3.1 is designed to help you think about your role in the supervisory process.

Exercise 3.1

A Personal Reflection on "Super-VISION"

1. Think back over your personal life experiences throughout your life, and identify three experiences that were life-altering events.

   _____

   _____

2. Note the themes that are apparent in these recollections. Who are the significant people? What role do they play in your life? Which of these individuals still play a significant role in your life? What impact do they have on your personal/professional life?

   _____

   _____

3. What values do you feel are most significant in guiding your decisions?

   _____

   _____

4. How have these values, beliefs, and events influenced your counseling theory?

   _____

   _____

5. What factors will play an impact on your supervisory style?

   _____

   _____

6. Think about your experiences during the time you received supervision. What were the qualities of your supervisor that were most beneficial to you?

   _____

   _____

7. What were some of the traits your supervisor possessed that hindered your growth?

   _____

   _____

8. What were some of the supervisory activities that were most helpful?

   _____

   _____

9. What were some of the experiences you did not receive that would have been helpful to you?

   _____

   _____

FOR THE SUPERVISEE

A person's expectations about a situation influence whether the experience is regarded positively or negatively. As a supervisee, reflecting on who you are and your role within the profession provides an opportunity to assess your expectations of supervision. Exercise 3.2 is designed to assist in thinking about your expectations of supervision.

Supervisors of school counselor trainees want to know what is supposed to happen in supervision, what supervisors and supervisees actually do, how the trainee grows, and how supervision influences counselees and others with whom trainees interact (Watkins, 1998). Borders and Brown (2005) stated that the supervisory process is similar to the counselee—

Exercise 3.2

Who Am I As a Counselor-in-Training?

1. Who are some of the significant people who have influenced your life?

   _____

   _____

2. What are some of the experiences you have had that led you to the profession of school counseling?

   _____

   _____

3. What values and beliefs help guide your decision making?

   _____

   _____

4. How might these values and beliefs interfere with your counseling ability?

   _____

   _____

5. What qualities are you looking for in a site supervisor?

   _____

   _____

6. What specific skills do you want your site supervisor to teach you?

   _____

   _____

7. How do you respond to feedback that you may receive that could be less than favorable?

   _____

   _____

counselor relationship in that a close facilitative relationship based on trust is desired (Holloway & Wolleat, 1981, as cited in Fernando & Hulse-Killacky, 2005).

There are several considerations in choosing a supervisory model. These include the number of years of experience as a school counselor, the school setting and structure, supervisor training and style, multicultural issues including race and ethnicity, gender, sexual orientation, the needs of the supervisor, and so on. Developmental, theory-specific, and integrated supervisory models (Bernard & Goodyear, 2004) are summarized in this chapter.

A DEVELOPMENTAL MODEL OF SUPERVISION

People have numerous experiences throughout life, and their strengths, values, and beliefs help them discover who they are. Through supervision, one gains a better understanding of the school counseling profession, including a greater insight into one's strengths, areas that need to be improved, and how one has grown cognitively, affectively, and behaviorally. Developmental models of supervision rely heavily on understanding self and others, personal motivational levels, and individual autonomy (Russell-Chapin & Ivey, 2004). Although each developmental model emphasizes some training aspects over others, they all describe individual behavior change across time, give attention to the factors that facilitate change (Stoltenberg & Delworth, 1987), and note the changes that occur in the supervisory relationship.

Stoltenberg and Delworth's (1987) integrated developmental model (IDM) is the most widely used model of counselor development because it describes typical trainee behavior at different levels and appropriate supervisor responses to the trainees at each level (Bernard &

Goodyear, 2004). The IDM is the developmental model summarized in this chapter. In this model trainee development occurs through three levels, with changes in three areas: self- and other awareness, motivation, and autonomy (Stoltenberg, McNeill, & Delworth, 1998).

Level 1 supervisees are new to the field, with limited direct experiences in counseling. The trainee's primary affect can be described primarily as confusion and anxiousness, with a marked dependency on the supervisor. The trainee shows little self-understanding (Borders & Brown, 2005; Stoltenberg et al., 1998) at this level. Typical supervisor and trainee behaviors at this level are found in Table 3.1.

The Level 2 trainee has more experience and is feeling more comfortable as a trainee. There is a gradual change in the focus from self to that of the counselee; this occurs as the trainee is exposed to more diverse individuals with multiple concerns. The trainee vacillates between autonomy and dependency and in levels of motivation as he or she experiences success and frustration (Stoltenberg et al., 1998). Skill flexibility and a sense of humor are more frequent at this level than during the initial stage. Typical behaviors of the trainee and supervisor are found in Table 3.2.

At Level 3 the trainee is better able to make decisions and has a greater ability to empathize and understand the counselee's view. The trainee is more motivated to learn new approaches and is better able to integrate skills and understanding, which leads to increased autonomy (Stoltenberg et al., 1998). Typical trainee behavioral traits are in Table 3.3, with appropriate suggestions for supervisors working with trainees at this level.

The developmental models are based on the trainee's developmental level, experience, skills, and confidence. Several books that describe developmental models in more detail include *Counselor Supervision: Principles, Process, and Practice* (3rd ed.), published by Brunner-Routledge (Bradley & Ladany, 2001). The chapter by Peggy Whiting, Loretta Bradley, and Kristen Planny titled "Supervision-Based Developmental Models of Counselor Supervision" provides more specific information on developmental approaches. In addition, the book by Cal Stoltenberg, Brian McNeill, and Ursula Delworth titled *IDM Supervision: An Integrated Developmental Model for Supervising Counselors and Therapists* (1998), published by John Wiley, thoroughly discusses this approach and is discussed in greater detail in chapter 4. Theory-specific models view supervision as meeting trainee needs using the same process as identified counseling models, whereas the integrated models address trainee needs by identifying the supervisory role that will best meet these needs (Fernando & Hulse-Killacky, 2005).

THEORY-SPECIFIC SUPERVISION MODELS

Supervisors who adhere strictly to a specific counseling theory such as cognitive–behavioral, control, solution-focused, and so on may view supervision as being similar to the counseling process and as a result supervise from the same theoretical orientation. Too often, individuals make the erroneous assumption that if an individual is an outstanding counselor, he or she would also be an exceptional supervisor. This is not always the case. For instance, if a supervisor depended solely on psychoanalytic theory, supervision would focus on such issues as the

Table 3.1

Level 1 Behaviors

Trainee	Supervisor
Anxious/insecure	Encourages autonomy
Dependent on supervisor	Nonjudgmental
Little insight/focus is primarily on self	Directives provided
Black-and-white thinking	
Apprehensive but highly motivated	Structure provided
Imitates supervisor	Supportive and encouraging

Table 3.2

Level 2 Behaviors

Trainee	Supervisor
Conflict between autonomy/dependency	Provide an autonomous environment
Motivation fluctuates	
Overconfident/overwhelmed	Less structure provided
More focus on the counselee	Specific skills are taught
Recognition of need for more skills	Directive when trainee is uncertain

trainee's early childhood experiences, defense mechanisms, or transference and counter-transference. A person-centered supervisor may focus on the areas of self-discovery and personal growth (Rogers, 1961, as cited in Russell-Chapin & Ivey, 2004) in a supervisory environment that provides the conditions of genuineness, empathy, and warmth using a nondirective style.

A benefit of the theory-specific approach is that if the supervisee and trainee share the same philosophy, the supervisor can model the technical aspects of this theory so that the trainee will be able to practice and adapt with feedback (Cyc-Online, 2001). The downside of this model is that the trainee may not have the opportunity to practice and adapt other theoretical approaches that may be more suitable with various counselees. Specific books in which the reader can obtain more information on this theoretical approach include *The Supervisory Relationship: A Contemporary Psychodynamic Approach* (2001) by Mary Gail Frawley-O'Dea and Joan E. Sarnat, published by Guilford Press. The *Handbook of Psychotherapy Supervision* (1997) by C. Edward Watkins, published by John Wiley, is another reference.

The integrated approach to supervision combines the theory-specific and developmental models. This model is discussed in the remainder of this chapter because of its relevance to school counseling supervision.

INTEGRATED MODELS

A supervisor using an integrated approach will take on different roles throughout the supervisory process (Bernard, 1997; Hess, 1981; Williams, 1995). The *discrimination model* developed by Janine Bernard is one example of an integrated approach to supervision in that the supervisor assumes one of three roles: teacher, counselor, or consultant, depending on the function and focus of supervision. Roles change several times during a single session (Bartlett, 1983) as a result of the knowledge that the supervisor is trying to convey.

The Teacher Role

The role of the teacher is chosen when the supervisor has made the conscious choice to instruct the supervisee. As the trainee first begins his or her clinical experience, anxiety and

Table 3.3

Level 3 Behaviors

Trainee	Supervisor
Increased confidence	More collegial with sharing information
More insight	Confrontational in some areas
More motivated	Discriminatory role chosen based on trainee needs
Conditional dependence on supervisor	More consultative
Goals set by trainee	Encouragement to self-evaluate

uncertainty are common characteristics. Supervisees report that they want their supervisor to be directive (Rabinowitz, Heppner, & Roehlke, 1986, as cited in Williams, 1995), knowledge-able, instructional by providing techniques and structure (Ronnestad & Skovholt, 1993, as cited in Whisenhunt, Romans, Boswell, & Carlozzi, 1997), and supportive (Carifio & Hess, 1987, as cited in Williams, 1995). In a teaching role, supervisors help trainees find solutions to problems that they are encountering, allow trainees to make mistakes that facilitate self- and professional discovery, and allow trainees to apply knowledge to an actual setting (Williams, 1995).

The Counselor Role

The counselor role is assumed when the trainee's personal needs are interfering with the counseling process or the growth of the counselee. The focus is on assisting the trainee with personal issues that may interfere with productive counseling. This role is not without critics who believe that the process of supervision and counseling should remain separate (Williams, 1995). Williams suggested to these skeptics that supervisors can ethically handle this dilemma by exploring with the trainee how these personal issues interfere with his or her performance as a counselor and discussing strategies that may resolve these concerns.

The Consultant Role

A consultant role is assumed when the supervisor believes that providing options rather than solutions better facilitates trainee learning. When the trainee is able to identify his or her personal needs, the supervisor is in a better position to help the trainee with problem solving (Williams, 1995). The supervisor as a consultant provides the trainee with the freedom to think through situations and make decisions, and the supervisor allows flexibility and independence in working out problems. As a consultant, the primary role is attending to the interactions between the trainee and the individuals with whom he or she assists.

The supervisor determines the role that will best provide the trainee with the skills and knowledge that are needed. However, some theorists believe that there is a fourth role the supervisor should assume, that of evaluator (Williams, 1995).

The Evaluator Role

The evaluator is often regarded as the least favorable of all the supervisory roles. It is never easy to provide negative feedback to trainees, and too many supervisors avoid this task by offering glowing comments and exceptional grades (Williams, 1995). This procedure does not help the trainee grow personally or professionally, and when areas to improve are not targeted, it eventually proves detrimental to other individuals who work with the trainee, and later when the trainee becomes a counselor. Evaluation should not take place only at the conclusion of a clinical experience; it should occur routinely (Williams, 1995). At some point the supervisor may have to make the decision as to how well the trainee is performing in various areas. In some cases the decision will need to be made about whether the trainee is appropriate for the profession (Johnston & Gysbers, 1967). Supervisees want and need feedback. In a study by Kadushin (1993, as cited in Williams, 1995), trainees identified the failure to provide feedback as the greatest supervisor shortcoming. The supervisor makes a conscious choice as to the role he or she is going to assume based on the trainee's performance in various focal areas, including process skills, conceptualization skills, and personalization skills (Bernard, 1997; Russell-Chapin & Ivey, 2004).

THE SUPERVISORY FOCAL POINTS

Process skills are the trainee's observable, intentional counseling behaviors that include *attending skills,* such as questioning, encouraging, paraphrasing, reflection, and summarization. Supervisees also need to effectively use *influencing skills,* such as feedback, advice, self-disclosure, interpretation, and logical consequences, that invite counselees to gain insight and take appropriate action. Furthermore, trainees can utilize skills that can direct discussion to areas that may affect the counselee, such as behavior, attitudes, environment, or other individuals (Nugent, 1994).

Conceptualization skills include the trainee's ability to understand the counselee's perspective, identify themes, choose interventions, and recognize counselee goal attainment (Bernard, 1997). Understanding and hypothesizing about what is going on with the counselee before, during, and after counseling sessions is a skill that takes time and practice and that can be learned through supervisor probes and inquiry.

Personalization skills include the ability of the trainee to listen to supervisor feedback, adapt behaviors based on this information, assume responsibility for learning, and strive for greater personal growth (Bernard, 1997).

Table 3.4 outlines the various supervisory roles (teacher, counselor, consultant, or evaluator) within each of the skill foci (process, conceptualization, and personalization skills). The supervisor assumes different roles when focusing on the trainee's skills. The role that is chosen depends on what the trainee needs.

When the supervisor instructs the trainee about various issues, then the supervisor can be viewed as a teacher (Stoltenberg & Delworth, 1987). If the supervisor explores the trainee's personal issues that may interfere with counseling, then the supervisor may be seen as a counselor. When the supervisor offers the supervisee assistance to benefit a third person (student, teacher, parent), then the supervisor may be seen as a consultant. If the supervisor provides an assessment and corrective feedback, then the supervisor may be seen as an evaluator (Williams, 1995).

With the major roles the supervisor assumes, it is not unusual for the supervisor to ask, "What role do I enact when, and at what time?" According to Williams (1995), several questions guide this decision based on the skill foci, counselee, and setting:

- Is the focus on the counselee or personal feedback on ability?
- Should the focus be on learning new skills?
- Is learning new skills the focus of feedback?
- Is understanding the counselee the area of concern?
- What suggestions would improve the trainee's skill?
- To whom do I compare the trainee's ability?

Table 3.4

Role of Supervisor and Skill Focus

Focus	Teacher	Counselor	Consultant	Evaluator
Process skills	Instructing trainee about skills of reflection, para-phrasing	Teaching the trainee who has difficulty using silence as a therapeutic skill	Instructing trainee about using creative techniques in counseling sessions	Providing feedback on the use and effectiveness of skills used by the trainee
Conceptualization skills	Assisting trainee to look at session themes	Probing trainee's personal thoughts about the counselee	Providing tasks for trainee to practice prior to a problematic session	Assessing how well the trainee works through the counseling stages
Personalization skills	Inquiring about trainee's anxiety in working with adolescent females	Asking probing questions about trainee's thoughts and feelings in a session	Supplying resources and situations for the trainee to contemplate personal beliefs and values	Providing feedback to trainee regarding personal growth and areas on which to work

Whatever supervisory role is chosen will affect the trainees' sense of self-efficacy and will be based on the needs of the supervisees and supervisors (Goodyear & Bernard, 1998, as cited in Fernando & Hulse-Killacky, 2005). Exercise 3.3 is designed as an aid for the supervisor in identifying the role that he or she most commonly assumes. More effective supervision occurs when a role is assumed to center attention on a specific skill.

The role with the highest number of responses in Exercise 3.3 may give you an indication of the role in which you are most comfortable. Supervisors are most effective when they perform each of these roles because the trainee is shortchanged when only one or two of the roles are selected.

There are a number of supervisory models from which to choose. Deciding what supervisory model to choose depends on issues such as your own orientation to the world, perception of change, years of experience as a school counselor, multicultural training, and the needs of the trainee.

SUMMARY

Numerous theories of supervision guide the supervision process. When supervisors do not have training in supervision, school counselor trainees may not receive a premium experience.

Exercise 3.3

Identifying the Supervisor Role

To help you identify the role you are most comfortable as a supervisor, think back to a time when you provided supervision for a school counselor trainee. Place an "X" next to the activities that best characterize you in this situation.

1. _____ Identifies appropriate tasks
2. _____ Provides emotional support
3. _____ Attends to the trainee's style of counseling
4. _____ Assesses trainee goal attainment
5. _____ Helps trainee establish goals
6. _____ Provides time for trainee to process feelings
7. _____ Observes trainee's activities
8. _____ Checks whether trainee implemented interventions
9. _____ Suggests interventions
10. _____ Gives trainee a chance to analyze feeling toward a counselee
11. _____ Collaborates with counselee
12. _____ Follows up on trainee's progress
13. _____ Models interventions
14. _____ Explores trainee's personal identification with counselees
15. _____ Allows trainee leeway in planning activities
16. _____ Provides trainee with feedback
17. _____ Explains rationale for strategy
18. _____ Works with trainees on difficulties within the school setting
19. _____ Experiments with various intervention methods
20. _____ Helps trainee access strengths and weaknesses
21. _____ Provides and discusses reading materials
22. _____ Paraphrases and clarifies trainee's stories
23. _____ Provides options rather than answers
24. _____ Conducts regular evaluation sessions

A. Add up the number of "X's" you have next to Numbers 1, 5, 9, 13, 17, 21: _____
This number corresponds to your role as a teacher. (This role is assumed when the supervisor chooses to instruct the trainee.)

B. Add up the number of "X's" you have next to Numbers 2, 6, 10, 14, 18, 22: _____
This number corresponds to your role as a facilitator/counselor. (This role is assumed when the supervisor assists the trainee in looking at personal issues affecting his or her performance.)

C. Add up the number of "X's" you have next to Numbers 3, 7, 11, 15, 19, 23: _____
This number corresponds to your role as a consultant. (This role is assumed when the supervisor provides options to allow the trainee to make his or her own decisions.)

D. Add up the number of "X's" you have next to Numbers 4, 8, 12, 16, 20, 24: _____
This number corresponds to your role as an evaluator. (The supervisor chooses this role when a judgment is made about the trainee's performance.)

Furthermore, relationships may be less effective when developmental issues are not recognized and addressed. This chapter summarizes developmental, theory-specific, and integrated supervision models. Supervision is more than providing a supervisee with the types of activities normally performed by a professional school counselor. This relationship includes attending to the needs of the counselee by assuming various training roles, particularly when focusing on the trainee's counseling process, conceptualization, and personalization skills.

REFERENCES

Bartlett, W. E. (1983). A multidimensional framework for the analysis of supervision of counseling. *The Counseling Psychologist, 11*, 9–17.

Bernard, J. M. (1997). The discrimination model. In C. E. Watkins (Ed.), *Handbook of psychotherapy supervision* (pp. 310–327). New York: Wiley.

Bernard, J. M., & Goodyear, R. K. (2004). *Fundamentals of clinical supervision* (3rd ed.). Boston: Pearson.

Borders, L. D., & Brown, L. L. (2005). *The new handbook of counseling supervision*. Mahwah, NJ: Erlbaum/Lahaska Press.

Bradley, L. J., & Ladany, N. (Eds.). (2001). *Counselor supervision: Principles, process, and practice* (3rd ed.). Philadelphia: Brunner-Routledge.

Cyc-Online. (2001, January). Supervision models. *The International Child & Youth Care Network, 24*. Retrieved October 17, 2004, from http://www.cyc-net/cyc-online/cyc-1001-supervision%20 models.html

Fernando, D. M., & Hulse-Killacky, D. (2005). The relationship of supervisory styles to satisfaction with supervision and the perceived self-efficacy of master's level counseling students. *Counselor Education and Supervision, 44*, 293–304.

Frawley-O'Dea, M. G., & Sarnat, J. E. (2001). *The supervisory relationship: A contemporary psychodynamic approach*. New York: Guilford Press.

Hess, A. K. (1981). *Psychotherapy supervision: Theory, research, and practice*. New York: Wiley.

Johnston, J. A., & Gysbers, N. C. (1967). Essential characteristics of a supervisory relationship in a counseling practicum. *Counselor Education and Supervision, VI*, 335–340.

Nugent, F. A. (1994). *An introduction to the profession of counseling* (2nd ed.). New York: Merrill.

Russell-Chapin, L. A., & Ivey, A. E. (2004). *Your supervised practicum and internship: Field resources for turning theory into action*. Belmont, CA: Thomson.

Stoltenberg, C. D., & Delworth, U. (1987). *Supervising counselors and therapists: A developmental approach*. San Francisco: Jossey-Bass.

Stoltenberg, C. D., McNeill, B., & Delworth, U. (1998). *IDM supervision: An integrated developmental model for supervising counselors and therapists*. San Francisco: Jossey-Bass.

Watkins, C. E. (Ed.). (1997). *Handbook of psychotherapy supervision*. New York: Wiley.

Watkins, C. E. (1998). Psychotherapy supervision in the 21st century: Some pressing needs and impressing possibilities. *Journal of Psychotherapy Practice and Research, 7*, 93–101.

Whisenhunt, B. J., Romans, J. S., Boswell, D. L., & Carlozzi, A. F. (1997). Counseling students' perceptions of supervisory modalities. *The Clinical Supervisor, 15*, 79–90.

Williams, A. (1995). *Visual and active supervision: Roles, focus, technique*. New York: Norton.

CHAPTER 4

The Supervisory Process From a Developmental Perspective

THE PURPOSE of this chapter is to

- summarize developmental supervision
- help the trainee and supervisor have a better awareness of the growth that occurs during supervision
- discuss supervisory strategies that focus on self- and other awareness, motivation, and autonomy

My supervisor amazed me. I watched her work with elementary-age children and it seemed as if she could work miracles with them. I wanted to be just like her. I tried to do everything that she did. I used her worksheets, and I even structured my counseling sessions as she did. She seemed to like this relationship until I started doing things a little differently—more like my own style of working with children. It was at this time that I noticed a change in our relationship. She would resolve issues that I felt I should have solved, and I noticed that she just didn't seem as friendly as she had when I first started. I kept asking her if I was doing anything wrong, and she assured me that I hadn't. Yet, I left the internship feeling as if I had done something to jeopardize our relationship.

The statement above is from a student after she completed her internship in an elementary school. What she and her supervisor did not recognize were the stages of growth and development that occur in both the trainee and supervisor during the supervision process. If both individuals had been aware of the professional developmental process, each probably would have left supervision feeling satisfied and productive. The previous chapter summarized several supervisor models. This chapter provides a more thorough discussion of supervision from a developmental perspective.

DEVELOPMENTAL SUPERVISION

There are a number of developmental models of supervision (Borders & Brown, 2005) that describe the behavioral, affective, and cognitive changes that occur in both the supervisor and the trainee across time, the reasons for these changes, and how growth can be encouraged (Stoltenberg & Delworth, 1998). Each developmental model varies in the number of stages, with typical supervisee behaviors that progress from simple to more complex. In addition, each model is based on the various roles and expectations (Locher & Melchert, 1997). The integrated developmental model (IDM) as proposed by Stoltenberg and Delworth (1998) reflects the most recent developmental model (Murray, Portman, & Maki, 2003). Some theorists (Bernard & Goodyear, 2004) consider the IDM as the most popular model of counselor development. Not only does the IDM describe trainee behavior at different levels and how supervisors can work with trainees as they gain more experience, but it also incorporates the developmental needs of the trainee into four levels. Various focus areas highlighted at each of the levels include self- and other awareness, motivation, and autonomy (Stoltenberg & Delworth, 1998).

THE DEVELOPMENT OF TRAINEES

Level 1: Orientation

The initial supervision session is the first time the supervisor and counselor meet with the goal of formulating the context for supervision and goal setting (Hess, 1986). If the supervisor creates a trustful environment, the trainee may feel comfortable in expressing feelings, setting goals, and asking questions. Supervisory guidelines, ethical and legal concerns, supervision procedure, and logistical considerations are additional topics to be discussed during the initial meetings (Pehrsson & Ingram, n.d.).

Trainees are highly anxious and often have a fear of saying or doing the wrong thing, and they have mixed feelings of excitement and apprehension as they work with a counselee for the first time (Borders & Brown, 2005). Their thinking tends to be rigid. For example, based on their knowledge of multicultural issues, the trainees may assume that Asian American counselees are interested in the math and science areas without regard to the individual counselee's culture. At this level the supervisee is highly motivated but insecure, with little insight into the counseling process. The supervisor needs to emphasize structure, instructional directives, and support (Chagnon & Russell, 1995). Most important, the supervisory contract needs to be negotiated that reflects both the trainee and supervisor goals (see examples of contracts in chapter 2).

Level 2: Transformation

During the middle stages of training there is noticeable skill improvement, with a greater understanding of counseling dynamics. As the supervisee becomes more comfortable with the counselor role, there is a realization that the supervisor is not an authority figure but rather a helper (Hess, 1986). Even though supervisees are now more aware of their strengths and weaknesses, they often feel as if they are on an emotional roller coaster. There is uneasiness when they are faced with new situations but also pride when they successfully complete a task (Borders & Brown, 2005). Trainees at this stage accept feedback more readily yet still desire a supportive environment in which to make decisions and to experiment with new strategies.

Level 3: Professional Direction

Level 3 is reached during the later stages of clinical experiences. The skills and strategies that have been successful form the foundation of the trainee's counselor identity (Hess, 1986). For instance, if the trainee has been successful with scaling techniques to determine counseling focus, this strategy will be used as a scaffold on which to build more strategies.

Level 4: Integrated

The final level is comparable with what has been defined as a "master counselor" (Murray et al., 2003). Some developmental models of supervision do not recognize this last stage as relevant to preservice supervision because most counselors who graduate from their degree program are primarily in the middle stages of development (Borders & Brown, 2005). The counselor at this advanced level is seen as an autonomous individual (Loganbill et al., 1982, as cited in Hess, 1986), capable of independent practice and able to seek supervision when needed.

AREAS OF FOCUS

As the trainee works through the four levels of development, the IDM places attention on various foci, including self- and other awareness, motivation, and autonomy.

Self- and Other Awareness

Just as counselors ask their counselees to self-evaluate, it is as important for supervisors to ask their trainees to self-reflect. It is a mistake to assume that this self-reflection will occur naturally (Wubbolding, Brickell, Loi, & Al-Rashidi, 2001). In the beginning the trainee is more focused on him- or herself, with many self-doubts expressed as "Am I doing this right?" or "What should I say/do next?" With experience the trainee better understands how counseling affects counselees, and he or she has a greater ability to comprehend the counselee's emotional and cognitive states. Wubbolding (1998, as cited in Rosenthal, 1998; Wubbolding et al., 2001) provided several reflection questions the supervisor can ask:

- Are you headed in the direction you would like to go?
- Are your specific actions effective in getting what you want?
- Does your belief about change help or detract from your ability to work with counselees?
- Are your beliefs in line with the mission of the supervision site?
- Is your present level of commitment the best it can be?
- How can you increase the quality of your services?

Motivation

The trainee's enthusiasm fluctuates when exposed to various experiences and successes. Success often leads to a higher motivational level and a drive to try something new. Readiness for tackling new tasks is a mixture of the perception of task difficulty, willingness to take risks, and other past experiences (Thompson, 2004). However, when the trainee attempts a new activity that did not produce the expected results, the motivational level may decrease when confronted with a new situation.

Autonomy

In the beginning stages, trainees have a strong need to be advised and instructed (Stoltenberg, McNeill, & Delworth, 1998). However, with success and experience, the trainee will seek greater independence and autonomy in decision making.

When the supervisor sustains a higher level of functioning than the supervisee, an optimum learning environment is maintained. This gap both encourages and challenges the trainee to move to a higher level of functioning (Borders & Brown, 2005).

Developmental processes do not just guide the supervisee; the supervisor also progresses through developmental changes that influence his or her affect, cognition, and behavior (Stoltenberg & Grus, 2004). Supervision development has not received much attention in the literature (Hess, 1986), yet an understanding of these stages may assist the supervisor with professional and personal awareness. As stated by a middle school counselor, "As a supervisor, I learned from my supervisee, as I hope she learned from me."

FOR SITE SUPERVISORS

The Developmental Stages of the Supervisor

It is important to recognize that supervisors go through various developmental stages as well, and they gain a better understanding of their identity as a supervisor as they progress through the stages. The developmental stages include the introductory, transformation, and identity consolidation stages.

Stage 1: The Introductory Stage

Once the clinical experiences have ended, the trainee is ready to enter the counseling profession and is considered as a colleague with equal status. At this point there is a role change, with an assumption that this neophyte is now able to assume the same responsibilities as experienced counselors and is therefore qualified to serve as a supervisor.

A natural tendency is to provide supervision in the same way that this individual had been supervised even though this may not be in the best interest of the trainee. Feelings of self-consciousness, unawareness of supervision resistance, uncertainty of when to intervene, and being uninformed of the various supervision stages and relevant research could jeopardize a productive relationship. Furthermore, the situation may be exacerbated when the trainee is older and more experienced in counseling skills than the supervising school counselor. With more experience and training, the supervisor may begin to view supervision as a professional responsibility, which could serve as a catalyst to seek more training (Hess, 1986).

Stage 2: Transformation
With more practice the supervisor begins to recognize what works and what does not work during supervisory sessions. The supervisor is now able to realize his or her impact on the trainee and is able to give the trainee useful feedback without fear of intruding into the trainee's personal issues. There is an awareness of the trainee's needs and the supervisory role (teacher, counselor, consultant, evaluator; see chapter 3) that best fits (Hess, 1986). A parallel process occurs during supervision. Just as the trainee develops a more integrated counselor identity, the supervisor also gains a better understanding of his or her identity as a supervisor.

Stage 3: Supervisor Identity Consolidation
During the final stage the supervisor is able to view the trainee's needs through a clearer lens, but disappointment will result if the supervisee believes his or her personal needs are unaddressed (Hess, 1986). To make certain that the trainee's expectations are met, the supervisor could ask, "What do you need to make this time more productive?" or "Is there something that I can do that would be more helpful?" Despite the supervisor's best efforts, the following situations are examples of how the trainee may express resistance and disappointment:

- The trainee may believe that the supervisor does not have much to offer if a supervisee has had counseling experience in other settings or if the supervisor is younger than the supervisee (Hess, 1981).
- Supervision may be viewed as confusing and an infringement on time if the supervisor lacks supervisory training and experience (Hess, 1981).
- The trainee or supervisor may express dissatisfaction by being late for appointments or neglect to schedule supervisory time (Hess, 1986).
- The trainee may introduce materials or strategies that contradict the information or advice previously provided by the supervisor (Hess, 1986).
- Supervision may be trivialized through small talk or through off-task behaviors.

When the supervisor notices these behaviors, refocusing the supervisory process by addressing the supervisee's needs and goals can assist the trainee.

FOR SITE AND PROGRAM SUPERVISORS

Supervisory Strategies Throughout the Process

Both the supervisor and trainee will grow and change as a result of their supervisory relationship. Administrative, clinical, and developmental supervision are different types of supervision that facilitate growth. Administrative supervision relates to the activities that focus on fulfilling school requirements and accountability (Spruill & Benshoff, 2000). Activities include scheduling guidance classes, documentation, and collaboration. Clinical supervision relates to the direct services the school counselor provides (Murray et al., 2003), such as using a particular counseling orientation, appropriately using skills, conceptualizing cases, and evaluating counselee progress. Developmental supervision promotes personal and professional growth. In a school setting, typical opportunities include an awareness of strengths, awareness and appropriate use of legal and ethical issues, and attending professional meetings

(Henderson, 1994). Unfortunately, clinical and developmental supervision have only received cursory attention not only because of the misconception that there is no need for this type of supervision in a school environment but also because of the lack of qualified individuals available to perform this type of supervision.

On the first day of one of my practicum classes, we were discussing class requirements and supervision expectations. All of these students were neophytes as none had a background in education outside of a fieldwork experience. The only experience any of them had in counseling was from the role-plays that took place in their counseling theories class. As the students were sharing the events of meeting with their site supervisor for the first time, I was surprised when one of these students revealed that her supervisor expected her to lead a study skills group during the second week of her practicum experience. Naturally, this student expressed anxiety and worry at the prospect of leading a group of seventh-grade students without any prior experience. She was not developmentally or professionally ready for this challenge. Supervisors need to ask themselves, "What activities are most appropriate at each supervisory level?" or "What procedures are most useful in focusing on the areas of self- and other awareness, motivation, and autonomy?" The following sections outline various supervisory strategies in the administrative, clinical, and developmental domains during the process.

Supervisor Strategies During Level 1 (Orientation)

During the orientation level, the supervisor plays a major role in providing a comfortable environment while structuring how supervision is to occur. The various supervisory roles identified in the discrimination model by Bernard (1979) are also included in this discussion, in addition to the evaluative task that is an additional supervisory responsibility.

The supervisor takes on a teacher role when providing answers to trainee questions, instructing in techniques, or informing about school rules and regulations. The counselor role will be assumed when there is a need to facilitate the trainee's self-growth, the consultant role when providing options and alternatives (Pearson, 2004), and the evaluator role when providing feedback during the supervisory process.

Administrative Supervision During Level 1 (Orientation)

Administrative supervision includes structuring the sessions, providing time for the supervisee to discuss concerns, introducing the trainee to personnel, and informing him or her of the school policy and procedures. Essential questions to be addressed by the supervisor and trainee include the following:

1. What are the supervisee's goals?
2. What goals do I, as a supervisor, wish to accomplish?
3. What activities will assist in accomplishing these goals?
4. How often will we meet for supervision? When will these meetings occur? What procedures will be used for supervision?
5. Which sessions will be audiotaped or videotaped? What are the procedures for making use of the equipment?
6. What room(s) will be available for counseling sessions?
7. What are the procedures for dismissing a student from class? Returning a student to class?
8. What are the school rules?
9. What are the behavior management policies for the school?
10. What is the supervisor's scope of training?
11. What is the supervisee's scope of training?
12. What are the procedures to be followed for emergency situations? Who should be contacted?
13. What assessment tools will be used?
14. How are absences to be handled?

15. What is the dress code?
16. What procedures should be followed for contacting students? Parents? Teachers?
17. How will the teachers/administrators/parents/students be introduced to the trainee?

It is not unusual for supervisors to worry about whether their focus should be on the trainee or the counselee in making certain that both are receiving the best care possible (Hansen, Pound, & Petro, 1976, as cited in Bartlett, 1983).

Clinical and Developmental Supervision During Level 1 (Orientation)

Some supervisory models focus on case conceptualization, counseling skills, and administrative tasks, with little attention to self-awareness. Because inexperienced trainees are initially engrossed in their own thoughts and feelings and trying to figure out what to do, they often miss obvious counseling themes and dynamics presented by the counselee. The supervisor can ask the supervisee to practice various counseling skills followed by a discussion surrounding the impact of these efforts. Interpersonal process recall (IPR), developed by Norman Kagan (1990), is a supervision strategy that helps trainees become aware of these various counseling dynamics. The IPR steps include the following:

1. The supervisor reviews the tape or portions of the tape prior to the supervision session.
2. During the supervisory session, either the supervisee or the supervisor can stop the tape at any point. The feelings and thoughts of the trainee are discussed at the point where the tape was stopped. The supervisor asks relevant questions when he or she stops the tape. Because one goal is to move the trainee from focusing on self to a greater awareness of the counselee, several leading questions that may help this occur include (Cashwell, 2001):
   - What do you wish you had said to him or her?
   - What prevented you from saying that?
   - If you could do it over again, how would you tell him or her what you are thinking?
   - How did you want him or her to see you?
   - What were your feelings/thoughts at that time?
   - What do you think is the real issue?
   - Does the counselee remind you of anyone in your life?

Areas of Focus During Level 1 (Orientation)

Self- and Other Awareness

During the orientation stage the trainee is more concerned about him- or herself rather than the counselee. Sometimes these trainees are frustrated when they believe that their supervisor is "prying into their sessions." However, once trainees are sensitive to the supervisor's concern about vicarious liability, they are more likely to engage in an honest discussion (Pearson, 2004).

Motivation

In the beginning the trainee is motivated to put learning into practice. As the supervisee experiences success, confidence increases, but in other situations the trainee may realize that additional skills are needed to work successfully with other counselees with different concerns. Motivational levels among trainees vary. Some trainees will view the experience simply as a requirement that needs to be met, and others will view the experience as an opportunity to grow and learn (Pearson, 2004). Supervisees may inspire the trainee's willingness to learn through the following questions:

1. How can I assist you in making this a valuable learning experience?
2. What kinds of counselees do you consider the greatest challenge?
3. What are some of the counselee behaviors that are most problematic for you?

4. What do you hope to get out of supervision?
5. Are there any areas with which you would like more assistance?

The trainee is encouraged to listen to the counselee's narrative as a step in learning to focus on the counselee. The use of the HELPING model, an assessment adopted from Lazarus's multimodel model (BASIC ID), may help in this redirection (Baker, 2000; Schmidt, 1999):

H = *Health concerns.* Does the counselee have any medical issues, absences, tardiness, hospitalizations?

E = *Emotions.* Is the counselee able to identify emotions? Are emotions expressed congruent with what the counselee is saying?

L = *Learning.* What is the counselee's learning style? Do the grades match ability?

P = *Personal relationships.* Who are the counselee's friends? Who are the significant people in the counselee's life?

I = *Imagery and interests.* How does the counselee see him- or herself? What are the counselee's interests?

N = *Need to know.* What other information is needed to help this counselee?

G = *Guidance of behavior.* How well does the counselee understand the consequences of his or her behavior?

Imagery is an additional tool that helps the trainee to enter and understand the counselee's world. In a strategy adapted from Shorr (1983, as cited in Williams, 1995), the counselee can be asked to imagine his or her mother or father in the office. The trainee may be encouraged to ask the counselee, "What do you want to say to your mother or father?" followed with the question, "What is their reply?"

Autonomy

Supervisors, aware of the anxiety experienced by beginning trainees, can support the trainee through constructive feedback and encouraging the trainee to try new activities and skills. Structure and direction are highly desired in the beginning. To help the trainee become more autonomous, the supervisor can encourage the trainee to discuss areas of concern and to brainstorm alternative ideas for addressing these issues (Pearson, 2004).

Because trainees want to observe and model their supervisor during the beginning stage, it is not uncommon for the trainee to emulate the supervisor's behaviors during the initial stages. With more skill, the trainee will develop his or her own style and will be more willing to make decisions.

Supervisor Strategies During Level 2 (Transformation)

At this level the trainee is feeling a sense of pride in past accomplishments, but when new activities are introduced, anxiety resurfaces. Because counseling dynamics are better understood and modeled at this level, this is an ideal time for the trainee to practice advanced counseling skills.

Administrative Supervision

The supervisee can schedule appointments, design, and implement group counseling sessions without assistance. In addition, the trainee can take the initiative in developing evaluation procedures for showing how the school counselor is a significant contributor to the educational mission.

Clinical and Developmental Supervision

At this level the counselee's experiences help conceptualize how the school counseling program is integral to meeting K–12 students' needs. Trainees are now beginning to focus on the counselee's needs rather than themselves. As they reach this second stage, supervisors facilitate this shift by attending to the various areas of focus.

Areas of Focus in Level 2 (Transformation)

Self- and Other Awareness

The following questions can help in moving the supervisee to a new level:

- What counselees do you find yourself thinking about frequently?
- What are some of your thoughts, feelings, and behaviors when you think about this person?
- What are some of the dynamics that most confuse you?
- What are some of the things you have considered in trying to improve the counselee's behavior?
- What do you think the counselee is thinking/feeling when you ask that question?

Motivation

As before, motivational levels fluctuate from apprehension when engaging in a new activity to pride when success occurs. Supervisors can be inspirational coaches by providing professional opportunities for the trainee to work individually with teachers, set up conferences, and conduct in-service sessions. A professional identity develops when trainees are in a supervisory environment that allows for independence where confrontation can take place in a caring environment (Stoltenberg & Delworth, 1998).

Autonomy

As new tasks are planned and implemented, the trainee is anxious about performance, yet there is also a desire to be more independent (Chagnon & Russell, 1995). A supervision shift occurs from concerns about self to sensitivity to the counselee (Gaoni & Neumann, 1974, as cited in Hess, 1986), with a realization of how personal issues affect counseling. The supervisor can facilitate the shift to a more advanced level by asking the following questions:

- What is it about this activity that you find to be most difficult?
- What would help alleviate these concerns?
- What resources do you need?
- What are your thoughts and beliefs about this task?

Supervisor Strategies During Level 3 (Professional Direction)

Developing a counselor identity that integrates skills and knowledge is a hallmark of Level 3. The supervisor is viewed as a colleague, yet when the trainee feels unsure and hesitant to attempt new tasks, the supervisor is sought as a consultant. A professional identity is now a more comfortable fit.

Administrative Supervision

The trainee now has a better grasp of the school rules and procedures and is knowledgeable about the structure of the educational system. The trainee is able to contact teachers and parents, knows procedures for contacting students, and is able to arrange meetings and conferences without assistance. The trainee also has a greater awareness of why documentation of proceedings and meetings are helpful.

Developmental and Clinical Supervision

The trainee is able to focus on the needs of the counselee and has a better ability to recognize nonverbal communication, use more advanced counseling skills, apply various theoretical approaches to the different student concerns, and develop evaluative strategies for analyzing the effectiveness of tasks.

Areas of Focus in Level 3 (Professional Direction)

Self- and Other Awareness

Understanding how personal issues and relationships influence counseling is in the forefront during the final supervisory stages (Guest & Beutler, 1988, as cited in Stoltenberg, McNeill, & Crethar, 1994). The trainee has a better understanding of how to balance him- or herself with counselee awareness and how these interpersonal factors affect the counseling process.

Motivation

As more experience is gained, the trainee is more motivated, recognizes his or her scope of training, and is able to refer counselees without feeling incompetent (Stoltenberg & Delworth, 1998). The trainee is also better able to examine the counseling process, identify strategies that were productive, and evaluate the strategies that were not as effective. The supervisor can assist the trainee by asking the following questions in examining theory and techniques (Williams, 1995):

- What are your most common counseling techniques?
- What are the most common dynamics you see happening between you and the counselee?

Autonomy

Trainees are encouraged to advocate for themselves, remain flexible, and take the initiative to ask for anything that they need to make the supervisory process even more successful. The supervisee is now considered more responsible for his or her learning and growing as well as self-assessment. Using a technique from solution-focused counseling, the supervisor can help the trainee to examine the sessions as if he or she were a "fly on the wall." What is happening? What are people doing? How are individuals different as a result of the counseling process? One creative supervisory technique is to ask the supervisee to "draw a picture as to how you believe the counselee is feeling about you, and how would you like it to be?" (Williams, 1995).

SUMMARY

This chapter focuses on the supervisory process from a developmental model. Although there are various developmental supervisory models that describe the trainee's professional and personal growth through stages, the IDM, developed by Stoltenberg et al. (1998), is highlighted in this chapter. The trainee progresses through a series of levels with growth occurring in the areas of self- and other awareness, motivation, and autonomy. Various supervisory strategies facilitate understanding throughout these stages.

As the trainee grows through the various strategies used by the supervisor, the supervisor also matures in understanding and skills during this process. Three stages have been identified by Hess (1986) that explain the growth that naturally occurs within supervisors.

REFERENCES

Baker, S. B. (2000). *School counseling for the twenty-first century* (3rd ed.). Upper Saddle River, NJ: Merrill.

Bartlett, W. E. (1983). A multidimensional framework for the analysis of supervision of counseling. *The Counseling Psychologist, 11,* 9–17.

Bernard, J. M. (1979). Supervising training: A discrimination model. *Counselor Education and Supervision, 19,* 60–68.

Bernard, J. M., & Goodyear, R. K. (2004). *Fundamentals of clinical supervision* (3rd ed.). Boston: Pearson.

Borders, L. D., & Brown, L. L. (2005). *The new handbook of counseling supervision.* Mahwah, NJ: Erlbaum/Lahaska Press.

Cashwell, C. S. (2001, October). IPR: Recalling thoughts and feelings in supervision. *CYC-Online, 33.* Retrieved from http://www.cyc-online/cycol-1001-supervision.html

Chagnon, J., & Russell, R. K. (1995). Assessment of supervisee developmental level and supervision environment across supervisor experience. *Journal of Counseling & Development, 73,* 553–558.

Henderson, D. (1994). *Supervision of school counselors.* Greensboro, NC: ERIC Clearinghouse on Counseling and Student Services. (ERIC Document Reproduction Service No. ED372353)

Hess, A. K. (1981). *Psychotherapy supervision: Theory, research, and practice.* New York: Wiley.

Hess, A. K. (1986). Growth in supervision: Stages of supervisee and supervisor development. *Clinical Supervisor, 4,* 51–67.

Kagan, N. I. (1990). IPR: A validated model for the 1990s and beyond. *Counseling Psychologist, 18,* 436–440.

Locher, B. T., & Melchert, T. P (1997). Relationship of cognitive style and theoretical orientation to psychology interns' preferences for supervision. *Journal of Counseling Psychology, 44,* 256–260.

Murray, G. C., Portman, T. A. A., & Maki, D. R. (2003). Clinical supervision: Developmental differences during preservice training. *Rehabilitation Education, 17,* 19–32.

Pearson, Q. M. (2004). Getting the most out of clinical supervision: Strategies for mental health. *Journal of Mental Health Counseling, 26,* 361–373.

Pehrsson, D. E., & Ingram, M. A. (n.d.). *Supervision. A guide for beginning counselors.* Retrieved October 17, 2004, from http://www.shsu.edu/_piic/summer2001/pehrssoningram.htm

Rosenthal, H. (1998). *Favorite counseling and therapy techniques: 51 therapists share their most creative strategies.* Washington, DC: Accelerated Development.

Schmidt, J. J. (1999). *Counseling in schools: Essential services and comprehensive programs* (3rd ed.). Needham Heights, MA: Allyn & Bacon.

Spruill, D. A., & Benshoff, J. M. (2000). Helping beginning counselors develop a personal theory of counseling. *Counselor Education and Supervision, 40,* 70–80.

Stoltenberg, C. D., & Delworth, U. (1998). *Supervising counselors and therapists: A developmental approach.* San Francisco: Jossey-Bass.

Stoltenberg, C. D., & Grus, C. (2004). Defining competencies in psychology supervision: A consensus statement. *Journal of Clinical Psychology, 60,* 771–785.

Stoltenberg, C. D., McNeill, B. W., & Crethar, H. C. (1994). Changes in supervision as counselors and therapists gain experience: A review. *Professional Psychology, 25,* 416–449.

Stoltenberg, C. D., McNeill, B., & Delworth, U. (1998). *IDM supervision: An integrated developmental model for supervising counselors and therapists.* San Francisco: Jossey-Bass.

Thompson, J. M. (2004). A readiness hierarchy theory of counselor-in-training. *Journal of Instructional Psychology, 31,* 135–142.

Williams, A. (1995). *Visual and active supervision.* New York: Norton.

Wubbolding, R. E., Brickell, J., Loi, R., & Al-Rashidi, B. (2001). The why and how of self-evaluation. *International Journal of Reality Therapy, XXI,* 36–37.

CHAPTER 5

Supervision Integrated to the ASCA National Model

Carol A. Dahir

THE PURPOSE of this chapter is to

- summarize the American School Counselor Association (ASCA) National Model
- provide supervisors with the opportunity to reflect on the integration between their school counseling program and the ASCA National Model
- present supervisors with the opportunity to determine activities within the ASCA National Model for supervisees

REALITY CHECK: FROM THEORY TO PRACTICE

Graduate students come to our school sites prepared and enthusiastic to discuss and debate the merits of comprehensive school counseling programs and describe what the ideal scenario for implementation should look like. They have an unbridled passion to act as counselors, advocates, leaders, collaborators, and consultants to maximize opportunities for students to acquire academic, career, and personal/social development skills that all students need to succeed.

Those of us who received our school counseling credentials before the release of the National Standards for School Counseling Programs (Campbell & Dahir, 1997) and the Transforming School Counseling Initiative (Education Trust, 1997) or the publication of the ASCA National Model (ASCA, 2003) experienced a more traditional approach to graduate preparation. As the school counseling profession moves to embrace these new directions and paradigms, the challenge for the supervisor is seeking a harmonic balance of providing opportunities to help trainees experience all aspects of implementing a comprehensive school counseling program while refining their counseling and intervention skills. As supervisors, it is our responsibility to prepare the next generation to apply their knowledge and abilities in a meaningful way and lead the way to improve our schools.

TRANSFORMING SCHOOL COUNSELING

The school counseling program plays an essential role in school improvement efforts, and the school counselor's role as a systemic change agent through leadership, advocacy, collaboration and teaming, and assessment and use of data underpins the Transforming School Counseling Initiative (Education Trust, 1997). Through intentional efforts, school counseling has moved from a service-driven model to a data-driven and competency-based model. The school counseling program is now in a critical position to effectively complement academic rigor with affective development.

FOR PROGRAM AND SITE SUPERVISORS AND TRAINEES

What Interns Need to Know and Be Able to Do: Implementing the National Standards

Since the debut of *A Nation at Risk* (National Commission on Excellence in Education, 1983), the education and business communities and the public and private sectors regularly deliberate the outcomes of American public education. The current school improvement agenda, the No Child Left Behind Act of 2001, evolved from the educational reform movement, which originated in 1991 as America 2000 (U.S. Department of Education, 1991) and was reauthorized as Goals 2000: The Educate America Act of 1994. As part of this effort, the development of national standards was undertaken across all academic disciplines that continue to influence how teachers teach and how students learn. Phrases such as "higher academic achievement," "increasing student potential," "rigorous academic preparation," and "accountability" are commonly heard in communities across the United States.

ASCA determined that, like the academic subject standards, the development of school counseling standards would define what K–12 students should know and be able to do as a result of participating in a school counseling program (Campbell & Dahir, 1997). The standards confirmed the continued importance of the three widely accepted and interrelated areas of student development, and nine standards emerged from the research: academic development, career development, and personal/social development. (Campbell & Dahir, 1997). Table 5.1 summarizes the ASCA standards for school counseling programs.

The National Standards for School Counseling Programs (ASCA, 1997) tied the work of school counseling programs to the mission of schools and encouraged school counselors to assume a leadership role in school reform (Bowers, Hatch, & Schwallie-Giddis, 2001).

National standards-based school counseling programs help students develop attitudes, knowledge, and skills in academic, career, and personal/social development that are needed in today's and tomorrow's world.

Table 5.1

National Standards for School Counseling Programs

Domain		Standard
Academic	A	Students will acquire the attitudes, knowledge, and skills contributing to effective learning in school and across the life span.
	B	Students will complete school with the academic preparation essential to choose from a wide range of substantial postsecondary options, including college.
	C	Students will understand the relationship of academics to the world of work and to life at home and in the community.
Career	A	Students will acquire the skills to investigate the world of work in relation to knowledge of self and to make informed career decisions.
	B	Students will use strategies to achieve future career goals with success and satisfaction.
	C	Students will understand the relationship among personal qualities, education, training, and the world of work.
Personal/social	A	Students will acquire the knowledge, attitudes, and interpersonal skills to help them understand and respect self and others.
	B	Students will make decisions, set goals, and take necessary action to achieve goals.
	C	Students will understand safety and survival skills.

Note. From *Executive Summary: The National Standards for School Counseling Programs,* by the American School Counselor Association, 1997. Copyright 1997 by the American School Counselor Association. Reprinted with permission.

Moving the Profession Forward: The ASCA National Model

With the continued progression of school improvement and standards-based education, the ASCA developed the ASCA National Model (ASCA, 2003). The ASCA National Model integrates the three widely accepted and respected approaches to program models: comprehensive, developmental, and results-based (Myrick, 2003).

Comprehensive school counseling programs facilitate the *new vision* of the school counselor (House & Hayes, 2002; House, Martin, & Ward, 2002). The outside frame of Figure 5.1 represents the skills of leadership, advocacy, collaboration, and systemic change promoted by the Transforming School Counseling Initiative (Education Trust, 1997) to help every student succeed academically. The inside of the figure depicts the four interrelated quadrants (foundation, delivery system, management system, and accountability) that are the essential components of successful and effective comprehensive school counseling programs (ASCA, 2003). Each of these quadrants, discussed below, is integral to implementing a comprehensive school counseling program.

The Foundation

The foundation of the program reminds school counselors of the importance of developing a proactive *belief* system that ensures that every student will benefit from the school counseling program. School counselors are reminded to align their work with the school mission statement for student success. The foundation addresses the *what* of the program, discussing what every student should know and be able to do (ASCA, 2003, p. 22) based on the National Standards.

Figure 5.1

The ASCA National Model

Note. From *American School Counselor Association National Model: A Framework for School Counseling Programs,* by the American School Counselor Association, 2003. Copyright 2003 by the American School Counselor Association. Reprinted with permission.

Beliefs and Philosophy

Beliefs and philosophy are inextricably related. What school counselors believe about students, families, colleagues, and community strongly influences how they work with students. Consider the following examples when developing belief statements:

- All students can learn and achieve.
- School counselors collaborate for student success.
- Every student is entitled to an equitable education.
- School counseling programs balance academic, career, and personal/social development.
- Every student needs a plan to focus on his or her future and educational goal.

Exercise 5.1 helps school counselors to consider their belief statements.

The Mission Statement

A mission statement describes the purpose for the school counseling program and, in alignment with the school's mission, is committed to providing every student with the skills needed to become lifelong learners and productive members of society. The mission statement publicly displays the commitment of school counselors to collaborate with colleagues and ensure that every student benefits from the educational opportunities offered in each school system (see Exercise 5.2).

Integrating the ASCA National Standards

ASCA's National Standards for School Counseling Programs (ASCA, 1997) established goals, expectations, support systems, and experiences for all students. The National Standards offer

Exercise 5.1

Belief Statement

Write a sample belief statement(s) below:

_____

_____

_____

Exercise 5.2

Mission Statement

Write your school's mission statement here:

_____

_____

How does your work connect to the mission statement in your school building?

_____

_____

school counselors, administrators, teachers, and counselor educators a common language to promote student success through school counseling programs, which is readily understood by colleagues in schools who are involved in school improvement and the implementation of standards across other disciplines. Each standard is followed by student competencies that identify student learning outcomes. Student competencies define the knowledge, attitudes, or skills students should obtain or demonstrate as a result of participating in a school counseling program. Competencies are the pathway to documenting and demonstrating student growth and progress development to the achievement of the nine standards. As key components of the foundation, the National Standards lay the groundwork to ensure that every student benefits from the school counseling programs and raises the level of expectation of the outcomes for students. The standards make excellence in school counseling possible.

FOR SITE SUPERVISORS

Aligning With the National Standards

Take the time to examine the activities and strategies that you use with your students and align each with the National Standards. Copy the following chart (Exercise 5.3) that includes elementary school (ES), middle school (MS), and high school (HS) and begin to map your services

Exercise 5.3

The Intern's Involvement in Exploring a Developmental School Counseling Program

Name(s) _____ School(s) _____ Grade _____

School Improvement Issue: Improve student grades

Domain: Academic _____ Career _____ Personal/Social _____

Standard: Academic _____ Career _____ Personal/Social _____

Student competency	Grade level	Activity	Expected results	Connection to school improvement (accountability)
	ES	Students establish goals to improve grades and create a plan as to how to achieve this. Every student reviews her/his plan with report card grades.	Every student has a written plan. Report card shows improvement in grades.	The school building's report card shows more students achieved higher grades (*A*s and *B*s) than in the previous school year.
	MS	Students demonstrate how using time and task management improves their grades. Student with teachers and parents check agenda/planner daily.	Every student uses the planner/agenda book daily. Student report card shows improvement in grades. Homework and assignments are completed on time.	The school building's report card shows more students have passed courses than in the previous school year.
	HS	Students establish a 4-year academic plan that is articulated with future career goals. Every student reviews her/his report card each quarter and the 4-year academic plan.	Every student develops a written plan with a career goal. Student report card shows improvement in grades.	Data each quarter show improvement in the number of students passing courses. Annual data show more students passed courses than in the previous school year.

so that they are aligned with the National Standards. You will use this information as the foundation for your comprehensive program.

Delivery System

The delivery system quadrant helps us examine methods for delivering a school counseling program. By carefully examining current practice and student needs as revealed by school improvement data, school counselors can determine the amount of time they need to spend on each of the following important areas:

1. School counseling curriculum (e.g., structured groups, classroom guidance)
2. Individual student planning (e.g., advising, assessment, placement, academic, career and personal/social goal setting, and follow-up)
3. Responsive services (e.g., individual and group counseling, consultation, and referral)
4. System support (e.g., program management, coordination of services, community outreach, and public relations)

School Counseling Curriculum
The school counseling curriculum is a sequential, standards-based instructional program designed to assist all students acquire, develop, and demonstrate competencies in three content area domains: academic achievement, career employability, and personal/social development. The cooperation and involvement of school faculty and administration are essential for effective, successful curriculum implementation. In most circumstances, the curriculum is intended to serve the largest number of students possible through large-group meetings and classroom presentations. The curriculum gives attention to particular issues or areas of concern in the school building or district, such as conflict resolution.

The curriculum design and development include the following strategies: (a) creating a scope and sequence that help to define and clarify the topics and competencies taught at each grade level and (b) articulating what students should *know, understand,* and be able to *do* as a result of the curriculum (Exercise 5.4).

Classroom instruction. This element involves school counselors designing, teaching, and assessing the impact of standards-based lessons and presentations that meet the academic, career, and personal/social developmental needs of each student (Exercise 5.5).

Cross-content/interdisciplinary curriculum. This element encourages counselors to become part of an interdisciplinary team and integrate the school counseling curriculum objectives across the total school curriculum (Exercise 5.6).

Large-group instructional activities and presentations. This element conveys information in a variety of ways by offering group activities, workshops, assemblies, and meetings to accommodate student needs and interests (Exercise 5.7).

Individual Student Planning
Successful students take ownership for their academic and affective learning and development. Individual student planning provides opportunities for students to plan, monitor, and evaluate their progress. Activities can include but are not limited to working with students to set and monitor goals, develop a career plan, establish behavioral goals, create an educational plan, and understand, interpret, and apply testing and assessment information in a meaningful way to present and future plans. Individual student planning can involve parents, personalizes the educational experience, and helps students to develop a pathway to realize their dreams.

Individual student planning consists of ongoing, systematic activities that assist students with planning, managing, and monitoring their academic, personal/social, and career/employability goals. These activities are counselor directed and delivered on an individual or small-group basis. Each student is provided with the information, encouragement, and support needed to work toward his or her personal goals. Parents or guardians are frequently included in these activities. Implementation strategies include the following:

Exercise 5.4

Identifying Intern Activities Within the Curriculum

List key topics that you and your intern could deliver in a sequential and developmental manner across the grade levels in your building.

_____

_____

_____

Exercise 5.5

Intern Involvement in Classroom Instruction

List the grade levels/key faculty members that you and your intern might partner with to develop the classroom lessons.

_____

_____

_____

Exercise 5.6

Intern Involvement in Interdisciplinary Curriculum

List two or three curriculum or schoolwide initiatives that would benefit from the contributions you and your intern can offer (e.g., Character Education).

_____

_____

_____

Exercise 5.7

Large-Group Instructional Activities

List some important topics that you and your intern can deliver to a large group.

_____

_____

_____

- *Individual/small-group appraisal:* Counselors assist students and parents/guardians with analysis and evaluation of student abilities, interests, aptitudes, and achievements. Test results, career surveys, extracurricular activities, grades, and hobbies are examples of resources and data used to assist with identification of educational and career goals.
- *Individual/small-group session:* Counselors work with students using personal/social, educational, and career/labor market information in helping them to plan their long- and short-range educational and career goals.
- *Student monitoring:* Counselors monitor student progress on a regular basis as the students progress in school and develop appropriate interventions as needed.

- *Consultation:* Counselors partner with parents/guardians and other educators to assist students, and they plan and execute academic, career, and personal goals.
- *Referral/placement:* Counselors collaborate with students, school faculty, and families to assist with transition from grade to grade, school to school, school to work, college, and post-high school placements.
- *Portfolio development:* Counselors assist students with portfolio development to document personal achievements, competencies, extracurricular accomplishments, and long-range goals.

Exercise 5.8 helps supervisors evaluate their school's individual planning component.

Responsive Services

When school counselors proactively address student-related concerns such as peer pressure, resolving conflict, family relationships, personal identity issues, substance abuse, motivation, and achievement challenges, they deliver responsive services. Included in responsive services are interventions necessary to help at-risk students succeed, individual and group counseling, consultation, referrals to community agencies, crisis intervention, and management and prevention activities. Crisis, school building and faculty concerns, parental trepidations, community matters, and student requests can dominate the impetus for response and intervention. Implementation strategies and outreach include the following:

- *Individual/small-group counseling:* Counselors counsel students with identified needs/concerns or students who request counseling. This is an opportunity to discuss or clarify needs and guide therapeutic intervention. The school counselor must act ethically at all times in accordance with the ASCA Code of Ethics and federal, state, and local laws and policies with respect to confidentiality, suspected cases of abuse, and threats of harm or violence.
- *Consultation:* Counselors work collaboratively with students, parents, teachers, and community members to develop a broad base of support and help for students.
- *Referrals:* Counselors consult with and make referrals to community agencies to assist students facing personal crisis outside the scope of the school counseling program.
- *Schoolwide prevention/intervention programs:* Counselors collaborate with all faculty, students, staff, and community-based organizations to expand responsive service outreach.
- *Crisis counseling:* Counselors provide short-term prevention and intervention counseling and support to students and school staff dealing with crisis.
- *Crisis prevention and management plans and school response teams:* School crisis plans guide school prevention, intervention, and management of crisis response. Staff crisis training establishes readiness to meet student or school needs in emergency situations.
- *Student support services team:* Counselors collaborate with student services staff to plan interventions for the academic, social, and emotional needs of identified students.

Exercise 5.9 helps supervisors evaluate the responsive services of the school.

Exercise 5.8

Intern Involvement in Individual Student Planning

Identify three different ways that you and your intern can use individual planning with the students in your school building.

1. _____

2. _____

3. _____

Exercise 5.9

Intern Involvement in Responsive Services

Your trainee/intern can list the many responsive services that are delivered in your school building and to whom they are intended.

_____

_____

_____

_____

_____

_____

System Support

School counselors, when engaged in system support, offer ongoing sustenance to the school environment through the organization, delivery, management, and evaluation of the school counseling program. Support activities assess (a) how effectively program delivery achieves the system's goals and mission, (b) the degree to which school counseling programs are aligned with school and district mandates and state and federal education reform legislation, and (c) the impact of program services on students and school community. Oftentimes system support consists of indirect services that are not delivered directly to students. For example, hosting an advisory committee helps to inform the program's direction and provides a sounding board for discussion about what is working, what needs to change, and how the comprehensive school counseling program can better support student success. Indirect services may include professional development to faculty, serving on school committees, and coordinating safe school initiatives that are essential to impact systemic change and support the "new vision" of transformed school counseling (Ripley, Erford, & Dahir, 2002). System support strategies include the following:

- *Program coordination leadership:* This provides direction, vision, and accountability for school counseling programs. Ongoing consultation with administration and colleagues will foster understanding of departmental mission, goals, action plans, initiatives, and calendars.
- *Advisory council:* The council is a small, representative community group that partners with the school counseling program to identify and assess needs, establish goals, and provide support and advocacy for the counseling program.
- *Public relations and community outreach:* Public relations activities keep the community updated about counseling programs and establish community partnerships.
- *Staff development:* Ongoing, systematic professional development program will assist in assessing counselors' competence to implement the counseling program.

Exercise 5.10 asks school counselors to assist trainees in learning about their school's system support, and Exercise 5.11 assists trainees in examining the comprehensive school counseling program's delivery system.

Management System

The comprehensive school counseling program must be efficiently and effectively managed. In the management system quadrant, supervisors and interns address the *when* (action plan and calendar), the *why* (use of data), *who* will implement (management agreement), and *on what authority* (management agreement and advisory council) the school counseling program

Exercise 5.10

Intern Involvement in System Support

Your trainee/intern can list at least three examples of system support in your school.

1. _____

2. _____

3. _____

Exercise 5.11

Intern Involvement in Comprehensive School Counseling Program

Examine all the different ways that the comprehensive school counseling program is delivered in your school. Ask your trainee/intern to categorize three of your activities and services in each area of the delivery system.

School Counseling Curriculum

1. _____

2. _____

3. _____

Individual Student Planning

1. _____

2. _____

3. _____

Responsive Services

1. _____
2. _____
3. _____

System Support

1. _____

2. _____

3. _____

is delivered. The ASCA National Model encourages school counselors to include key elements to manage the program. Some of the key elements include the following.

Management Agreements

Management agreements are to be established annually between school counselors and the principal. The counselor develops a draft of the agreement, reviews it with the principal, then reviews the document, and together they arrive at consensus as to priorities, timeline, and implementation. When the principal and school counselors agree on program priorities and implementation strategies, the school counseling program is more likely to produce the desired results for students.

Advisory Council

An advisory council is a representative group of people who are appointed or who volunteer to both advise and assist the school counseling program. Council membership should reflect the community's diversity and can include school staff, parents, school board members, students, and business and community representatives.

Use of Data

Student achievement data analysis monitors that all students have equity and access to a rigorous academic curriculum and identifies academic gaps. Counselors suggest systemic changes in policy and procedures to enhance academic achievement based on data. The use of data to effect change within the school system is integral to ensuring students' success. School counselors should be proficient in the collection, analysis, and interpretation of data.

School counselors monitor student progress through collection of three types of data:

1. *Student achievement data:* standardized test scores, grade point average, graduation rate, promotion/retention rates, and other data.
2. *Achievement-related data:* course enrollment patterns, discipline referrals, suspension rates, attendance rates, parent/guardian involvement, participation in extracurricular activities, and so on.
3. *Standards- and competency-related data:* percentage of students with 4-year plan on file, percentage of students participating in job shadowing, percentage of students setting and meeting educational goals, percentage of students fulfilling the competencies as determined by the school counselors, school improvement team, and advisory council.

Action Plans

For effective delivery of services, school counselors must develop a plan of action detailing annual program activities as a means of addressing how desired results will be achieved. Action plans usually contain the following:

- domain, standard, and school improvement goals
- student competency
- description of the activity
- curriculum/materials being used in the activity
- timeline
- means of evaluation
- measurable outcomes
- person responsible
- number of students involved

Program Audit/Self-Study

Annual program audits determine the degree to which the school counseling program is being implemented in alignment with the model. Audit results often suggest changes in the school counseling program and the master calendar for the following year.

Use of Time

ASCA recommends that school counselors spend the majority of their time in direct service to students. Gysbers and Henderson (2000) were more specific in their recommendation for time distribution, suggesting that school counselors spend 80% of their time in direct service to students and 20% in program management. While the amount of time counselors should spend delivering services in each component area remains relative to the individualized needs of each school, ASCA provides recommendations as shown in Table 5.2.

Calendars

School counselors should develop and publish a master calendar of program events and activities that help to facilitate involvement of stakeholders in the school counseling program. These can also be great public relations tools.

Table 5.2

Sample Distribution of Total School Counselor Time Within the Delivery System Component

Delivery System Component	Elementary School % of Time	Middle School % of Time	High School % of Time
Guidance curriculum	35–45	25–35	15–25
Individual student planning	5–10	15–25	25–35
Responsive services	30–40	30–40	25–35
System support	10–15	10–15	15–20

Note. From *Developing and Managing Your School Guidance Program* (3rd ed.), by N. C. Gysbers & P. Henderson, 2000, p. 53. Copyright 2000 by the American Counseling Association. Adapted with permission.

Although the management of the school counseling program is coordinated by school counselors, many activities are shared by the entire staff. Collaborative management activities that establish, maintain, evaluate, and refine can include the following:

- planning and organizing tasks
- evaluation
- follow-up and program revision activities
- collaborating with teachers about program operation
- conducting needs assessments
- promoting program awareness and student goals.

Exercise 5.12 examines how the school counseling program is managed.

Accountability System

Accountability is sharing responsibility to collectively remove barriers that impede learning and involves all of the critical players in a school setting. Accountability is the result of intentional efforts to close the achievement gap and meet the goals of school improvement. School counselor accountability is a collaborative act of advocacy to ensure that every student has the opportunity and access to a quality education.

The ASCA National Model encourages school counselors to collect and analyze data, use data-driven decision making, and make evaluations focusing on student achievement that contribute to the school and system improvement goals. The accountability component of the ASCA National Model shows the relationship of the school counseling program to the instructional program. School counselors use their specialized training to show how the school counseling program moves school improvement data in a positive direction.

Exercise 5.12

Intern Involvement in School Management

Ask your trainee to identify the many ways that the counselors in your school manage the school counseling program. What areas of the management system would benefit from improvement?

_____

_____

_____

Data can present a picture of the current status of student needs and achievement issues and can be used to develop practices that can lead students to higher levels of success. Data inform, confirm progress, and reveal shortcomings in student performance. School counselors can collect and analyze student data to inform and guide the development of a comprehensive school counseling program based on schoolwide issues.

A six-step accountability process called MEASURE confirms the impact of the school counseling program on critical data, those elements of the school report card that are the backbone of the accountability movement (Dahir & Stone, 2003). MEASURE supports the accountability component of the ASCA National Model and moves school counselors from a "counting tasks" system to aligning the school counseling program with standards-based reform. MEASURE is a way of using information such as retention rates, test scores, and postsecondary rates to develop specific strategies for connecting school counseling to the accountability agenda of today's schools. MEASURE is an acronym for:

Mission: connect the comprehensive K–12 school counseling program to the mission of the school and to the goals of the annual school improvement plan

Elements: identify the critical data elements that are important to the internal and external stakeholders

Analyze: discuss carefully which elements need to be aggregated or disaggregated and why

Stakeholders – Unite: determine which stakeholders need to be involved in addressing these school improvement issues and unite to develop strategies

Reanalyze: examine your results or your impact and rethink and refine the strategies, refocus efforts as needed

Educate: show the positive impact the school counseling program has had on student achievement and on the goals of the school improvement plan

Exercise 5.13 uses the MEASURE system to evaluate the school improvement plan.

Exercise 5.13

Intern Involvement in the MEASURE System

Your intern/trainee can collaborate with the counselors in your building and develop a MEASURE to connect your work to the school improvement plan in your school.

MEASURE: Mission, **E**lements, **A**nalyze, **S**takeholders–**U**nite, **R**eanalyze, **E**ducate
A Six-Step Accountability Process for School Counselors

Name and Address of School:
Name of Counselor Leading the Initiative:
Principal:
Enrollment:

School Demographics:
Caucasian/Non-Hispanic
African American
Hispanic
Asian
Other
Free-reduced lunch
English as a second language

(Continued)

Exercise 5.13 *(Continued)*

Intern Involvement in the MEASURE System

Step 1: **M**ission

> **Mission**
> Connect your work to your school's mission
>
> **Your mission statement is:**

Step 2: **E**lements

> **Current Critical Data Element**
> What indicator of school success are you trying to positively impact? Grades? Test scores? Attendance? Promotion rates? Postsecondary going rate?
>
> The school counselor as part of the leadership team identified these critical data elements to try to impact:

Step 3: **A**nalyze

> Analyze the data to see what they reveal, to identify the problem areas, to establish your baseline, and to set your goal. It may be necessary to disaggregate the data, e.g., race, ethnicity, gender, socioeconomic status, teacher assignment.
>
> | Baseline: Where is this data element currently? | Goal: Where do you want the data element to be in a year? |
> | --- | --- |

Step 4: **S**takeholders – **U**nite

> **Develop an Action Plan**
> School counselors, as managers of resources, join existing groups of stakeholders, such as the school improvement team, or bring other stakeholders and resources into the task of creating and implementing an action plan. Strategies are developed that will change systems as well as impact individual students and targeted groups of students.
>
> Impacting systems means (a) replicating successful programs and interventions; (b) identifying barriers that adversely stratify students' opportunities to be successful learners; and (c) developing strategies to
> * change policies, practices, and procedures
> * strengthen curriculum offerings
> * maximize the instructional program
> * enhance the school and classroom culture and climate
> * provide student academic support systems (safety nets)
> * influence course enrollment patterns to widen access to rigorous academics
> * involve parents and other critical stakeholders (internal and external to the school)
> * raise aspirations in students, parents, teachers, and the community
> * change attitudes and beliefs about students and their abilities to learn

(Continued)

Exercise 5.13 *(Continued)*

Intern Involvement in the MEASURE System

Stakeholders	Strategies Connect your strategies to the American School Counselor Association (ASCA) National Standards and the ASCA National Model. **Beginning date:** **Ending date:**
School Counselors	
Teachers	
Administrators	
Students	
Technology Staff	
Student Services Staff	
Local Colleges	
Community Agency Members	
Parents	
Teacher Assistants	
School Improvement Team	
Local Business Community	

Step 5: **R**eanalyze, Reflect, and Revise

Reanalyze Restate the baseline data. Where are the data after the action plan? Did the strategies have a positive impact on the data? Restate the baseline data: Data after action plan: Impact:	**Reflect and Revise** Reflect on why the stakeholders were successful or unsuccessful. Revise the action plan so that progress can be made and you can continue to get better results. Which of the strategies worked? Which strategies should be replaced? Added? Based on what you have learned, how will you revise the action plan?

Step 6: **E**ducate

Promote and publicize the results of your work. Develop a report card for your own program to let the internal and external school members know your work is connected to the mission of the schools and to student success. The School Counseling Program Accountability Report Card (SPARC) is a way to do this.

Note. From *School Counselor Accountability: A Measure of Student Success,* by C. Stone & C. Dahir, 2004. Copyright 2004 by Pearson Education. Adapted with permission.

WORK FROM A PROGRAM PERSPECTIVE

Working closely with your intern/trainee will help her or him to better understand how the ASCA National Model helps school counselors to move theory into practice and respond to the needs and goals of the entire school community. School counselors coordinate the objectives, strategies, and activities of a comprehensive school counseling program to meet the academic, career, and personal/social needs of all students (ASCA, 1999). When guidance and counseling is conceptualized, organized, and implemented as a program, it places school counselors in the center of education and makes it possible for them to be active and involved (Gysbers & Henderson, 2001).

Using the ASCA National Model (ASCA, 2003) and the specific state or local adaptation encourages counselors to provide both prevention and intervention programs and to create a model of collaboration that integrates the expertise of school counselors, other pupil services personnel, business, and community into the total program. It also ensures that the program is current with the needs and expectations of education agenda and societal issues (ASCA, 2003).

SUMMARY

When supervisors and interns/trainees use a comprehensive programmatic model, no longer will the trainee report that there is disconnect between theory and practice and express disappointment and frustration that classroom concepts are not carried over to the supervisory experience. Using the ASCA National Model as the foundation to the internship experience provides the trainee with the ability to understand and learn how to design, implement, and evaluate a comprehensive school counseling program and connect the work of the school counselors to the needs of 21st-century students and schools.

REFERENCES

American School Counselor Association. (1997). *Executive summary: The National Standards for School Counseling Programs.* Alexandria, VA: Author.

American School Counselor Association. (1999). *Position statement: The role of the professional school counselor.* Alexandria, VA: Author.

American School Counselor Association. (2003). *American School Counselor Association national model: A framework for school counseling programs.* Alexandria, VA: Author.

Bowers, J., Hatch, T., & Schwallie-Giddis, P. (2001, September/October). The brain storm. *ASCA School Counselor, 42,* 17–18.

Campbell, C., & Dahir, C. (1997). *Sharing the vision: The National Standards for School Counseling Programs.* Alexandria, VA: American School Counselor Association.

Dahir, C., & Stone, C. (2003). Accountability: A m.e.a.s.u.r.e. of the impact school counselors have on student achievement. *Professional School Counseling, 6,* 214–221.

Education Trust. (1997). *Working definition of school counseling.* Washington, DC: Author.

Goals 2000: The Educate America Act of 1994, Pub. L. No. 103-227.

Gysbers, N. C., & Henderson, P. (2000). *Developing and managing your school guidance program* (3rd ed.). Alexandria, VA: American Counseling Association.

Gysbers, N. C., & Henderson, P. (2001). Comprehensive guidance and counseling programs: A rich history and a bright future. *Professional School Counseling, 4,* 246–256.

House, R. M., & Hayes, R. L. (2002). School counselors: Becoming key players in school reform. *Professional School Counseling, 5,* 249–256.

House, R. M., Martin, P. J., & Ward, C. C. (2002). Changing school counselor preparation: A critical need. In C. D. Johnson & S. K. Johnson (Eds.), *Building stronger school counseling programs: Bringing futuristic approaches into the present* (pp. 185–208). Greensboro, NC: ERIC Counseling and Student Services Clearinghouse.

Myrick, R. D. (2003). *Developmental guidance and counseling: A practical handbook.* Minneapolis, MN: Educational Media Corporation.

National Commission on Excellence in Education. (1983). *A nation at risk: The imperative for educational reform.* Washington, DC: Author.

No Child Left Behind Act of 2001, H.R. 1.

Ripley, V., Erford, B., & Dahir, C. (2002). Planning and implementing a 21st century comprehensive, developmental professional school counseling program. In B. Erford (Ed.), *Transforming school counseling* (pp. 63–119). Columbus, OH: Merrill Prentice Hall.

Stone, C., & Dahir, C. (2004). *School counselor accountability: A measure of student success.* Upper Saddle River, NJ: Pearson Education.

U.S. Department of Education. (1991). *America 2000: An education strategy.* Washington, DC: Author.

PART III

Current and Emerging Supervisory Issues and Techniques

CHAPTER 6

Critical Issues in Multicultural Supervision

THIS CHAPTER is written for supervisors and trainees and addresses

- the influences of culturally different supervisors and supervisees
- the multicultural stages in supervision
- creative strategies for addressing multiculturalism in supervision
- specific multicultural competencies

Gary Roosevelt was proud of his accomplishments as an African American school counselor. Mr. Roosevelt grew up in a poor, rural farming community in Indiana and was the first member of his large family to attend and graduate from college. This was an achievement that was no small feat because he worked two jobs while he was enrolled full-time at a local college. Mr. Roosevelt was a teacher of students with special needs before he reached his goal of becoming a high school counselor. After 15 years as a professional school counselor, he had formed a great partnership with the professors at the university who trained individuals for the profession of school counseling, and he frequently served as a supervisor for these trainees. Mr. Roosevelt felt comfortable in his supervisory role, but when an older, White male was assigned to him as a trainee, Mr. Roosevelt sensed tension and "distance" when he met with this trainee. He discussed these feelings with the program supervisor but was still unable to resolve his discomfort. Mr. Roosevelt decided to discuss these issues with his intern, and as a result he learned that the trainee felt that he would not have a quality supervisory experience because of Mr. Roosevelt's racial background and age.

FOR SUPERVISORS

Multicultural supervision is a relationship in which two or more culturally diverse individuals (such as those described above) are involved in a relationship with the purpose of enhancing the trainee's growth and education while attending to the welfare of the counselee (Bernard & Goodyear, 1997, as cited in Garrett et al., 2001). The supervisor, counselor-in-training, and the counselee with whom this trainee works each brings cultural factors into the relationship that cannot be ignored (Hird, Cavalieri, Dulko, Felice, & Ho, 2001). Because the United States includes a history of oppression, this historical impact may influence what occurs between the counselee and counselor. Therefore, it stands to reason that it will also affect what happens between the supervisor and the trainee.

Professional and personal growth occur during supervision, as does an understanding of how multicultural issues affect counselees, trainees, and supervisors (Constantine, 1997). As the face of U.S. culture becomes more diverse, professional school counselors have an obligation to integrate multicultural training into the supervisory process (Gainor & Constantine, 2002). When supervisors are perceived as having more cultural awareness than the trainee, they are perceived as more influential (Ladany, Brittan-Powell, & Pannu, 1997). Despite this responsibility, multicultural awareness in supervision is relatively new (D'Andrea & Daniels, 1997), and because many supervisors have not been trained in diversity issues, there is often a lack of awareness of beliefs and values as well as a lack of knowledge of different cultural groups (Garrett et al., 2001).

When diversity is not discussed in supervision, those with the least personal, cultural, or socioeconomic power pay the biggest price (Hird et al., 2001). In one study, respondents revealed that if cultural concerns had been discussed early in supervision, the experience would have been more meaningful (Constantine, 1997, as cited in Garrett et al., 2001).

Supervision may be difficult when supervisees are as knowledgeable or even more knowledgeable about multicultural issues than their supervisors (D'Andrea & Daniels, 1997). Supervisors have a responsibility to assess their own multicultural competencies, foster a relationship with supervisees who are able to teach multicultural issues, learn about multicultural issues through training sessions, or consult with minority community role models (D'Andrea & Daniels, 1997).

Most school counselor training programs require at least one course in multicultural issues. However, because this is a relatively new inclusion in most counselor education programs, many supervisees have a greater understanding of diversity issues than do their supervisors. In a study by Ladany et al. (1997), the ability to discuss racial identity was related to the supervisory foci, the strength of the supervisory relationship, and multicultural competence. For instance, the majority supervisor without multicultural knowledge may perceive the minority supervisee as resistant to self-disclosure and engage in feedback, unwilling to investigate his or her behavior, and overly reliant on him or her (Fong & Lease, 1997).

FOR SUPERVISORS AND TRAINEES

Culturally Different Supervisors and Supervisees

If the supervisor does not establish a climate of trust, it is difficult for supervisees to self-disclose and self-reflect (Day-Vines et al., 2005). However, in a study by Watkins, Terrel, Miller, and Terrell (1989, as cited in Fong & Lease, 1997), Black counselees who were in counseling with a White counselor viewed their counselor as not having the ability to help them. If these same findings were applied to supervision, Black trainees would have trust issues with White supervisors, have lower expectations, and be uncomfortable in revealing personal issues.

Furthermore, Sue and Sue (1990, as cited in Fong & Lease, 1997) examined communication styles among diverse supervisory pairs. Whites are often characterized as having loud hurried speech, quick answers, a task-oriented focus, and prolonged eye contact when listening but less when talking. This style contrasts with Native Americans, African Americans, and Asian Americans, who may speak in softer, slower, subtle tones and have less direct eye contact and an unassertive manner. These differences may create misinterpretation and inaccurate assumptions (Fong & Lease, 1997). The following scenario provided by Song Lee, a counselor education doctoral student at North Carolina State University, is an example of how cultural factors may influence supervision.

Megan has been in Dr. Lin's counseling practicum class for 5 weeks. Dr. Lin is an Asian American female instructor, and Megan is a middle-class White female. During supervision, Megan did not speak much, although she is a talkative person outside of practicum class. Her counseling skills have not been improving in the same pace as her classmates. She also had not been implementing suggestions from Dr. Lin in her counseling sessions. A few of her counselees (from low socioeconomic backgrounds) had canceled two sessions in a row. She believed her counselees' resistance to counseling was due to their lack of motivation.

During one of the group supervision sessions, Dr. Lin directed the group of students to process how they were doing with their counselees. While another student, Kate, a Mexican female, was processing her frustrations, Megan let out a sigh and wanted Kate to role-play the situation. Dr. Lin acknowledged Megan's idea but redirected Kate to finish processing before the class engaged in any role-playing. As Kate was about to finish sharing her feelings, Megan disregarded Dr. Lin's redirection and asked Kate to role-play with her again. This time, Megan moved her chair and positioned herself in front of Kate. Kate appeared stunned but went along with Megan.

In the scenario, could it be that Megan disregarded Dr. Lin's instruction because of Dr. Lin's cultural membership? Or could it be that Megan viewed counseling from a Eurocentric viewpoint and disregarded other views and perspectives?

Gender Issues in Supervision

Gender is another powerful consideration particularly in regard to biases in expectations or actions that might occur in supervision. As a counselor educator at a small liberal arts college, a superintendent from a local elementary school who was interested in hiring for a school counseling position contacted me for names of qualified candidates to fill this vacancy. I recommended a young male graduate whom I felt was an excellent candidate. This recommendation was met with silence, and after a few moments the superintendent stated that he had not even considered the possibility of a male school counselor working with primary-age students. Could this same belief negatively influence a supervisory session between cross-gender or same-gender supervisors and supervisees? Some researchers (Granello, 2003; Wester, Vogel, & Archer, 2004) answer with a resounding "yes!"

In a study by Wester et al. (2004), male supervisees working with male supervisors were more likely to view the partnership negatively, possibly owing to the competitive interactions for some men. This study suggests that more attention needs to be placed on expectations of gender roles and ability to express feelings. In a study by Granello (2003), both male and female supervisors asked for more opinions, suggestions, and evaluations from male supervisees than female supervisees. However, female supervisees praised or supported supervisors of both genders more often than did male supervisees. These studies suggest that supervisors need to be aware of the different strategies used with male and female supervisees. Furthermore, Paisley (1994) revealed that sexual harassment and involvement with trainees are likely to be perpetuated by trainees who become sexually involved with their supervisors.

Other Issues in Supervision

Sexual orientation is another critical factor that may affect the supervisory relationship. The following scenario provided by Shamshad Ahmed, a counselor education doctoral student at North Carolina State University, illustrates this point.

Rita is a 40-year-old Middle Eastern female intern at the university counseling center. Her supervisor, John, is a 52-year-old White male. In the first meeting, John informed Rita of the policies and of the weekly supervision meetings. Rita did not feel comfortable asking questions and agreed with everything that he conveyed to her. In the second meeting, Rita shared with John her uncomfortable feelings working with a White, gay male counselee. Rita didn't feel comfortable that the counselee talked openly about his sexual preferences and drug issues. When she discussed the case and expressed her uncomfortable feelings, John gave her a puzzled look, which made Rita feel even more uncomfortable.

Age differences between the supervisor and trainee are also considerations in a supervisory relationship. For example, older male supervisees were asked for evaluations and opinions six times more often than were older female supervisees (Granello, 2003).

It is vital that a trustful atmosphere is adopted in which personal feelings and thoughts can be expressed between the supervisee and supervisor, and even with the counselee, if appropriate. It is vital that counselors are aware of their knowledge, attitudes, and skills when working with culturally different individuals. The multicultural competency checklist in Figure 6.1 provides a guide for assessing one's own competence in addressing these issues with a supervisee.

I. Counselor Awareness of Own Cultural Values and Biases	Yes	No	Need More Training
A. Attitudes and Beliefs			
1. I am aware of my own values and respect individual differences.			
2. I am aware of how my own cultural background and experiences and attitudes, values, and biases influence counseling relationships.			
3. I am able to recognize the limits of my competencies and expertise.			
4. I am comfortable with differences that may exist between myself and others in terms of race, ethnicity, culture, and beliefs.			
B. Knowledge			
1. I have specific knowledge about my own racial and cultural heritage and how it personally and professionally affects my definitions of normality–abnormality and the process of counseling.			
2. I possess knowledge and understanding about how oppression, racism, discrimination, and stereotyping affect me personally and in my work.			
3. I possess knowledge about my social impact on others.			
C. Skills			
1. I seek out educational, consultative, and training experience to improve my understanding and effectiveness in working with culturally different populations.			
2. I am constantly seeking to understand myself as a racial and cultural being and am actively seeking a nondiscriminatory identity.			
II. Counselor Awareness of Counselee's Worldview			
A. Attitudes and Beliefs			
1. I am aware of my negative emotional reactions toward other racial and ethnic groups that may prove detrimental in my professional abilities.			
2. I am aware of my stereotypes and preconceived notions that I may hold toward other racial and ethnic minority groups.			
B. Knowledge			
1. I possess specific knowledge about the life experiences, cultural heritage, and historical background of culturally different individuals.			
2. I understand how race, culture, ethnicity, and so forth may affect personality formation, vocational choices, manifestation of psychological disorders, help-seeking behavior, and the appropriateness or inappropriateness of counseling approaches.			
3. I understand and have knowledge about sociopolitical influences that impinge upon the life of racial and ethnic minorities.			
C. Skills			
1. I continually familiarize myself with relevant research and the latest findings regarding mental health and mental disorders of various ethnic and racial groups.			

Figure 6.1

Supervisor Checklist for Multicultural Competencies

(Continued)

C. Skills	Yes	No	Need More Training
2. I am actively involved with minority individuals outside of the counseling setting (community events, social and political functions, celebrations, friendships, neighborhood groups, and so forth) so that my perspective of minorities is more than an academic or helping exercise.			
III. Culturally Appropriate Intervention Strategies			
A. Attitudes and Beliefs			
1. I respect others' religious and/or spiritual beliefs and values.			
2. I respect indigenous helping practices and minority community intrinsic help-giving networks.			
3. I value bilingualism and do not view another language as an impediment to counseling.			
B. Knowledge			
1. I have a clear and explicit knowledge and understanding of the generic characteristics of counseling and therapy and how they may clash with the cultural values of various minority groups.			
2. I am aware of institutional barriers that prevent minorities from using mental health services.			
3. I have knowledge of the potential bias in assessment instruments and use procedures and interpret findings keeping in mind the cultural and linguistic characteristics of counselees.			
4. I have knowledge of minority family structures, hierarchies, values, and beliefs.			
5. I am aware of relevant discriminatory practices at the social and community level.			
C. Skills			
1. I am able to engage in a variety of verbal and nonverbal helping responses.			
2. I am able to exercise institutional intervention skills on behalf of my counselees.			
3. I am not adverse to seeking consultation with traditional healers and religious and spiritual leaders and practitioners in the treatment of culturally different counselees when appropriate.			
4. I take responsibility for interacting in the language requested by the counselee and, if not feasible, make appropriate referral.			
5. I have training and expertise in the use of traditional assessment and testing instruments.			
6. I attend to as well as work to eliminate biases, prejudices, and discriminatory practices.			
7. I take responsibility in educating my counselees and their families to the processes of psychological intervention, such as goals, expectations, legal rights, and my counseling orientation.			

Figure 6.1 *(Continued)*

Supervisor Checklist for Multicultural Competencies

Multicultural Stages in Supervision

According to Sue and Sue (1999, as cited in Russell-Chapin & Ivey, 2004), when supervisors have developed an awareness of individual differences, gained insight into their own values and beliefs, have knowledge about the counselee's perspectives, and have gained a more advanced stage of racial identity, positive counselee growth is more likely (Kwan, 2001, as cited in Russell-Chapin & Ivey, 2004). Supervisors who have not had cultural sensitivity training may find it beneficial to consult with minority colleagues about multicultural issues in supervision, in addition to seeking continued education.

Carney and Kahn's (1984, as cited in D'Andrea & Daniels, 1997) model of multicultural counselor development explains that the supervisory relationship is challenged when supervisors and supervisees are operating at different multicultural stages. These stages are critical for both the supervisor and the trainee, and each may find him- or herself in one of the five stages described below.

Stage 1

At this stage there is little knowledge of multicultural counseling. The supervisor's role is to create a supportive, structured environment in which both trainees and supervisors are encouraged to explore ways that they or others have been influenced by minority group membership. Supervisees are also encouraged to explore this concept with their counselees (Leong & Wagner, 1994, as cited in D'Andrea & Daniels, 1997). The following questions help both the supervisors and supervisees in their understanding of multicultural functioning in interpersonal relationships.

1. How would I rate my level of understanding in terms of culture, ethnicity, and race?
2. What do I understand about the impact of cultural, ethnic, and racial factors on the counseling process?
3. How much do I understand people from diverse cultural, ethnic, and racial backgrounds?
4. How much education have I received regarding multicultural issues?
5. What experiences have I had that have assisted in my understanding of multicultural issues?
6. How would I rate my ability to provide culturally sensitive counseling services?
7. What are my biases about the trainee's or supervisor's race? (Constantine, 1997, as cited in Hird et al., 2001)
8. What are some of my values that may interfere with counseling or supervising an individual from a different background? (Constantine, 1997, as cited in Hird et al., 2001)

Stage 2

At this stage, there is an increased awareness of cultural/ethnic/racial issues, but there continue to be limitations in understanding how cultural/racial identity influences the counseling process. Values and beliefs, eye contact, personal space, attitudes toward those in authority, rules defining touching, nonverbal communication, and gender roles are all cultural variables influencing interpersonal relationships (Kluckhorn & Strodtbeck, 1961, as cited in McNeill & Horn, 1995).

A discussion surrounding how the supervision or counseling relationship is influenced by differences in backgrounds and how various techniques can be adapted for culturally diverse counselees facilitates a greater awareness of cultural sensitivity. In addition, learning about differences in values, beliefs, and behaviors is also beneficial for effective relationships. For example, some Native American, Asian, or Hispanic trainees may find it difficult to accept the competitive nature of graduate school because their culture values group harmony (McNeill & Horn, 1995). Or an African American raised in a poor inner-city neighborhood may be conflicted when supervised by a supervisor from this same racial group who espouses values that are contrary to the trainee's belief system (McNeill & Horn, 1995). The following questions can prepare for movement into the next stage.

1. What values and beliefs are important to you and why? (Goodenough, 1981, as cited in Garrett et al., 1997). (This question is intended to focus on the disparity of values and beliefs that may exist between the supervisor and trainee.)
2. Tell me what you perceive is happening in this session. Or, I'm experiencing tension right now and I was wondering if you are also feeling this tension, and how you would like to resolve it? (This question is intended to interpret the dynamics or interpersonal supervisory concerns in supervision.)

Stage 3

This stage is marked by the conflicting feelings one has about working with individuals from diverse backgrounds. On the one hand, there is excitement about this experience; on the other hand, there may be anxiety about one's limited experiences with diversity. Supervisors can help trainees and maybe even themselves by acknowledging conflicting feelings or by processing counseling dynamics using interpersonal process recall (IPR), a strategy developed by Kagan (1980, as cited in Cashwell, 1994). The following questions are designed to develop personal insight into thoughts, feelings, and behaviors that may occur in a relationship among individuals:

1. Is there anything you wish you had said?
2. What do you think the reaction would be if you had asked that question?
3. What were some of your thoughts during the session?
4. How do you want to be viewed in this relationship?
5. What are some of your values/beliefs that influenced you during the session?
6. Were you aware of any particular feelings? Thoughts? Behaviors?
7. How do you think your beliefs and values are different from the trainee or counselee?
8. Does this individual remind you of any particular person in your life who would create these feelings or thoughts?

Stage 4

At this stage there is increasing knowledge about diversity, and a wide variety of counseling or supervisory techniques have been developed. Supervisees are able to pick and choose the counseling strategies that would be most effective with their counselees, and supervisors are aware of effective supervisory strategies to use with their trainee. Also at this stage there is more recognition of the factors that contribute to problems such as power, socialization, and other differences. For instance, supervision and counseling are often viewed as a relationship in which there is a power differential. As discussed earlier in this chapter, because of socialization, males in our society tend to have more power than females. Ignoring these gender differences disregards any meaningful discussions that may impede the counseling or supervisory session, yet maximizing these differences could also lead to misleading conclusions (Paisley, 1994).

Different cultural/ethnic groups engage in various communication patterns that are more conducive to listening rather than talking. Culturally aware individuals are less apt to mislabel this style as a lack of interest or resistance and will instead adapt strategies compatible to the worldview of those with whom they interact (McNeill & Horn, 1995). Continued self-reflection and evaluation are instrumental to the maintenance and enhancement of multicultural awareness. The following questions can serve as continual reminders:

1. What is my preferred mode of communication? Does this type of communication help or hinder my relationship with others?

2. What strategies do I use to help the counselee or trainee work toward goals? Are these strategies based on my needs or those of the counselee?
3. What do I want in terms of outcome? Is this the same expectation as that of the counselee/trainee?

Stage 5

At this final level there is a greater awareness of the impact of culture on counseling and supervision, with an increased tendency to advocate for counselees or trainees. Supervisors are now serving in more of a consultant role by encouraging the trainee's advocacy efforts and serving as a sounding board (Gainor & Constantine, 2002). Trainees are serving in the same role with their underrepresented counselees. As advocates, the counselor-in-training or professional school counselor is better able to make certain that appropriate services are available for *all* individuals.

As awareness and behaviors change, individuals become more culturally sensitive. Creativity is a powerful vehicle for building trust and promoting self-efficacy (McCollum & Green, 2005), yet there is little information on the creative process, supervision, and multicultural issues. The next section describes creative approaches that may promote cultural responsiveness.

FOR PROGRAM SUPERVISORS

As noted in the previous section, supervisors have the duty to be prepared for difficulties that may arise between the supervisees and with themselves. Creative supervisory strategies may assist trainees to express their uniqueness and act as a bridge for supervisees to carry these same strategies into counseling sessions. Exercises 6.1, 6.2, and 6.3 are adapted from suggestions by McCollum and Green (2005).

SUMMARY

For too many years counselors in all settings viewed counseling from a Western perspective, a belief that often created unproductive counseling with unsatisfactory results. Supervisors who

Exercise 6.1

The Ball Toss

This exercise is designed to link supervision responsibilities with movement. In an informal setting, a soft ball is tossed between the supervisor and supervisee with the purpose of engaging in a comfortable conversation. When the supervisor is holding the ball, he or she states supervising responsibilities. The ball is then tossed to the supervisee, who relates his or her responsibilities in supervision. This process continues until each has stated his or her roles and expectations are learned. This activity promotes an informal atmosphere as a warm-up for a more professional conversation about supervisory responsibilities.

Exercise 6.2

Representing My Culture

Discussing one's cultural background can be difficult, particularly if an individual holds a belief that sharing personal details is taboo. In this exercise, the supervisor arranges different types of objects representing all aspects of nature, people, animals, and things on a table. Each supervisee is asked to choose an object and to share what that object represents from his or her cultural perspective. For instance, one supervisee from India chose a replica of the Statue of Liberty that symbolized the freedom that she did not experience in her country but was important to her and her family. This relaxed method of sharing can lead to a more in-depth discussion of cultural considerations.

Exercise 6.3

My Story

Supervisees can be invited to share a story about an event that best represents their culture, or a story about a time they learned something about themselves or others as a result of a cultural incident. For example, several years ago I had the opportunity to teach in Japan. Not knowing how to read or write Japanese presented difficulties when I did not have the benefit of an interpreter. On one occasion, the male dean of the college, another male instructor, and myself just completed dinner with some Japanese businessmen. Afterward the Japanese hosts invited the men to a bar to celebrate our accomplishments. Although they extended the same invitation to me, it was quite clear that my presence at the celebration was not really wanted because they had already called a taxi that was waiting to take me back to my hotel. It was on this occasion I became aware that the spoken language was not as important, because the actions alone represented the influence of males in this culture.

Note. From *Creative Skills Approach to Multicultural Supervision,* by J. J. McCollum and E. Green, 2005, from a paper presented at the meeting of the Association of Counselor Education and Supervision, Pittsburgh, PA. Adapted with permission.

are culturally effective are better able to provide meaningful supervision. Cultural differences have significant implications in regard to dynamics such as self-reflection, disclosure, nonverbal behaviors, and communication styles. Gender differences may also create an unsuitable relationship if attitudes and knowledge that could impair the relationship are not explored. It is vital that both the supervisor and supervisee understand the process of multicultural supervision and the various developmental stages through which both of these individuals progress. Creative use of supervision activities is a nonthreatening way to initiate a discussion of culture and how it influences relationships.

REFERENCES

American Counseling Association. (2005). *Cross-cultural competencies and objectives.* Retrieved October 24, 2005, from http://www.counseling.org/Content/NavigationMenu/RESOURCES/MULTICULTURALANDDIVERSITYISSUES/Competencies/Competencies.htm

Cashwell, C. (1994). *Interpersonal process recall.* Greensboro, NC: ERIC Clearinghouse on Counseling and Student Services. (ERIC Document Reproduction Service No. ED372342)

Constantine, M. G. (1997). Facilitating multicultural competency in counseling supervision: Operationalizing a practice framework. In H. L. K. Coleman & D. B. Pope-Davis (Eds.), *Multicultural counseling competencies: Assessment, education and training, and supervision* (pp. 310–324). Thousand Oaks, CA: Sage.

D'Andrea, M., & Daniels, J. (1997). Multicultural counseling supervision: Central issues, theoretical considerations, and practice strategies. In H. L. K. Coleman & D. B. Pope-Davis (Eds.), *Multicultural counseling competencies: Assessment, education and training, and supervision* (pp. 290–309). Thousand Oaks, CA: Sage.

Day-Vines, N., Craigen, L., Dotson-Blake, K., Douglass, M., Grothaus, T., Holman, A., & Wood, S. (2005, April). *Broaching the subject of race, ethnicity and culture during the counseling process.* Paper presented at the American Counseling Association Annual Convention, Atlanta, GA.

Fong, J. L., & Lease, S. H. (1997). Cross-cultural supervision: Issues for the White supervisor. In H. L. K. Coleman & D. B. Pope-Davis (Eds.), *Multicultural counseling competencies: Assessment, education and training, and supervision* (pp. 387–403). Thousand Oaks, CA: Sage.

Gainor, K. A., & Constantine, M. G. (2002). Multicultural group supervision: A comparison of in-person versus Web-based formats. *Professional School Counseling, 6,* 104–111.

Garrett, M. T., Borders, L. D., Crutchfield, L. B., Torres-Rivera, E., Brotherton, D., & Curtis, R. (2001). Multicultural superVISION: A paradigm of cultural responsiveness for supervisors. *Journal of Multicultural Counseling and Development, 29,* 147–159.

Garrett, M. T., Borders, L. D., Crutchfield, L. B., Torres-Rivera, E., Brotherton, D., & Stone, G. L. (1997). Multiculturalism as a context for supervision: Perspectives, limitations, and implications.

In H. L. K. Coleman & D. B. Pope-Davis (Eds.), *Multicultural counseling competencies: Assessment, education and training, and supervision* (pp. 263–289). Thousand Oaks, CA: Sage.

Granello, D. H. (2003). Influence strategies in the supervisory dyad: An investigation into the effects of gender and age. *Counselor Education and Supervision, 42,* 189–202.

Hird, J. S., Cavalieri, C. E., Dulko, J. P., Felice, A. D., & Ho, T. A. (2001). Visions and realities: Supervisee perspectives of multicultural supervision. *Journal of Multicultural Counseling and Development, 29,* 114–130.

Ladany, N., Brittan-Powell, C. S., & Pannu, R. K. (1997). The influence of supervisory racial identity interaction and racial matches on the supervisory working alliance and supervisee multicultural competence. *Counselor Education and Supervision, 36,* 284–304.

McCollum, J. J., & Green, E. (2005, October). *Creative skills approach to multicultural supervision.* Paper presented at the meeting of the Association of Counselor Education and Supervision, Pittsburgh, PA.

McNeill, B. W., & Horn, K. L. (1995). The training and supervisory needs of racial and ethnic minority students. *Journal of Multicultural Counseling and Development, 23,* 246–258.

Paisley, P. (1994). *Gender issues in supervision.* Greensboro, NC: ERIC Clearinghouse on Counseling and Student Services. (ERIC Document Reproduction Service No. ED372345)

Russell-Chapin, L., & Ivey, A. (2004). Microcounseling supervision: An innovative integrated supervision model. *Canadian Journal of Counselling, 38,* 165–176.

Wester, S. R., Vogel, D. L., & Archer, J. (2004). Male restricted emotionality and counseling supervision. *Journal of Counseling & Development, 82,* 91–98.

I thank Shamshad Ahmed and Song Lee, doctoral students in counselor education at North Carolina State University, Raleigh, who contributed to this chapter.

CHAPTER 7

Working With the Difficult Trainee

Marianne Woodside and Tricia McClam

THE PURPOSE of this chapter is to

- identify the problems that may arise during the practicum or internship
- suggest ways to approach these issues that support the roles and responsibilities of the faculty supervisor, the school counseling site supervisor, and the counseling trainee

Working with difficult trainees in school counseling practicum and internship experiences is challenging. This chapter identifies these challenges and describes three ways to approach the issues. A collaborative relationship between the site supervisor and the faculty supervisor provides a constructive framework for addressing issues. This positive context is helpful when addressing difficulties related to motivations, expectations, and unprofessional behavior. All require attention from both faculty and site supervisors. Application to the clinical experiences, orientation for supervisors and students, and the development of an educational plan contribute to mutual understandings and expectations. When dealing with difficult issues, helpful program policies include a four-step process described in this chapter. Students are encouraged to apply the concepts introduced to a detailed case study.

> Eleanor Fisher has an appointment with Chuck Taylor, one of her practicum supervisees. She dreads their supervision time together because Chuck is often late and inattentive and denies any difficulties or challenges he faces at his school site. In fact, he canceled their last supervision meeting, and she has not seen him in 2 weeks. As the time approaches for the appointment today, she finds that *she* would like to cancel the meeting, sensing that it is going to be a waste of her time. Dr. Fisher wonders when she should call Chuck's school supervisor, Ms. Rodriguez, with her concerns about his performance.

This scenario illustrates one issue that might arise during practicum or internship. Students like Chuck Taylor present special challenges for a supervisor, and it is in the best interest of everyone involved to address problems and concerns. It benefits trainees as they begin to build and hone the skills necessary to become effective school counselors. Considering the welfare of the counselee in the helping process is also important. Trainees who are incompetent, uncaring, and ineffective have the potential to do harm. Finally, it is in the supervisor's best interest to deal with difficult or challenging trainees because an interesting phenomenon occurs as the supervisor actually finds that he or she is adopting some of the very same behaviors as the trainee—dreading appointments, being late, being inattentive, and sometimes canceling or just not showing up for supervision.

The supervisor has an ethical as well as a legal obligation to provide honest feedback to the school counseling trainee. To maintain the integrity of the school counseling program, faculty and site supervisors want to train the very best students to join the ranks of other school counselors. Working with school counseling trainees requires professional behavior on the part of supervisors, modeling the behavior that trainees emulate.

There are three components to consider when addressing difficult issues: the context of collaboration in which supervision occurs, the initial difficulties one might encounter in the initial weeks of practicum and internship, and challenging issues for which initial difficulties are merely symptoms or early warnings. These components and a discussion of policies and procedures are followed by a case study and discussion questions.

WORKING COLLABORATIVELY

In reality, the practicum and internship experiences are a collaborative effort between the faculty supervisor and the school counseling site supervisor. Throughout the experience, the importance of collaboration is apparent. The strengths of collaborative work include a shared responsibility for practicum and internship experiences, a willingness to understand the multiple perspectives of both supervisors and the trainee, and joint decision making. The faculty supervisor assumes a leadership role as well as responsibility for developing a collaborative atmosphere in which supervision occurs.

What helps establish a positive atmosphere? Four characteristics support effective collaboration. First, there must be a common goal. Within a school counseling context, the faculty supervisor and the school counseling site supervisor commit to make the practicum or internship an excellent learning experience for the trainee and to provide help for the school and its students. Second, respect and trust are essential for effective collaboration. Mutual respect is especially important when supervisors have different perspectives; each becomes the "expert" with knowledge and skills related to his or her role and to the site in which he or she works. For example, the faculty supervisor understands the overarching goals of the practicum and internship experiences as well as the education and training the trainee receives prior to working in the school. The school counseling site supervisor brings information about the context of the school and the needs of its students. The trainee bridges the environments of the school and the university or college.

The third characteristic of working together is effective communication. Both supervisors learn to talk and listen to each other. The fourth significant feature of collaboration is willingness for each supervisor to ask for assistance, provide assistance, or receive it. All of these characteristics build a sense of community and reduce the isolation of supervision.

The result of collaboration is a cohesive partnership between the two supervisors that provides a foundation for supervision, especially when dealing with difficult or challenging trainees. Problems or concerns may surface at any time during the clinical experience, and a collaborative approach is an effective way to address them.

A particularly vulnerable time for a school counseling trainee is at the beginning of the clinical experience. A number of problems may occur related to motivations and expectations, reluctance or resistance, as well as problems associated with problem behavior such as being overly demanding, unmotivated, or egocentric. Unprofessional conduct may also arise as an issue. The collaborative relationship between supervisors provides a concrete effort to address any problems. A discussion of these difficulties follows.

Motivations and Expectations

Mara has always known she wanted to be a school counselor, especially since she worked with the school counselor when she was in middle school. She felt important when working in the front office, calling parents to verify absences, and conversing with the principal and vice principal. There were also times when she heard information about other students that she thought was interesting. Although she had been warned about confidentiality, she felt a sense of power when she knew about people or situations that others didn't.

People choose a career in the helping professions for a number of reasons. Among them are the desire to help others, self-exploration, control, and the very experience of being helped. On the surface these appear to be acceptable and even laudable motivations for this career choice; however, they may also have negative effects.

A major reason for wanting to be a counselor is the desire to help others. Feeling worthwhile when helping to resolve the problems or conflicts that others face or when improving their conditions or situations is a powerful motivator. In fact, contributing to the well-being of others is often a stronger motivation than salary. Where caution is necessary is when the desire to be helpful takes precedence over the counselee's wishes, values, and needs. A counselor may know exactly what actions a counselee needs to take to improve the family situation, school performance, or uncontrollable anger, but it is the counselee who must make the decision and take the action.

A second motivation that influences career choice is the desire for self-exploration. Courses in psychology, sociology, child and family studies, social work, and counseling are often popular choices for college students who want to learn more about themselves, understand behavior, and gain insights into their own attitudes and beliefs. If this need for self-exploration becomes more important than the counselee's needs, then trouble may result. If this desire remains unexplored and unchecked, then the counselor may become the counselee and the counselee may become the counselor, or there may suddenly be two counselees.

The desire to exert control is usually expressed by individuals as an interest in management or administration. Caring, competent people are needed in administrative positions in schools, agencies, and government, and who better to understand the challenges of the counseling profession than one of its own. Unfortunately, the desire to control or dominate counselees or other counselors may be cloaked as an administrative aspiration. Individuals with a strong need to control are probably not suited for the helping professions. Mara's feelings about confidential student information are an indication of this desire for power and bear further exploration.

Finally, it is human nature to want to be like those who have helped us in some capacity. For example, an influence on Mara's career choice was probably the school counselor with whom she worked. No doubt she modeled some important skills and professional behavior that impressed Mara. This motivation, however, can lead to some unrealistic expectations. Reflections about the experience of being helped are usually positive when the counselor is competent and caring and the counselee is cooperative and motivated. Unfortunately, not all counselors and counselees are like this, so this expectation may lead to disillusionment, discouragement, and frustration.

How should a supervisor respond to issues related to student motivations? First, exploring a trainee's motivations and expectations is critical and should occur prior to any clinical experience. If necessary, the identification of alternative ways of meeting personal needs may be appropriate. These may include a referral for therapy, the exploration of professional development opportunities, or both. Developing supportive peer relationships may also be helpful as students work together to face the challenges of a professional school setting. Finally, the exploration of motivations and expectations should be a topic of discussion among trainees at the beginning of their practicum or internship experience, in either group or individual supervision or both.

Both the faculty and the school site supervisor have a responsibility to facilitate the exploration of motivations. A concerted effort by both supervisors ensures that it will occur and that they address any concerns. Supervisors also assume responsibility for any decision making about steps to be taken if issues remain unresolved. Sometimes, the acknowledgment that the chosen profession and the student are not a good fit leads to counseling the student out of the program. Other times, the exploration of motivations and expectations may lead to the identification of the trainee's unresolved issues.

<u>Reluctance and Resistance</u>

Throughout the semester, Dilip has been chronically late for individual supervision, has canceled three times, and is inattentive when he does show up. At the elementary school where he is doing his internship, he is chronically late and manages to avoid one-on-one meetings with the school counselor. When confronted about his behavior by either supervisor, he admitted that he does not need supervision, sees no value in it, and has experienced no problems.

One of the main challenges of working with a trainee like Dilip is recognizing reluctance or resistance. Although the causes of reluctance and resistance are similar, reluctance occurs at the beginning of the relationship and is characterized as a hesitancy to participate in supervision. Resistance, on the other hand, may occur at any time in the relationship. What these two have in common is the similarity of causes and behaviors. For example, negative attitudes about supervision, including seeing neither benefits nor need, may cause either to occur. Some trainees perceive supervision as admission of weaknesses, mistakes, or both. For others, it translates to feelings of discomfort, embarrassment, and being threatened. The resulting behaviors include missing appointments, inattentiveness, denial of problems, silence, and supervisor rejection.

There are a number of strategies that a supervisor might use when faced with these behaviors. One is to recognize and discuss the trainee's feelings about supervision and the supervisory relationship. It may also be helpful to explore the trainee's perceptions, ideas, and expectations for supervision. This would be an appropriate time to explain the goals and process of supervision and the nature of the relationship. In a sense, demystifying the supervisory process may reduce feelings of threat and discomfort.

Other strategies to counter resistance may also be effective. For example, an immediate strategy is changing the pace or the topic under discussion. The supervisor may need to move more slowly or even abandon a topic until a later meeting, perhaps when more trust and rapport have been established. Silence presents different challenges because it can have different meanings. It is the supervisor's responsibility to evaluate the meaning of silence and any accompanying behavior. Is it resistance? Is the counselee reflecting on what has been said? Is the trainee waiting for the supervisor to provide direction?

A key to dealing effectively with reluctance or resistance is recognizing it and addressing it. Dilip is an example of a resistant trainee. If these same behaviors were present at the beginning of the semester, then we might characterize Dilip's behavior as reluctance. In this case, an explanation of supervision and a discussion of the expectations, perceptions, and feelings of both the supervisor and Dilip might be helpful in building a relationship and countering behaviors that prohibit Dilip from benefiting from the practicum or internship experience.

<u>Problem Behaviors</u>

A number of behaviors may appear throughout the practicum and internship that, if not addressed, may result in frustration, anger, disappointment, or dissatisfaction on the part of the supervisors or the trainee. Three are introduced here.

Problem 1: Overly Demanding Behavior

Chandra has been in both individual and group supervision for the past 2 weeks. During that time she has "dropped in" on her supervisor four times each week outside of office hours and has stayed after each of the two weekly group supervision meetings to talk with her supervisor. She has called the supervisor at home once on a Saturday and once on a Sunday. In all these encounters, she is talkative and does not give her supervisor a chance to talk. She describes her practicum experience in great detail. The information she provides is more about the concrete situations and less about her reflection. She voices concern and states she wants to learn but does not appear to seek or hear feedback.

Chandra is an example of an overly demanding trainee. She monopolizes the supervisor's time both in the office and in group supervision, schedules unnecessary appointments, calls the supervisor at home, and bombards the supervisor with e-mails. It is almost as if she is with the supervisor all day—and even into the evening and weekends. Causes of this behavior may be dependence on the supervisor about what to do or a need for attention, approval, or both. This student behavior will not change without some type of intervention. Failure to address this demanding behavior will lead to supervisor frustration, anger, and inattentiveness.

An important strategy for dealing with the overly demanding trainee is to establish boundaries. Some supervisors may assume that students understand the boundaries of a supervisor–supervisee relationship. Others may address this issue at the beginning of the semester in a syllabus review. Although it is preferable for a discussion to occur at the beginning of the semester for all students, it may also require reinforcement later in the semester. For the particularly needy student, a one-on-one conference may be necessary to confront the overly demanding behavior directly. Setting strict limits about meeting frequency and times, calling outside office hours, and "dropping by" will lead to a much more productive supervising relationship.

It is also likely that this behavior will carry over to the practicum or internship site. This is another situation that illustrates the advantages of a collaborative approach between faculty and school counseling site supervisors. If there is effective communication between both supervisors, then this behavior can be addressed on two fronts. This joint effort may include establishing boundaries and modeling professional behavior.

Problem 2: Lack of Motivation

Josh shows up for supervision because it is required, but he rarely participates. He meets with counselees because it is required but has yet to produce a tape of a counseling session. In fact, his site supervisor reports that he shows up but does nothing until directed to do so.

Josh is an unmotivated trainee. His goal is to meet the required number of hours of counselee contact and supervision and to graduate. He is not interested in learning, participating, or changing. In group supervision, the other members of the group do all the work. In individual supervision, it is the supervisor who does the work. Josh is simply present. The results of this behavior are that both group members and the supervisor believe that the unmotivated trainee is not assuming any responsibility, and they are resentful and frustrated. All are beginning to dread any meetings where Josh is present.

This is another behavior that may occur at the school site as well and is best addressed by a joint effort of the two supervisors. With trainees like Josh, at some point, probably sooner than later, either one or both supervisors will have to confront Josh with his behavior and construct some type of contract that specifies exactly what Josh must do to succeed. Involving Josh in writing the contract that includes a schedule or a format for individual supervision, counselee hours, and group supervision is one strategy to increase his participation. Another approach is for the supervisor to establish boundaries about what he or she is willing and able to do. Doing all the work in supervision lets Josh off the hook and reinforces his lack of motivation to do anything.

Problem 3: Egocentrism

Sue is really committed to her internship experience. She appears to be the model trainee; she demonstrates professional behaviors such as arriving at her school on time, addressing ethical issues such as confidentiality and dual relationships, participating in the supervisory process, and submitting paperwork in a timely manner. But when she talks about the students with whom she works, she identifies each of them by recalling her own experiences in school. The pattern of speech is, "Well, I can see Terry is angry; I would have been mad, too; in fact, I had a similar situation occur to me when I was in school."

Sue illustrates an egocentric approach to counseling. In each encounter, Sue's response is focused on herself, not on the other. It does not matter if she is in a casual conversation with students, classroom guidance activities, or individual counseling sessions. Trainees who are egocentric are unable to see multiple perspectives. They attribute counselee motivations without asking the counselee, they establish goals and directions based on their own preferences, and they use methods and techniques that would work for them.

This is a serious problem that may have consequences for the counselee if not addressed immediately. In Sue's case, the egocentrism is masked by other appropriate behaviors, a respectful attitude toward supervision, and an appearance of reflective practice.

When working with trainees who are egocentric, the supervisor needs to help the trainee refocus. Oftentimes role-plays and skill reminders such as active listening, paraphrasing, and asking for clarification remind trainees that their goal is to help students. Using a very structured approach to planning each counseling session also helps trainees engage themselves and students in the helping process.

Unprofessional Conduct

Two areas of focus encompass unprofessional conduct exhibited by trainees. The first occurs when trainees act unethically; the second occurs when trainees fail to disclose information vital to their placements.

Problem 1: Unethical Behavior

Rosa really loves being in high school again and is working in her old high school. She is captivated by the students, especially the seniors who really look up to her. She sees them everywhere: at the mall, at church, and at the football games. She knows their parents, too! The girls want her to attend their parties, and the boys have asked her out. She is really flattered by the attention. She spent last Saturday shopping, looking for just the right clothes to fit in and be noticed by her students. She is having more fun in high school this time around than when she attended the first time. Rosa maintains this new circle of friends because she is able to gossip with the girls about other students and teachers.

Difficult trainees present supervisory challenges if they act unethically. Prior to practicum or internship, all students complete a course in ethical, legal, and professional behavior in which they study the American School Counselor Association's (2004) ethical guidelines for practicing school counselors. These guidelines articulate school counselor responsibilities to students, parents, colleagues and professional associates, the school and community, diversity, and the profession. Chapter 10 provides a more detailed discussion on these ethical commitments. Several of these guidelines relate directly to the work of trainees in a school counseling setting.

School counselors work directly with children and youths and must be especially careful to protect and respect the rights of their students. Each trainee needs to be aware of potential dual relationships, especially because trainees may live in the same community in which the school is located. Rosa's placement is especially difficult because she already knows the school and the students. Counseling family members or close friends should be avoided if possible. The difficulty with dual relationships is lack of objectivity and conflict of interest. Confidentiality is difficult for the trainee, especially if the trainee knows or encounters students in another setting such as social or religious organizations or institutions. In "routine" conversation outside the helping relationship, the trainee may disclose information gained during a professional encounter. Negotiating the issues of confidentiality is difficult but must be a part of the trainee's reflective practice.

Issues of dual relationships and confidentiality provide the trainee with opportunities to make good ethical decisions. In Rosa's case she is taking advantage of the situation to meet her own needs rather than identifying potential ethical issues. In fact, her age and developmental level appear to be similar to the students she serves.

It is especially important for trainees to recognize their professional role and to distinguish it from a friendship. Tempting though it may be at times for the trainee to be "friends" with students in a school setting, establishing boundaries between professional and students is important. Both supervisors need to work with Rosa to outline her violation of ethical guidelines related to dual relationships and confidentiality. Explorations with her may help determine if she does not yet understand professional counseling behavior or if she has unresolved issues related to belonging or self-esteem.

Problem 2: Failure to Disclose

> Satchel is a recovering alcoholic unbeknownst to either his site or university supervisor. Because they were unaware of this, they honored his request to work at an outpatient mental health program for alcoholics housed on school grounds. As the semester progresses, Satchel engages in unprofessional self-disclosure, disregards boundaries, and does not follow school protocol. One example is talking about counselees in the teachers' lounge. He also establishes alliances with counselees outside of the setting by making counseling appointments at the local coffee house.

Satchel is a trainee with unresolved mental health issues, in this case, substance abuse. Often trainees will have unresolved issues that will affect their performance in practicum and internship. These issues may include but are not limited to the effects of a death, rape, therapy, and situational and developmental problems. Sometimes the very presence of these unresolved issues leads a student to a helping profession as a career choice. Nondisclosure of these issues creates problems for the faculty and school counseling site supervisors, the trainee, and the school. Certainly a primary consideration are the students who are at risk from the trainee's unprofessional behavior. The setting is in jeopardy as a placement for future students. An exploration of trainees' psychological well-being is necessary prior to a placement. The identification of unresolved issues at this point will prevent problems later in the placement and be an appropriate time for referral if necessary.

Students also need to disclose information if they have a criminal record, even if the adjudication was in their favor. This information must be conveyed to the program faculty and also to school personnel. School counseling programs and public and private schools may have policies and regulations that prohibit students' participation in the program or the school.

INITIAL DIFFICULTIES

In most school counseling programs there are certain times when either a formal or an informal assessment indicates initial problems or concerns such as motivation, resistance, reluctance, and others. Many programs address these at the application stage, orientation, and ongoing evaluation.

The *application to practicum and internship* is the point to begin the clinical experience. Trainees in the school counseling program initiate their application for practicum or internship. This application indicates that they have completed required coursework, met the insurance requirements, and signed the pledge of ethical commitment. Trainees read the practicum and internship manual carefully to familiarize themselves with the expectations and responsibilities they will assume.

During *orientation* trainees learn more about practicum or internship, visit several potential school sites, talk with trainees at various stages of clinical experience, learn about the stages of professional development and professional identity, and choose their school counseling site. They work with their future faculty and school counseling site supervisors to develop a Practicum/Internship Education Plan that spells out their goals, objectives, activities, and outcomes. This is a written document that establishes an agreement between both supervisors and the trainee. It is important that both supervisors collaborate in establishing a clinical experience that helps trainees develop a professional counseling identity and allows them to practice basic counseling skills.

Once the practicum or internship begins, supervision, one component of *ongoing evaluation*, starts. For programs approved by the Council for Accreditation of Counseling and Related Educational Programs (CACREP), students are supervised in various ways including the following: a minimum of 1 hour working with the school counseling site supervisor; a minimum of 1 hour working with the faculty supervisor; and a minimum of 1½ hours each week in group supervision class. Chapter 1 provides a more detailed description of CACREP criteria for practicum and internship. Supervisors search for ways to build on student strengths during the supervisory process. The midterm evaluation is an opportunity for the initial assessment of practicum and internship performance and a time to address any concerns that the faculty or site supervisor may have. Some of their concerns may indicate more serious issues.

REMEDIATION OF SERIOUS ISSUES

There are occasions when the practicum or internship application, orientation, and ongoing supervision and evaluation do not address the more serious issues that may arise. Challenges such as working with a trainee who is reluctant, resistant, overdemanding, or unmotivated may be symptoms of deeper or more serious issues. The supervisor has a number of responsibilities when working with a trainee with serious and unresolved issues, especially when it results in unprofessional behavior. Working in concert, the faculty and school counseling site supervisors follow four steps: (a) identification of difficult issues, (b) confrontation about the behavior and provision of written feedback about concerns, (c) development of implementation plan, and (d) continuation or removal from the placement or the program.

The first step, *identification of difficult issues,* occurs when the supervisor identifies what exactly is going on with the trainee in the placement. What are the problem behaviors? How are they affecting performance? How are they affecting students? The school? What has the site supervisor observed? There is no wrong time to discuss difficult issues that arise during the practicum and internship. Maintaining a balance between a discussion of strengths and a discussion of difficulties allows the supervisor to foster support and provide a foundation and climate for change.

A second step is to *confront the trainee about the behavior by providing oral and written feedback.* With serious concerns, supervisors must convey to the trainee the gravity of the difficulties. Providing feedback in writing indicates to the trainee the seriousness of the situation, the behaviors that are inappropriate, and the consequences of the trainee's behavior. All written feedback is placed in the trainee's central file, including the trainee's responses to the feedback provided.

The *implementation plan to address the difficult behavior* represents the third step in addressing serious issues. The faculty supervisor and the school counseling site supervisor develop this plan together and discuss the plan with the school counseling trainee. It is important to build on strengths and clearly articulate in behavioral terms what change is necessary. This plan includes positive behaviors expected of the trainee, awareness of the ethical and legal dimensions of the behavior, and the professional standards to which the trainee must adhere. Included are the consequences if the trainee docs not change his or her behavior.

It is also possible that the school counseling trainee has committed egregious mistakes, and part of the plan development is ascertaining if remediation is possible or if the *removal of the trainee* is in the best interests of all involved. These are difficult challenges for both the faculty and the school counseling site supervisor and require time and consultation with other school personnel and program faculty.

The case of Ariel illustrates how supervisors work with a challenging trainee. Questions follow that encourage you to critique the supervision and suggest the strengths and weaknesses of the supervisory process.

THE CASE OF ARIEL

Working with difficult trainees can be a challenge for the supervisor, but the experience can also be rewarding if the trainee responds positively to supervision. As you read this case, evaluate the timing of the intervention, the type of intervention, and the efforts at remediation.

The following individuals are involved in the case of Ariel:

Ariel Scarletti: trainee in school counseling practicum
Dr. Cho: Ariel's advisor
Dr. Bateson: the practicum faculty
Ms. Johnson: the school counseling site supervisor
Mia Chang: the doctoral student individual supervisor

Part I: Introduction to Ariel

Ariel is a trainee in a school counseling program. At age 29, she has spent over 7 years trying to decide about her career. Both of her parents work in the public schools; her father teaches math and English at the local high school where she attended. Her mother, now retired, was an elementary school counselor with 20 years of experience. Ariel is pleasant, is articulate, and works hard.

Part II: First-Year Summary

Dr. Cho is Ariel's advisor and has been for the past year. Ariel came to him first for assistance in planning her program of study. Actually the curriculum is fairly prescribed, so Dr. Cho uses the semester advising appointments as a way of getting to know trainees in the program. Ariel was accepted as a trainee in the spring, and she began the program in the fall. Because the school counseling program does not have interviews, Ariel was accepted on the basis of her written file. Her GRE scores were high, she had above-average reference letters, and her experience was relevant to counseling. She had worked as a waitress; she had 5 years of volunteer experience in the human services and appeared to be committed to helping others. Her letter of application summarized her search for a career.

Dr. Cho was impressed with Ariel, but he also believed that there was something not quite right. He could not put his finger on it. He taught her in one course during her first semester. She attended most classes but came late several times because she was traveling from work. He called on her, as well as others, and somehow what she had to say was just a little off the subject. For example, one day the discussion centered on the case of an Appalachian welfare mother who was struggling to make ends meet by working the welfare system. Ariel summarized the case by saying, "This is a case similar to the one we read in philosophy class. The welfare mother has an existential point of view and it affects how she views the system. It is obvious she does not take responsibility for her own life." Well, Dr. Cho knew that this was not really the point of the discussion, and he wondered about the relevance of relating a welfare mother to existentialism. In this case, the welfare mother's main concern is providing for her children.

In the spring, when all faculty reviewed the files, Ariel was barely discussed. That semester there were two trainees in the program who were not performing well in courses. Most of the discussion focused on these trainees: identifying the issues, generating alternative ways of working with them, and determining a plan of action for them for the late spring and the following fall.

Ariel applied for practicum in the spring of her first year of study. Because her mother was a school counselor, she was clear about the curriculum and also knew quite a bit about the position for which she was studying. In fact, she did study hard, but her mind was not always on what she was learning. She was reading books that her boyfriend was reading and trying to support him in his studies. Her relationship with him was not going well. She really wanted the relationship to last and felt that she was willing to do whatever it would take to keep him.

During this time Ariel was still attending classes and planning her summer studies. She interviewed for her practicum. She believed that she and her supervisor, Ms. Johnson, would get along famously. But she was not sure that she agreed with the theory that Ms. Johnson used with the difficult children with whom she worked. Ms. Johnson was trained as a behavioral specialist, and she had all of the students on behavioral contracts. But Ariel did not say anything to the supervisor or to her advisor. She just planned to work with Ms. Johnson in the fall.

Part III: The Second Year

Ms. Johnson works as a middle school counselor. She is currently supervising Ariel. She had interviewed Ariel in the spring and was excited to have a practicum trainee, her first in 5 years. She remembered that trainees take a lot of time to supervise, but she also remembered how much fun she had with the three trainees whom she had supervised previously. Dr. Bateson, the practicum supervisor, called Ms. Johnson and visited the school before the fall term. They both attended the same church and had been acquaintances for years. Dr. Bateson spoke well of Ariel.

Dr. Bateson began the group supervision during the first week of the term. There were four trainees enrolled in practicum. In spite of the work the previous spring and the summer, the trainees were not all ready for their practicum; however, Ariel was placed and working in the school the first week. In fact, she was so excited about her placement she began a week early. The other trainees had not enrolled until the first week of the term, and Dr. Bateson was busy locating supervisors and school sites for them. Joining the practicum team were two counselor education doctoral students, Mia Chang and Peter Smith. Dr. Bateson asked Mia to provide individual supervision for Ariel.

During the first class Dr. Bateson noticed an odd interaction with the trainees. Ariel seemed to be unwilling to listen to what the others had to say. She made judgments about her classmates, their placements, and the students with whom they worked. For instance, a classmate described one of her students as reticent. Ariel stated that the student had something to hide and was definitely not to be trusted. One student talked about using a mirror to talk to herself. Ariel indicated she thought this was stupid. Another classmate talked about her fears of encountering a student who talked about suicide. Ariel argued that those students were the most interesting and that she welcomed the challenge. Ariel also complained that she did not agree with the philosophy of the school or her site supervisor, Ms. Johnson. When asked to explain what she considered a mismatch, all she would say was that there were too many rules.

This type of interaction continued for the next 2 weeks. In addition, Ariel seemed unable to discuss her placement in specific terms. At the beginning of each class, the trainees summarized the events of the week, talking about their school counseling settings, describing students they had seen, and sharing information about group counseling and classroom guidance. Each of the other three trainees was reflective about school experiences and talked about the most significant challenges. In spite of probes from Dr. Bateson and questions from her classmates, Ariel talked about "the placement" going "all right." She described her activities the second week by saying, "Well, I work with students all morning. We're in group and one morning I led the group." After questions from others, she indicated, "We just do the routine things . . . students seem to respond well to me . . . nothing special . . . there's really nothing to say." The last statement she made was about philosophical difficulties. After class Dr. Bateson asked Mia about her supervision of Ariel. Mia indicated that Ariel did not seem to listen to the students. Mia also stated that Ariel seemed to believe she was establishing rapport when there was little evidence of it.

The fourth week Ariel continued to belittle the other trainees and their students during supervision. After multiple probing from Dr. Bateson, Ariel finally described an incident that occurred at school. After a group session focusing on anger management with eight 7th graders, one of the students asked Ariel what she did when she was angry. She reported that she had replied, "That is absolutely none of your business." Everyone in the group supervision was silent and stunned. Dr. Bateson asked why that response, but all Ariel did was repeat herself. She was unaware of the impact she was having on the group.

After the fourth session Dr. Bateson decided to meet with Ariel to discuss his observations and to share his concerns. After consulting with Mia, he wrote Ariel a letter outlining his observations based on his experience in group supervision and asked Ariel to come see him. He planned to give Ariel the letter during the meeting. The contents of the letter (see Figure 7.1) provided the focus for the meeting. It includes strengths, concerns, and a mid-semester plan.

TO: Ariel Scarletti
FROM: Dr. Bateson
SUBJECT: Practicum Performance
DATE: XX-XX-XXXX

The purpose of this letter is to provide you with an assessment of your performance in the Counseling Practicum from January 18th until February 28th. This formative evaluation marks four weeks in the semester, reflects observations of your performance in the group supervision class, and reflects on your work in your clinical setting gained from listening to your taped counseling sessions. The memo articulates the strengths demonstrated during your practicum experience and concerns about your performance in your clinical setting and group supervision, and identifies specific skills that you need to demonstrate between now and the end of the term.

Strengths

You have shown an enthusiasm for working in a clinical setting this semester. Evidence of this enthusiasm includes an early start at the placement, dependable attendance, and your desire to work with middle school students. After reviewing two of your tapes, Mia, your counseling intern supervisor, reports that your ability to reflect content and feelings represents the skill level of a beginning counselor. You have demonstrated an ability to normalize a student's feelings. To some degree, you are linking patterns between the student's present behavior and past behavior, although the links between past and present, at times, focus more on you making a statement about what you perceive rather than asking for the student's assessment of your perceptions.

Concerns

The concerns fall into four areas: a focus on self, an inability to establish rapport with fellow trainees and your students, doing work for the students, and difficulty responding to supervision. A discussion of these concerns follows.

A focus on self

You demonstrate a focus on self while working with your students and during group supervision. With the students you want to cover the material that you think is important rather than let the students lead. For example, in one tape, the student wanted to talk about an issue, but you stated that you did not want to talk about that issue. You changed the subject quickly. Another time you stated that you knew what the student wanted out of the session rather than letting the student tell you. In another part of the conversation, the student wanted to talk about a subject, but you told her that sounded like a "big" issue and you wanted only to talk about little issues.

During the group supervisory sessions you reported concerns with a student interaction and focused on your needs rather than the student's needs. For example, you said that when one student asked you, "What do you do when you get angry?" you did not use this as an opportunity to make a connection and explore with the student ways to manage anger; instead, you replied this was "not the student's business." Although your other classmates and the counseling intern supervisor tried to help you find alternative ways of responding to this student, many of which focused on involving the student in the exploration, you continued to focus on what you did not want to tell this student.

During the group supervision you also focus on yourself. I believe that positive interactions during group supervision occur when practicum trainees are able to share information about their work with students in very specific terms and other classmates and supervisors join the discussion in the following ways:

- Helping classmates explore more deeply the issues or situations being described
- Responding empathetically to classmate concerns
- Responding positively when trainees describe interactions and activities that worked
- Asking questions to understand the situation more clearly

Figure 7.1

Practicing Performance Assessment

(Continued)

- Presenting skill development opportunities
- Problem solving to help classmates plan for future sessions with their students

This positive interaction does not occur when you participate during group supervision. What does occur is a constant return to how you view issues and students without paying attention to other classmates and the situations they present. When others are talking about their placements, you do not show an interest in what is being discussed by asking exploratory questions, making empathetic responses, or helping problem solve for future counseling sessions. Your response is either about another subject that is not relevant to the discussion or it is a belittling judgment about the student (at the other placement). The focus of the conversation was on you, and the other trainees did not receive feedback or help from the group.

An inability to establish rapport with fellow trainees and students
Based on the tape of your counseling session, you did not demonstrate skills that help establish rapport. For instance, in one tape, after 30 minutes talking with the student, you had to ask the student her name again. Your intonation and content indicated that you conducted a question-and-answer session with the student rather than providing an opportunity for the student to talk about what was of interest to her. You also encouraged the student to seek the help of a "professional," indicating that the treatment she was receiving at the middle school was not legitimate. This does not foster student confidence and trust. You indicated to the student that she did not need to share details of a situation because you did not think that the details were important.

Doing work for the students
Working with students, you control the situation and do not help the students explore their own situations. For instance, you do not let students talk about what they want to talk about, rather you let them know when you want to change the subject and tell them you really do not want to hear the details. In one instance, the student talked about being ashamed of her suicide attempt; you told her to accept these feelings; she asked you how. And then you tried to explain how. This would have been the perfect opportunity to empathize with the difficulty of feeling shame and then helping the student explore ways of overcoming shame.

Difficulty responding to supervision
During the group supervision sessions, you are not able to contribute with specific information about your work at your practicum site. In class, you answer in very general terms about your experiences. In response to your generalities, your three other classmates, counseling intern supervisors, and I ask you questions trying to understand your experience, but many times you continue to talk about the experience in generalities like "it went fine" and "it was interesting," without providing information about content or feelings.

Summary
Ariel, you demonstrate an ability to reflect content and feelings that students express. However, you are limited in your ability to establish rapport with students and let the students talk about things important to them. You are also limited in your ability to listen carefully to your peers and help them think about their own experiences. You need to improve your ability to talk about students in a positive way. Finally, you need to develop the ability to discuss your clinical experiences in very specific terms and process the feedback that you receive during supervision.

On the next page I have begun a list of expectations I have for you over the course of the remaining 10 weeks of the semester. I hope that you will be able to add to this list of expectations. You will need to demonstrate these basic skills if you are to receive a passing grade in practicum. These expectations are in addition to the expectations spelled out in the practicum syllabus. Once you and I agree to this set of expectations, I will share them with Mia Chang, your counseling intern supervisor, and with Ms. Johnson, your school counseling site supervisor. You will have the support of all three of us as you continue to develop your counseling skills.

Cc: Ms. Johnson
        Mia Chang

Figure 7.1 *(Continued)*

Practicing Performance Assessment

The conference between Dr. Bateson and Ariel did not go particularly well. Dr. Bateson reviewed with Ariel her strengths and areas that needed improvement. Ariel expressed shock and dismay, stating that she was disappointed because her placement was going so well. Together they constructed a plan to address the areas of concern. The plan contained components such as objectives, a time frame, and activities. They both signed the plan (Figure 7.2).

Practicum in Counseling
Fall Semester

Student Interaction (as demonstrated by taped counseling sessions)
Allow student to establish agenda for counseling session.
Allow student to discuss incidents in detail.
Remember name of student.
Demonstrate empathy through voice intonation.
Use empathetic responses.
Reflect feeling and content with "I hear . . . " rather than "You were saying . . ."
Interpret without overexplaining.
Allow student to respond to your interpretation.
Avoid question and answer pattern.
Explore alternatives with student rather than push suggestions.
Let student tell you how she/he is feeling rather than you telling her/him.

Participation During Group Supervision
Pay attention to other classmates.
Ask helpful questions about classmates' experiences.
Respond empathetically to classmates.
Help problem solve.
Respond empathetically about other students or your own.
Provide explicit detail about your clinical experiences.

Student Signature   Faculty Supervisor Signature

_____   _____

Date   Date

_____   _____

Figure 7.2

Mid-Semester List of Expectations for Ariel Scarlatti

The next morning Dr. Bateson called Ms. Johnson to tell her about the conference with Ariel. His plan was to fax the letter and the plan to Ms. Johnson and offer to meet with both Ms. Johnson and Ariel together that week. Ms. Johnson answered the phone and thanked Dr. Bateson for calling, assuming that he was returning her phone call. Ms. Johnson indicated that she had called earlier, but Dr. Bateson had not yet checked his messages.

According to Ms. Johnson, Ariel was working with a sixth-grade girl who had been suspended twice for bringing drugs to school and was currently in in-school suspension (ISS) for verbally abusing a teacher. During the counseling session, Ariel turned off the tape recorder and then told the young girl not to worry about using drugs or getting in trouble. Ariel shared that she had abused drugs for years and claimed that it had not hurt her. She told the student that the school philosophy "sucked" and she needed to figure out how to get around the rules. Ariel told her she could help her get drugs and could teach her how to use them.

The ISS supervisor told Ms. Johnson that the student came back to ISS with a smug look on her face and reported that Ariel had given her some great advice and was definitely the one person at school who was on her side. The ISS supervisor contacted Ms. Johnson and passed this information along. That afternoon Ms. Johnson asked the student to come to her office; the student proudly relayed the information that Ariel had given her. She told Ms. Johnson that she had known all along that the school policy was bad. Ms. Johnson talked with the ISS supervisor again and then called a meeting with the principal, assistant principal, the head teacher, and the ISS supervisor. They all agreed that Ariel had violated both school policy and the counseling profession's ethical code, compromised the integrity of the school philosophy, and provided information to the student that placed that student in jeopardy. They did not want Ariel to return to the school.

Ms. Johnson called Ariel to her office and told her that she had violated school policy with her counselee in ISS. Ariel asked that she not call Dr. Bateson; she asked Ms. Johnson to give her a second chance. Ms. Johnson told her that she must call Dr. Bateson. They scheduled a meeting for the following day at 8:00 a.m. Ms. Johnson then sent Ariel home.

Dr. Bateson suggested that he and Ms. Johnson meet together first and then ask Ariel to join them. They arranged a meeting for the following morning. Ms. Johnson called Ariel to ask her not to report to the school until 9:00 a.m. In the meantime, Dr. Bateson consulted with faculty colleagues, the department head, and a member of the dean's staff. From the consultations he arrived at three scenarios for the next step: (a) ask Ariel to withdraw from practicum; (b) give Ariel an NC (no credit) for practicum; or (c) place Ariel in another site. He knew that he would be involved in remediation with Ariel unless she was asked to leave the program.

This case represents one of many scenarios that occur during school counseling practicum and internship. The questions in Exercise 7.1 encourage reflection on the challenges and issues of working with difficult trainees. Use the information in the earlier sections of the chapter, as well as other chapters of the text, to explore the issues associated with working with difficult trainees.

SUMMARY

This chapter identifies challenges that may arise during the practicum, internship, or both and suggests ways to approach these issues. Successful practicum and internship experiences require a collaborative effort between the faculty supervisor and the school counseling site supervisor. Characteristics of collaboration include establishing a common goal, respecting the expertise of each participant in the collaboration, and communicating effectively; all contribute to the working relationship. Both faculty and site supervisors may see difficulties surface at the beginning of the clinical experience related to motivations and expectations, reluctance or resistance, and problem behaviors such as being overly demanding or unmotivated. They may also identify unprofessional behavior, especially related to legal and ethical considerations.

Exercise 7.1

Thinking About Ariel

1. Describe prepracticum and beginning practicum activities used to prepare students for the practicum.
2. Outline any other steps for prepracticum and practicum that would have been helpful.
3. List five characteristics that describe Ariel.
4. Identify four issues that emerged during Ariel's practicum.
5. Describe the processes that Dr. Bateson and Ms. Johnson used to address the difficulties.
6. Outline three other activities or steps that either Dr. Bateson or Ms. Johnson could have taken.
7. Rewrite this case in a way that addresses issues you have with Dr. Bateson or Ms. Johnson's supervision or Ariel's performance as a practicum trainee.
8. Summarize Ariel's problems. Support with specific behaviors.
9. Identify a strategy to address each one.
10. Ariel's problems culminate with her involvement with the sixth-grade student. Describe Ariel's perspective of the situation. Describe the perspectives of the two supervisors.
11. As the case concludes, what recommendation would you make for Ariel? Support your recommendation.
12. Suppose *you* were working with Ariel and the recommendation was continuation in the program. Develop a plan that would prepare Ariel for a second chance for a more successful practicum experience.
13. Think about the responsibilities of supervising a practicum or internship student. What would you expect of the school counseling site supervisor? What expectations would you have for the faculty supervisor?
14. What are the skills one needs to be an effective supervisor, particularly with challenging trainees?

When issues and challenges arise during the clinical experience, supervisors can use established policies and procedures to guide their interventions. These policies and procedures include preventive measures that reduce the number of issues that supervisors might encounter. For instance, during the application to practicum and internship process and the orientation, students and site supervisors learn more about the practicum experience. This provides them with opportunities to ask questions, establish a relationship with supervisors, and develop an educational plan or contract that articulates their work on-site.

There are occasions when the practicum application, orientation, and ongoing supervision and evaluation do not address the more serious issues that may arise. The supervisor has a number of responsibilities when working with a trainee with serious and unresolved issues, especially when it results in unprofessional behavior. Four steps constitute a process to resolve issues: identification of problems, confrontation about the behavior and provision of written feedback about concerns, development of an implementation plan, and continuation or removal from the placement or the program. Resolution still remains a complicated and complex process that requires thoughtful reflection and action on the part of the faculty supervisor.

REFERENCE

American School Counselor Association. (2004). *Ethical standards for school counselors.* Alexandria, VA: Author. Retrieved from http://www.schoolcounselor.org/content.asp?contentid=173

CHAPTER 8

Supervision and Technology

Joel F. Diambra, Valerie A. Fulbright, and Daniel L. Fudge

THE PURPOSE of this chapter is to

- introduce technology terms
- explain and connect various applications and tools with supervision
- introduce the use of audio and video recordings
- discuss the advantages of digital format
- explain various forms of online communication
- summarize electronic portfolios, virtual reality supervision, and tools used to supervise using technology

FOR SUPERVISORS AND SUPERVISEES

Counselors in today's schools are required to deal with increasingly complex situations as compared with their predecessors. The increase in job demands places stressors on both the supervisor and the supervisee. Distance, underfunding, and time constraints all complicate vital communication. As a whole, school counselor trainees are fortunate in that they have access to innovative technological advances that their earlier counterparts did not.

TECHNOLOGICAL TOOLS IN SUPERVISION

It is important to recognize that the use of contemporary technology in supervision is truly an ever-changing and advancing field. Little research has been done investigating the efficacy of technology and school supervision. Studies have been done, however, in several related areas, including technology and instruction (Benigno & Trentin, 2000; Doyle, 2000; Eldredge et al., 1999; Hansen & Gladfelter, 1996; Huff, 2000; Johnson & Huff, 2000; Petracchi, 2000; Stadtlander, 1998), technology and counseling (Hayes, Taub, Robinson, & Sivo, 2003; Powell, 2004; Riemer-Reiss, 2000; Wall, 2004), and technology coupled with mentoring or supervision (Knouse, 2001; Manzanares et al., 2004; Page, Pietrzak, & Sutton, 2001; Petracchi & Patchner, 2001). Some studies show promising results. Petracchi and Patchner (2001) compared live instruction with interactive televised teaching. They found that social work students expressed no significant preference between these two forms of instruction. Hsiung and Tan (1999) studied the impact of a computer and Internet-based distance supervision hot line (DSHL) on the professional development of student teachers. They found that 100% of the student teachers responded in favor of DSHL and noted that student teacher and supervisor contacts increased using this means. In another study, Johnson and Huff (2000) investigated computer-mediated communication (CMC) with social work students at distant learning sites.

Results suggest that at the end of the experience students gave positive feedback about using technology and shared that they felt more capable of using CMC.

Ethical considerations, somewhat unique to technology use, must also be taken into account when communicating electronically (Herlihy, Gray, & McCollum, 2002). Maintaining confidentiality becomes a more difficult challenge with the use of some forms of technology. Fortunately, the American Counseling Association provides guidance for counselors in the use of technology in its 2005 *ACA Code of Ethics* (see Appendix C). Although this guidance is not directed toward supervision, much of the information can be applied to supervisory relationships.

Synchronous Versus Asynchronous

A discussion regarding communication using technology requires an understanding of *synchronous* versus *asynchronous* communication. Synchronous communication is when two or more parties present at the same time are able to interact, directly, in real time. Examples include an ear-to-ear discussion on the telephone or walkie-talkie, typing messages back and forth in an electronic chat room, or instant messaging. Both participants are able to talk or type and send a message while the other participant is able to receive the message at the same moment in time. This enables an electronic-based interactive discussion among two or more people all present at the same time. School counselor supervisors would use synchronous communication when interaction among participants needs to be immediate or live. For example, a trainee seeks guidance regarding his or her professional responsibility to warn an intended victim when the counselee describes a detailed plan to harm another student. This type of communication is time sensitive and potentially life threatening. Synchronous communication, therefore, is essential.

Asynchronous communication allows two or more parties to communicate, even when they are not all available and present at the same time. Examples of this include e-mail, discussion boards, and text messaging over cell phones. One participant sends messages, and these communiqué are made available to the recipients regardless of where the recipient is located. This message is stored and made available for the recipient to retrieve and respond to at a later time (Marjanovic, 1999). When immediacy is not critical, asynchronous communication provides a format by which supervisors or counselors can consider an array of responses and then construct and post an answer without having to interact in the moment.

Audio Recordings

Audio format is still useful and popular. Feist (1999) pointed out that audio recording provides helpful and candid information regarding a counselor's session. Most of us are familiar with portable Walkman players that replaced the cumbersome portable stereos popular in the 1980s. These small devices can be used with little to no hindrance in most daily activities. Walkman players made listening to analog cassette tapes convenient. The portable audio players changed to CD format when CDs became mass manufactured by Philips in 1980. Portable digital audio players such as Moving Pictures Expert Group 1 Audio Layer 3, commonly referred to as MP3, and iPod are gaining popularity. MP3 players allow the user to play audio "ripped" (typically music copied from a CD collection) or downloaded from the Internet. The iPod is marketed by Apple (Hewlett Packard also makes a version of iPod) and has a variety of additional options and uses. Basically, these devices use digital format and flash memory or tiny computer chip storage as a means of eliminating the need for CDs, and they boast the capacity up to 60 gigabytes (GB) of audio data. Users transfer digitally formatted music or other audio files (e.g., audio books) to their portable digital audio player, which can then be accessed quickly and listened to at their convenience.

Traditional analog recordings are quickly losing ground to digital recordings in a fast-paced electronic industry. This change affects counselors and counselor education programs. For supervision purposes, student counselors and supervisors often rely on audiotape recorded counseling sessions. These tapes are used for review and feedback. Tapes can be stopped and started, rewound, and fast-forwarded. These operations are extremely helpful for review and for creating time for reflection. Audio recorders are fairly unobtrusive, putting both counselor and counselee quickly at ease. With the advent of digital audio, recorders are much smaller in size and much greater in flexibility. Digital audiotape (DAT) recorders have not attained the popularity of DAT players. However, an iPod, for example, has the means to record as well as play digital audio. This suggests that digital audio recording will soon become commonplace and increasingly more affordable for counselors and supervisors. Additionally, technology is advancing quickly while combining tools to create multipurpose handheld instruments. For example, cell phones are being combined with personal digital assistants (PDAs) and portable digital audio players to create one multifunctional device. Using a cell phone to record digital audio and sending the recording via the Internet is already available to the public. Rather than write out process and case notes, school counselors and interns can audio record these notes using various methods. Additionally, upon reflection, supervisees can use audiotape to record thoughts and feelings they remember having during the session.

Podcasting is a process that makes sound files available online. This differs from Web casting and video conferencing in that files are downloaded remotely and automatically. Subscribers can use any digital audio player or personal computer to instantaneously receive and listen to sound feeds. The audio files can also be attached in e-mails as well as made available on the Internet. Digital audio is already being made available on Web sites and takes full advantage of this added convenience. Digital audio technology makes audiotaped sessions available to the supervisor within minutes and over great distances. This allows a supervisor–supervisee relationship to be conducted from different parts of the world, and also for geographically isolated counselors to connect with a supervisor at an urban university, for example.

Unfortunately, audio recordings do not capture all of the relevant dynamics necessary for quality supervision. Regardless of their format (i.e., analog or digital audio), audio recordings do not capture counselor or counselee affect, facial expressions, or body language. This shortcoming is ameliorated by the use of video recordings.

Videotaping

Both supervisors and supervisees identify videotaping as the most treasured form of technology (Goodyear & Nelson, 1997). Moreover, the supervisor can observe actual session dynamics in addition to listening to the session's audio recordings. Protinsky (1997) noted that, similar to audiotape, video can be manipulated (i.e., stopping, pausing, rewinding, replaying), making the process more useful than live observation. Also like audiotapes, videos can now be converted to or created directly in digital format. Digital video cameras are also readily accessible and are quickly making analog video cameras outdated. Even some digital still cameras allow recording of brief video movie clips. These are usually stored in *moving picture expert group* (MPEG) format, which can be uploaded to a personal computer or laptop, often with a simple click of a mouse and a basic *universal serial bus* (USB) cable, or even sent wirelessly via the Internet. Digital video can be shared in much the same way as audio files, including attachment by e-mail and through *file transfer protocol* (FTP) servers by way of the Internet. Digital recordings remain intact as duplication can occur without noticeable loss of quality.

Digital Video

Digital video, like digital audio format, allows recordings to be transferred via the Internet. This file sharing not only is convenient but also opens opportunities to receive expert supervision from any distance, or even to receive input from a supervisor in another country for a valuable cultural perspective that would otherwise be unavailable. Video clips can provide visual and auditory examples of applied concepts. For example, counselor educators at the University of Tennessee created two video clips to help train school counseling supervisors and prepare practicum and internship students. These clips are in video format and can be viewed by downloading RealPlayer; the supervisor type can be viewed at http://digitalmedia.utk.edu:8080/ramgen/10942.rm and the student clip at http://digitalmedia.utk.edu:8080/ramgen/10966.rm.

E-mail

E-mail, technically known as electronic mail, is a common word in nearly everyone's vocabulary today. E-mail is a very quick and efficient source of communication between as few as two people or as many as an entire group of recipients. Messages can be transmitted instantaneously with the touch of a button or the click of a mouse. Additionally, attachments (i.e., electronic files that may consist of text, data, pictures, movie clips, hyperlinks to Web sites, etc.) can be sent along with an e-mail. This makes e-mail an extremely effective and invaluable supervisory means of communication and information sharing.

Listserv

Listservs are becoming increasingly user-friendly and are popping up in a wide range of areas. A listserv, or electronic mailing list, includes one primary address to which a user can send an e-mail that is then forwarded to numerous subscribers at one time. A listserv makes life easy for the e-mail author who wants to reach a large audience interested in the topic as it makes and sends a copy to all the people who have subscribed. A large number of listserv sites were created at Kent State University Division of Information Services. Today, they host CESNET (Counselor Education and Supervision Network).

CESNET-L is likely the most well-known listserv concerning counselor education and supervision. ACESSCIN (American Counselor Education and Supervision School Counseling Interest Network) is a listserv, also managed through Kent State University, dedicated to school counseling. Both of these sites were established at Kent State University in the mid-1990s. These asynchronous, unmonitored forums provide a means whereby counselor educators, supervisors, and school counselors communicate, share resources, post job announcements, ask questions, request assistance, respond to colleagues, clarify positions, pose arguments, share teaching and supervision ideas, and more. Subscribers only need to provide an e-mail and password to be eligible to post messages. The site also includes "Subscriber's Corner," an interface whereby subscribers may view and manipulate their subscriptions. For counseling professionals, a listserv makes establishing an electronic social network with others within the same professional field readily possible and can literally span the globe.

A disadvantage is the large numbers of e-mails received from other members. This can be especially problematic and annoying when other members leave for vacation and set their computer to generate automated e-mail responses in their absence.

Discussion Boards

A discussion board provides a site in which subscribers can post, read, and respond to electronic messages. Also referred to as *discussion forums* or *message boards,* the creator has the opportunity to establish and post topics to direct user focus. Participants can respond independently to a forum topic providing a vast array of posted opinions or experiences from which readers can reflect and respond. Written and posted responses to a topic create an additional item to which participants can read and respond. Other participants can respond to a posting (e.g., comment or question), thus creating a linear "thread" of comments, questions, and responses to the original forum topic.

A more recently created forum, begun in January 2005, is the Counselor Education and Supervision Forum located at http://forums.delphiforums.com/cesforum/. The creators, Nick Piazza and Martin Ritchie, are counselor educators from the University of Toledo, Toledo, Ohio. The site mission is "the exchange of ideas and experiences between those professionals involved in the training or supervision of counselors at either the masters or doctoral level." Piazza and Ritchie created the forum "as many of the counselor education listservs were inundating their members with a huge volume of e-mails." The creators hoped that this type of forum would allow "members to read only those topics of interest and keep down the e-mail load" (personal communication, May 19, 2005). Messages can be posted in nine different topic folders ranging from "General" to "Supervision."

Instant Messaging and Chat

Instant messaging and chat essentially adapt an asynchronous discussion board format to a synchronous format. These are similar to having the supervisor and supervisee in the same room, albeit a virtual room that looks like a blank white computer document with a typed name or icon rather than the actual person. Each person types his or her words rather than speaking them. Once a thought is complete the "speaker" sends the message, enabling the receiver to read it. The recipient then types a response and sends it. This interchange can occur with multiple people at once. Some chat forums and instant messaging applications such as Yahoo! Messenger and ICQ offer voice chatting (imagine a speakerphone for your computer) with the click of a button as well as simultaneous Web cameras broadcasting for face-to-face communication.

Videoconferencing

Web cameras are quickly becoming a staple with most personal computer systems. Microsoft provides NetMeeting with most of their software packages. Simply use the "search" function on your system to determine if you already have NetMeeting. This is just one of a host of software programs that allow for real-time, person-to-person (visual and audio) videoconference supervision directly from two computers. The economic benefits and simplicity of use make Web cameras and videoconferencing software a handy tool for distance supervision.

Videoconferencing allows the supervisor and supervisee the ability to see each other. Visual contact adds physical affect, facial expressions, and other body language to the dialogue. Because much of communication is nonverbal, visual contact enhances the supervision process. Best practices in using videoconferencing have surfaced using the heuristic method. Some of these include the following:

- Make, distribute, and follow an agenda
- Prevent problems by ensuring the room and technology are set up properly and working
- Use a solid dark background
- Dress in solid colors but avoid wearing white or dark clothing (white causes glare and black soaks in light, making surrounding objects appear especially light)
- Avoid wearing shiny jewelry
- Limit movement or move slowly
- Maintain eye contact with the camera
- Introduce self before talking (name placards are an alternative)
- Avoid distracting noises
- Avoid excessive camera movement
- Use clear visual aids (Kettler, 2005; Peterson, 2004)

Johnson and Huff (2000) identified more generic terminology to describe the use of computers as a supervision aide: computer-mediated communication (CMC). CMC provides the supervisor more freedom to monitor supervisees at multiple sites all at once (Smart, 1999) and cultivates a sense of belonging among students (Folaron, 1995; Karayan & Crowe, 1997; Lattinig, 1994).

Other tools are sometimes made available within the videoconferencing software. For example, NetMeeting provides a toolbar with whiteboard, chat, sharing, file transfer, and remote desktop sharing. Whiteboard provides an interactive online chalkboard or grease board. Users can free draw, draw using shapes and lines, use various colors, and communicate while doing so. This feature can aid counselors in communicating to a supervisor in a classroom setting or career center arrangement using visual representations. Supervisors can erase and add to the drawing to suggest alternative strategies. The chat feature provides users with the ability to synchronously send typed messages to one another. The share feature allows meeting participants to view and work on files simultaneously. For example, the supervisor may have a consent form template that both the counselor and the supervisor can revise. All meeting participants can provide comments directly in the document. File transfer allows participants to access a browser and swap unopened computer files during a meeting. A supervisor may send a contract or policy, and a counselor may share daily journals. Remote desktop sharing enables users to access and control each other's computer desk top. Drawbacks exist too, however.

Using different software programs can cause connection glitches. Even using a different version of the same software can cause audio and video connections to not function properly. The video connection may come in slowly, out of sync with the audio, or in a choppy, blurry visual pattern. Operating these functions with inadequate or antiquated hardware can cause systems to freeze or crash entirely.

Current technology also makes group videoconferencing (i.e., multipoint face-to-face on-screen with several people simultaneously) possible. Counselor educators can utilize videoconferencing to conduct group supervision with a class of interns spread out across the city, country, or world. For school counseling and supervision, this provides the means for a number of counselor interns located at various schools across the state to still meet, face to face and ear to ear, with each other and their academic faculty supervisor. For school counselors who are supervising interns, videoconferencing can be used to connect with other school counselors who are conducting supervision to ask advice, discuss best practices, or get input regarding an ethical dilemma.

Blogs and LiveJournal

Tim Berners-Lee created the first blog (http://info.cern.ch/) in January 1992. Berners-Lee identified contemporary Web and computer programming events as they unfolded. The content of his site has been archived at the World Wide Web Consortium located at http://www.w3.org/History/19921103-hypertext/hypertext/WWW/News/9201.html.

A blog, also known as a *Weblog*, is an individually created Web site that serves as a publicly accessible journal for its creator. The author can make updates anytime she or he has computer and Internet access. Blog authors typically include links to related informational Web sites, other blog sites devoted to a similar topic, and Web resources (e.g., a Web site that provides free blog templates and Web site space). Visitors do not have the ability to change the content of the posted material. However, they are offered the opportunity to add comments to the original content. This affords the blog author the opportunity to receive a variety of input from a vast and diverse audience.

Fitzpatrick (2005) dubbed the name LiveJournal to his company (sold to another Web-based company, Six Apart, in 2005) and a template product very similar to those companies that provide online blog templates. Essentially, a LiveJournal is the same as a blog except that content and topics focus more on the author's personal thoughts, feelings, and experiences and less on links to related blog sites and Internet sources. However, this may simply be semantics as both blogs and LiveJournals typically capture and reflect the unique character of the author.

In school counseling supervision, a blog (or LiveJournal) can serve as an online journal to reflect a supervisee's experiences, thoughts, feelings, and professional development. This may simply replace a traditional handwritten or typed journal. In pastoral counselor training a process called *verbatim* is used to help train pastors to develop clinical skills. The pastor in training is asked to create a transcript of a session as he or she remembers it and can add beliefs, feelings, opinions, and so on as he or she creates and reviews the transcription.

Advantages to using a blog rather than a handwritten journal are the ease of making revisions and the ability to publicly post and make available the journal to a supervisor or larger audience. It also provides the opportunity for outside input. Disadvantages include the emphasis of maintaining counselee confidentiality and the legal ramifications of posting counselee-sensitive material in a public forum. Therefore, blogs might best be used to journal and share the counselor's own journey of professional development and to post generic situations, questions, challenges, and triumphs for a supervisor to read and respond.

Wikis

Howard "Ward" Cunningham created the first wiki on March 25, 1995. It has been referred to as the Portland Pattern Repository, People Projects and Patterns, the WikiWikiWeb, or Wiki for short. *Wiki wiki* in Hawaiian means "quick" or "super-fast." Its creation was intended for computer programmers to share information on key people, collaborate on computer language-related projects, and identify and share complicated computer language patterns.

A wiki can be considered a collective or group blog. Multiple authors are able to collaborate by modifying posted online content. Much like a blog, a wiki allows information to be shared readily in a public format. Unlike a blog, a wiki allows many different users to become coauthors of the content. Information is collected from any number of sources and people. Visitors are able to post information or edit and revise previously posted material. This format is especially useful for collaborative projects and ongoing dynamic communication needs. A wiki can be ever-changing, always a work in progress, conducive to keeping continually changing information up-to-date (e.g., state or national legislative actions on a hot counseling-related bill), developing interactive ideas (e.g., brainstorming or creating a schedule of career day events with numerous planners or exhibitors), and formulating or enhancing group responses to vague situations (e.g., an ambiguous ethical situation). Advantages include diverse simultaneous perspectives and a forum for flawed information to be corrected quickly. Disadvantages include the potential loss of critical or correct information when erroneous revisions are made by different participants as well as loss of individual ownership of an idea.

Both blogs and wikis can be created with restricted access by unauthorized users. Even novice creators, using a free public server (e.g., blogger.com), can keep their blog from being indexed in the server archives, preventing the public from learning their blog Web address. This lessens the likelihood that any random Web surfer can intentionally locate or stumble on a particular undisclosed blog site. More restrictive measures can be implemented when creators pay to use a server or use their own server. This security is the same for wiki creators.

Blogs are a rich data source for researchers interested in studying the school counselor–student or school counselor development. Wikis also provide researchers a unique opportunity to investigate the creation and morphing of ideas from a collective group of counselors engaged in collaborative electronic brainstorming. Securing a blog or wiki from unauthorized users establishes a forum whereby confidentiality can be more readily maintained, thus making these forums ideal for counselor supervision.

Laptops

Laptop computers, more recently referred to as notebooks, provide the full power and storage capabilities of a desktop computer, including a full-size screen and keyboard, in an ultra-light, convenient package that runs on battery power or an AC adapter. Most new notebooks come with wireless fidelity (Wi-Fi) Internet capabilities built in. These electronic tools provide unique opportunities for contemporary supervision. However, laptops may become antiquated as handheld personal digital assistants and cell phones combine to make on-the-go computing more expedient.

Cell Phones and Personal Digital Assistants (PDAs) and Personal Media Players (PMPs)

Many supervisors and student counselors have already used or thought of using cell phones as a supervision tool. It provides convenient, synchronous audio contact between two or more people. Message centers provide callers with the ability to leave a message anytime, day or night. Voicemail allows access to messages from the press of a button directly from your cell phone. Text messaging is a less intrusive way to communicate using cell phone technology. Rather than have a supervisor observe a student counseling through a one-way mirror and knocking on the door or calling on a land-line phone, the supervisor can less obtrusively text message brief notes with information and prompts.

Handheld PDAs or Smartphones have entered the marketplace integrating a handheld computer organizer with a cell phone. Most appear to be color-screen cell phones with a tiny keyboard. PDAs make wireless e-mail, text messaging, Web browsing, and digital camera and video readily available. Additionally, PDAs allow users to synchronize with existing compatible computer software packages, quickly launch applications, add memory, and install additional software applications all while on the move. In May 2005 *LifeDrive* was introduced by *palmOne*, a mobile manager boasting 3.85 GB of usable storage and the ability to store and access an impressive collection of functions, "1,200 office documents; 6,000 emails; 1,000 photos; 300 songs; two and a half hours of video; 50 voicemails; 10,000 contacts; and 10,000 appointments" (retrieved May 18, 2005, at http://www.pdabuzz.com/). This technology allows supervisees and supervisors to virtually carry their entire office in the palm of their hand. State-of-the-art cell phones now allow live video sharing or videoconferencing phone to phone; there is no need to videoconference from a laptop or desktop computer. Technology now makes face-to-face supervision possible from anywhere at anytime.

Electronic Portfolios (ePortfolios)

Portfolios are fast becoming a staple for demonstrating academic competence in education and training programs (Barrett, 2005). Electronic portfolios, or *ePortfolios*, are simply portfolios created and presented using electronic media. Tosh and Werdmuller (2004) identified three benefits derived from ePortfolios: an education instrument for the student, a supervision tool for academic programs and faculty, and an instrument or means to expand employment opportunities.

Counselor educators and supervisors can use different software (e.g., Microsoft Word or PowerPoint) to create electronic templates infusing accreditation standards as portfolio subheadings or guidelines. Tracking and guiding the development of a school counseling student's ePortfolio provides the supervisor with evidence of counselor development and is an ideal opportunity for providing feedback to supplement professional deficiencies and give suggestions for further professional growth.

Electronic format has several advantages over written portfolios: convenience, portability, flexibility, and cost. Students can conveniently make available or transport electronic portfolios. Simply add it to a personal/professional Web page, burn it to a CD or digital video disc (DVD), save it on a jump drive, or send it as an e-mail attachment—no more lugging a 10-pound portfolio in a three-ring binder to interviews. They are flexible in that they allow the creator the ability to incorporate graphics, digital audio, and digital video. For example, a video of a successful mediation between two quarreling elementary students, middle school orientation to an assembly of incoming sixth graders, and a college/career fair planned and implemented for graduating high school students are powerful visual demonstrations of school counselor knowledge, skills, and values. Cost is marginal as student counselors revise and save the portfolio electronically, thereby avoiding recurring costs associated with revising, re-creating, and making multiple copies of a paper document.

Demonstrating academic requirements in an ePortfolio format also provides an engaging capstone assignment. A student with an ePortfolio, complete with resumé, electronic artifacts demonstrating professional knowledge, skills, values, and links to the student's clinical LiveJournal entries or a blog, can leave a strong impression on a prospective employer.

Virtual Reality Supervision

Virtual reality therapy (VRT) or virtual reality exposure therapy (VRET) opens a whole new world to counseling supervision. Already, VRT is being used to successfully treat counselee anxiety, phobias, posttraumatic stress disorder, fear of public speaking, agoraphobia, and claustrophobia (Carlin, Hoffman, & Weghorst, 1997; Garcia-Palacios, Hoffman, Carlin, Furness, & Botella-Arbona, 2002; Garcia-Palacios, Hoffman, Kwong See, Tsai, & Botella-Arbona, 2001; Hodges, Anderson, Burdea, Hoffman, & Rothbaum, 2001). Advancing on Joseph Wolpe's notion in the 1950s of systematic desensitization, the process of recalling anxiety-producing events into the counselee's imagination and using relaxation techniques to dissipate anxiety, virtual reality makes the counselee's imagination a reality, virtually. Computer software programs, or "virtual world software," are created that mimic anxiety-producing events for the counselee. By using computer programming combined with virtual reality technology, events are produced much like a motion picture with movement and sound. The counselee can experience these events, virtually, in gradual increments approaching reality coupled with implementing relaxation techniques, until the anxiety-producing effect dissipates and the counselee is ready to be exposed to a real-life experience.

Why can't VRT be adapted to virtual reality supervision (VRS)? It is natural for student counselors to experience fear and anxiety when beginning practicum and internship experiences. It is possible to create virtual world software to imitate and bring shape, sound, and movement to these stressful first counseling encounters. This type of technology is well suited to decrease anxiety in fledgling counselors experiencing counseling-related fears.

Additionally, the use of VRS to provide ongoing counselor training by way of virtual counseling sessions and critical moments or ethical dilemmas that occur in counseling settings may be possible. What is it like to have a counselee make sexual advances toward you, as their counselor? How would you respond? It may be uncomfortable to role-play this type of scenario in a classroom full of counseling students. But, virtual reality may offer a different training and supervision tool by making these situations come to life. Counselors can actually practice experiencing and reacting to these types of challenging situations before they actually occur.

ONLINE ETHICS

Counselors' and supervisors' interactions are guided by the *ACA Code of Ethics* (American Counseling Association, 2005) with special attention to Section F: Supervision, Training, and Teaching (refer to Appendix C). In addition, Section A.12: Technology Applications addresses online communication (refer to Appendix C). Although online guidelines focus on couselor–counselee relationships, the tenets apply to the supervisor–counselor relationship. Highlights include informing users of technology limitations and maintaining confidentiality.

Uninvited third-party hackers may try to eavesdrop on private electronic communication. Encryption and firewall technology offer two safety measures. Encryption technology helps prevent unwanted third-party intruders from understanding the communiqué. Encryption changes data to unfamiliar symbols. To make sense of the encrypted data, users must translate the symbols back to familiar data (i.e., text, audio, or video data). A password or key is required for those who want to translate the encrypted file, and the password or key is only made available to authorized participants. A firewall is equivalent to a lock on a door. It only permits access to users who have the proper key or access card. It protects private data in one network from outside users from a different network. Firewall technology also provides safety filters to prevent potentially dangerous material from entering and endangering the system. Firewalls can alert authorized users to intrusion attempts and record intruder data. These two features allow supervisors, counselors, and supervisees to take reasonable measures to maintain and protect confidential electronic communication.

Professional ethics provide guidelines for protecting counselees, supervisees, counselors, and supervisors. Posting professional ethics on interactive supervision Web sites, especially ethics that pertain to electronic communication, helps to ensure participants are aware of the potential hazards and dangers associated with electronic communication.

CAUTIONS, DISADVANTAGES, AND POTENTIAL DRAWBACKS

After discussions about existing and futuristic technology that can enhance supervision, it seems prudent to mention that users may experience problems. Several problems associated with technology have been addressed within earlier sections of this chapter. However, in order that adventurous supervisors and supervisees are not surprised by potential drawbacks, some of the more common challenges, such as cost, viruses, availability, and compatibility, are briefly discussed here.

Cost is always a consideration. Although many of the technology ideas presented are readily available, adding hardware or software to existing equipment may mean additional cost. The expense to gain and maintain Internet access must be considered too. To lower expense, shop around for the best deal. Ironically, many of the best deals can be found via the Internet. Free software upgrades are often made available online.

High-speed Internet capability is not available in all settings. Some rural, mountainous areas or older school buildings, for example, may not be "wired" for high-speed Internet connection. This makes running large amounts of data (e.g., video and audio streaming) cumbersome, disjointed, and annoyingly slow.

Computer viruses, unknowingly acquired via the Internet or through file sharing, can damage hardware and software. Viruses can also interrupt connections and cause data or file transfer problems. Virus protection packages are a critical safeguard for all computer users. The ability to set your system to receive automatic updates makes maintenance relatively painless.

Technology also requires electrical or battery power. Although a basic problem, it is a problem experienced frequently. Do you remember the last time you gave or received a gift that required batteries only to discover "no batteries included"? How about the last time your cell phone cut off because the battery died? Electric power sources are not always readily available. Counselors who have conducted Outward Bound or wilderness ropes courses can attest to this. Planning ahead to ensure an electrical source is available or batteries are charged and in sufficient supply creates one more supervision step. Although mentioned earlier, software makers, in an attempt to correct shortfalls and improve their product, constantly change or upgrade their product. Newer versions of the same software package may not be completely compatible with earlier-made versions. Incompatibility may result in a malfunction of a specific tool within the package or even prevent one system from acknowledging and connecting to the other.

Incompatibility exists across differently skilled supervisors and counselors too. Teaching or supervising people who are on different ends of the continuum when it comes to understanding and using technology can pose unique challenges and frustrations for both parties. The following excerpt from a school counseling intern's e-mail to her supervisor highlights potential technology-related challenges. After several successful postings, the student attempted to write and post her required weekly journal to her private blog. Twice her attempts failed, and her text was lost and unrecoverable. The intern wrote to her faculty supervisor:

> For the second time in two days I have typed my entire journal entry into the [blog] site . . . it could not be completed because of internal server error. This is so frustrating and time wasting that I am ready to scream. I have too many other things to do to attempt this again today. I long for the pre-computer days when writing something like this long hand could take 15–20 minutes rather than several hours. (A. Bagge, personal communication, October 3, 2005)

After further investigation, the supervisor identified the problem: The student had used a different browser to access the blog. For some reason the browser she used was incompatible with the blog site. This thwarted her efforts to post her journal and cost the student a great deal of time and aggravation. Although the supervisor used the incident as a teaching/learning opportunity, this example is a pragmatic illustration of the types of problems and challenges supervisors, counselors, and interns may confront when using technology in supervision.

SUMMARY

Technological advances provide creative and convenient tools and applications to enhance and make supervision possible for school counselor students, professional school counselors, supervisors, and counselor educators. Digital audio and video formats make possible the immediate transfer and sharing of counseling tapes. The Internet provides a wealth of readily accessible resources, a network of like-minded professionals, and a virtual interactive meeting place anytime of the day or night. Although challenges and problems are inherent in using technology, the benefits outweigh the drawbacks. Technology is here to stay, and the possibilities are endless. Technology continues to advance at light speed. Future advances will only serve to make the unimaginable commonplace, to make virtual reality, reality.

REFERENCES

American Counseling Association. (2005). *ACA code of ethics*. Alexandria, VA: Author.

Barrett, H. C. (2005). *Researching electronic portfolios and learner engagement*. Retrieved May 25, 2005, from http://electronicportfolios.com/reflect/whitepaper.pdf

Benigno, V., & Trentin, G. (2000). The evaluation of online courses. *Journal of Computer Assisted Learning, 16,* 259–270.

Carlin, A. S., Hoffman, H., & Weghorst, S. (1997). Virtual reality and tactile augmentation in the treatment of spider phobia: A case study. *Behavior Research and Therapy, 35,* 153–158.

Doyle, D. J. (2000). Paradigm shift: Visual communication and empowerment. In J. A. Chambers (Ed.), *Selected papers from the 11th International Conference on College Teaching and Learning.* Jacksonville: Florida Community College, Center for the Advancement of Teaching and Learning.

Eldredge, G. M., McNamara, S., Stensrud, R., Gilbride, D., Hendren, G., Siegfried, T., & McFarlane, F. (1999). Distance education: A look at five programs. *Rehabilitation Education, 13,* 231–248.

Feist, S. C. (1999). Practice and theory of professional supervision for mental health counselors. *Directions in Mental Health Counseling, 9,* 105–120.

Fitzpatrick, B. (2005). *Big news . . . Six Apart and LiveJournal!* Retrieved May 26, 2005, from http://www.livejournal.com/users/news/82926.html

Folaron, G. (1995). Enhancing learning with email. *Journal of Teaching in Social Work, 12,* 3–18.

Garcia-Palacios, A., Hoffman, H. G., Carlin, C., Furness, T. A., & Botella-Arbona, C. (2002). Virtual reality in the treatment of spider phobia: A controlled study. *Behaviour Research and Therapy, 40,* 983–993.

Garcia-Palacios, A., Hoffman, H. G., Kwong See, S., Tsai, A., & Botella-Arbona, C. (2001). Redefining therapeutic success with VR exposure therapy. *CyberPsychology and Behavior, 4,* 341–348.

Goodyear, R. K., & Nelson, M. L. (1997). The major formats of psychotherapy supervision. In C. E. Watkins Jr. (Ed.), *Handbook of psychotherapy supervision* (pp. 328–344). New York: Wiley.

Hansen, N. E., & Gladfelter, J. (1996). Teaching graduate psychology seminars using electronic mail: Creative distance education. *Teaching of Psychology, 23,* 252–256.

Hayes, B. G., Taub, G. E., Robinson, E. H., & Sivo, S. A. (2003). An empirical investigation of the efficacy of multimedia instruction in counseling skill development. *Counselor Education and Supervision, 42,* 177–189.

Herlihy, B., Gray, N., & McCollum, V. (2002). Legal and ethical issues in school counselor supervision. *Professional School Counseling, 6,* 55–61.

Hodges, L. F., Anderson, P., Burdea, G., Hoffman, H. G., & Rothbaum, B. O. (2001). VR as a tool in the treatment of psychological and physical disorders. *IEEE Computer Graphics and Applications, 21,* 25–33.

Hsiung, C. T., & Tan, N. J. (1999, March). *A study of creating a distance supervision hot line.* Paper presented at the meeting of the National Association for Research in Science Teaching, Boston, MA.

Huff, M. T. (2000). A comparison study of live instruction versus interactive television for teaching MSW students critical thinking skills. *Research on Social Work Practice, 10,* 400–416.

Johnson, M. M., & Huff, M. T. (2000). Students' use of computer-mediated communication in a distance education course. *Research on Social Work Practice, 10,* 519–532.

Karayan, S., & Crowe, J. (1997). Student perceptions of electronic discussion groups. *T.H.E. Technological Horizons in Education Journal, 24,* 69–71.

Kettler, M. (2005). *Tips or best practices for effective videoconferencing.* Retrieved May 26, 2005, from http://www.ecu.edu/itcs/vc/tips.htm

Knouse, S. B. (2001). Virtual mentors: Mentoring on the Internet. *Journal of Employment Counseling, 38,* 162–170.

Lattinig, J. K. (1994). Diffusion of computer-mediated communication in a graduate social work class: Lessons from "the class from hell." *Computers in Human Services, 10,* 21–45.

Manzanares, M. G., O'Halloran, T. M., McCartney, T. J., Filer, R. D., Varhely, S. C., & Calhoun, K. (2004). CD-ROM technology for education and support of site supervisors. *Counselor Education and Supervision, 43,* 220–231.

Marjanovic, O. (1999). Learning and teaching in a synchronous collaborative environment. *Journal of Computer Assisted Learning, 15,* 129–138.

Page, B., Pietrzak, D., & Sutton, J., Jr. (2001). National survey of school counselor supervision. *Counselor Education and Supervision, 41,* 142–151.

Peterson, C. (2004). Making interactivity count: Best practices in video conferencing. *Journal of Interactive Learning Research, 15,* 63–75.

Petracchi, H. E. (2000). Distance education: What do our students tell us? *Research on Social Work Practice, 10,* 362–376.

Petracchi, H. E., & Patchner, M. E. (2001). A comparison of live instruction and interactive televised teaching: A 2-year assessment of teaching an MSW research methods course. *Research on Social Work Practice, 11,* 108–117.

Powell, B. (2004). New study finds phone therapy helpful for depression. *E-News From Washington, 4,* 30.

Protinsky, H. (1997). Dismounting the tiger: Using tape in supervision. In C. L. Storm & T. C. Todd (Eds.), *The reasonably complete systemic supervisor resource guide* (pp. 298–308). Needham Heights, MA: Allyn & Bacon.

Riemer-Reiss, M. L. (2000). Utilizing distance technology for mental health counseling. *Journal of Mental Health Counseling, 22,* 189–203.

Smart, J. F. (1999). Issues in rehabilitation distance education. *Rehabilitation Education, 13,* 187–206.

Stadtlander, L. M. (1998). Virtual instruction: Teaching an online graduate seminar. *Teaching of Psychology, 25,* 146–148.

Tosh, D., & Werdmuller, B. (2004). *Creation of a learning landscape: Weblogging and social networking in the context of ePortfolios.* Retrieved May 25, 2005, from http://www.eradc.org/papers/Learning_landscape.pdf

Wall, J. E. (2004). Assessment and technology—Allies in educational reform: An overview of issues for counselors and educators. *Measurement and Evaluation in Counseling and Development, 37,* 112–128.

CHAPTER 9

Creative Approaches to Supervision

Susan Norris Huss

THE PURPOSE of this chapter is to

- identify key elements in successful supervision in the time-challenged world of the practicing school counselor
- provide some nontraditional concepts and techniques to enhance the supervision experience for both the supervisor and the supervisee

"All my supervisor does is talk to me." "All my supervisor does is ask me questions." "I can't remember everything we talk about in supervision because we cover so much." These are all common comments heard from supervisees during their clinical experiences. Just as traditional counseling theories that rely on "talk therapy" are not always the most effective approach in counseling, traditional "talk supervision" may not be the most effective approach to supervision.

FOR SITE AND PROGRAM SUPERVISORS

School counselor supervision is a challenging and extremely important element in the development of professional school counselors. There is a need for training for those in the field who are training professional school counselors as well as those practicing professional school counselors who find themselves supervising trainees. Reflection and relationship are the two *R*s that need to be addressed in the supervisory experience.

RELATIONSHIP

It is an accepted belief that the single most important factor in a successful supervision experience between a supervisor and a supervisee is the creation of a trusting environment (McNamee & McWey, 2004; Newald-McCalip, Sather, Strati, & Dineen, 2003). Patton and Kivlighan (1997) stated that the relationship is an essential element in supervision efficacy and effectiveness. Newald-McCalip et al. also suggested that it is important for the supervisee to be engaged in the process from a position other than the traditional expert–novice position often held in traditional supervision relationships. It is further suggested that it is beneficial to ask supervisees what they view as appropriate supervision and to consult with them about how this process could lead to self-supervision. The ideas presented in this chapter were selected partly because they provide opportunities for the supervision relationship to develop into a positive element of the supervision experience.

REFLECTION

Despite the need to expand beyond "talk supervision," it is important to remember the significance of intentional talk supervision as well as the development of supervision "self-talk." Reflection is considered a key component in the professional development of counselors-in-training. Reflection means pondering about what happened, about what did not happen, about what one wants to happen, and about what one could do differently.

Ward and House (1998) proposed a supervision model that integrates reflective learning theory into the development of the supervisee and the supervision relationship. In this framework counselors-in-training are encouraged to reflect on their discomfort in professional experiences that highlight the reflective learning process; the framework also provides a context for the critical analysis of base assumptions and beliefs about counselees, change, and one's practice.

One of the difficulties with the concept of pondering is that it takes time, and in a fast-paced world, one tends to want to come up with responses immediately and is not willing or able to allow time for the beneficial art of pondering that can provide insight and answers. The following strategies facilitate the practice of contemplation.

The Sand Hourglass

A sand hourglass is suggested as a tool to make this pondering time more comfortable. This is a concrete visual item giving the supervisee time to truly reflect rather than feeling the pressure to come up with the right answer immediately. Because some people need longer than others, various timers could be available. This may also make the supervisee and perhaps even the supervisor more comfortable with silence, which is an important counseling skill.

The Sandtray

Another suggestion for increasing the benefit of pondering is the use of the sandtray. By allowing both the supervisor and the supervisee to draw in sand while working on an issue—be it a counseling issue, a counselee issue, or a supervisee issue—a possible solution, connection, or insight might occur (Williams, 1995).

This time issue needs to also be considered in the selection of the models to be used in supervision. I believe that solution-focused supervision is the most effective model for providing nontraditional creative supervision techniques.

SOLUTION-FOCUSED SUPERVISION

Solution-focused brief counseling is being used more and more in the school setting because of its efficiency and efficacy. Solution-focused supervision could be used for the same reason, and it lends itself to the use of "props" to enhance the learning. Solution-focused supervision encourages the needed trusting environment because it concentrates on the creation of solutions (Juhnke, 1996) rather than telling the supervisee what he or she did wrong and also allows the supervisee to identify what is already working.

Solution-focused supervision also lends itself to the use of nontalking techniques. The *miracle question* creates the basis for the solution and is a picture (which could actually be drawn by the supervisee) of that solution. The miracle question provides an opportunity to think about life without the problem. For example, "Suppose a miracle occurred while you were sleeping, and when you woke up, all your problems were solved. What would be different?" McNamee and McWey (2004) suggested the use of *bilateral art* to facilitate clinical supervision. This technique engages both the dominant and nondominant hands in the process of creating images in response to opposing cognitions or emotions. If a supervisee is having difficulty in creating the picture with solutions, this bilateral art technique could be used.

Another solution-focused concept in supervision is the identification of barriers to the completion of the goal. *Road signs* could be used to define what barriers might be in place to keep the supervisees from reaching the solution (*detour, road closed ahead, bumpy road*). Another road sign could be used to signify the designated time for the goal to be reached. For example, in Michigan when there is road construction, signs are placed along the way that indicate how much longer until the construction ends (e.g., *only three more miles of construction*). These signs can also be a creative means to designate the number of weeks left in supervision, particularly when the trainee is behind in assignments.

The use of solution-focused supervision represents quasi-postmodern and constructivist ideas (Britton, Goodman, & Rak, 2002) that can be easily integrated into other styles of supervision. It also lends itself to concrete and nontalking techniques.

TECHNIQUES USING CONCRETE ITEMS

Jacobs (1992), in his practical book on creative counseling techniques, stated that creative techniques add variety to counseling and help to prevent burnout. I believe the same is true in supervision. Further, Jacobs provided seven additional reasons for using creative counseling techniques that are just as valuable for the supervision process: (a) to make the concepts more concrete, (b) to heighten awareness, (c) to dramatize a point, (d) to speed up the counseling (supervision) process, (e) to enhance learning because people are visual learners, (f) to enhance learning because people learn through experience, and (g) to focus on the session (p. 3). For these reasons the use of creative supervision may be more beneficial than traditional supervision, with the added bonus of facilitating insight. A few examples of creative supervision techniques are provided below to help spur further creativity on the part of the supervisors and even the supervisees.

The Turtle

The use of a turtle in supervision represents the belief that "if you are going to make progress you are going to have to take risks" (stick your neck out just like a turtle). There are turtle puppets that actually have a movable head and legs that can retreat within the shell or stick out. Turtles can also be used to illustrate that there are times (such as when one is overanxious or maybe even impaired) when one needs to pull into one's shell for a bit and ponder, rethink, or just plain rest (e.g., the ethic of self-care).

Toolbox

A toolbox such as those used to contain either gardening tools or carpenter tools can be introduced at the beginning of the supervision process with the plan that it will be full or at least will contain more tools by the end of the supervision experience. Initially, the skills the counselee believes he or she has mastered can be put in the box using pictures, words, or some object to symbolize the skill. During the individual supervision sessions, each tool (skill) can be examined to see if it needs some repair, cleaning, or adaptations before putting it away again. This can also determine goals for the supervisee. And, of course, as new skills are developed, they can be added to the box. This approach helps supervisees realize that all skills need continuous attention, supports the fact that they already have skills, and allows them, as well as the supervisor, to determine which skills need more attention.

Common Household Objects

To get both the supervisee and the supervisor to start thinking of counseling uses for common everyday objects in more concrete terms, and to realize it is relatively easy to do, take a dozen everyday objects usually found on or in a desk (e.g., pen, marker, breath mints, rubber band, mechanical pencil, paperweight, stapler, staple remover). In group supervision each person selects one item. The person is then instructed to describe how the item might be used as a supervision (counseling) tool. The items are selected until all are gone. This demonstrates that any item can be used to make a concept more concrete. For example, a rubber band can be used to hold things together, to demonstrate that tension is needed for it to work (discomfort leads to growth), and to show that too much tension can cause it to break; this illustrates that one needs to stretch one's thinking about counselees' beliefs, or one needs to stretch to grow and develop the skills to put in one's toolbox.

The Empty Chair

The infamous *empty-chair technique* from Gestalt therapy (Perls, 1969) can be used with many variations in supervision to assist counselors-in-training to develop their skills in using chairs in their counseling. For example, the supervisee sits across from the empty chair, assumes the role of the supervisor, and talks to the chair as he or she believes the supervisor would talk to him or her as the supervisee. This technique can facilitate conversation that might be difficult, and it can also allow the supervisor to see issues the supervisee is dealing with that the supervisee has not been able to verbalize because of the potential of blurred roles (e.g., the supervisor as the evaluator).

Chairs

Chairs could also represent alternative solutions to difficulties the supervisee is having. If a supervisee is having problems telling the counselee what to do, the supervisor can stand on a chair with the supervisee kneeling in front. The supervisor may then begin to "tell the supervisee" what he or she needs to do. Afterward, the trainee will process the experience, his or her feelings, and who owned the decision.

SUPERVISION MAP

A visual chart or map to direct the session may be helpful to both the supervisee and the supervisor. The picture representation shown in Figure 9.1 provides structure and encourages input from both participants. The Supervision Meeting Outline provides a visual form that not only gives this activity structure but can also be documentation of the session.

The "Topics for Today" are drawn from the "Goals" of the last supervisory session. New items can be added to it at the beginning of each session. The "Strengths" portion enables both the supervisor and the supervisee to identify skills, interactions, or observations, specifically those related to the goals of the week that went well since the last supervision session.

The "Needs Attention" section provides for the identification of what needs to be worked on from both the supervisor's and the supervisee's perspective and may be turned into "Goals" to be reached. If solution-focused supervision is being used, it is during "Needs Attention" and "Goals" that the miracle question and the subsequent question "What else would be happening?" can be asked and discussion occurs. This is where the bulk of the time is spent in the session. This is also where identification of strategies for how the goals are going to be reached is determined as well as the barriers that are present that can impede reaching those goals.

The "Ethical Issues" portion provides the necessary opportunity to continuously work on, become aware/sensitive to, and be comfortable with the ambiguous ethical perspective of the school counseling profession. The last two ". . . would like to mention" sections provide the opportunity for both the supervisor and the supervisee to note things that they would like to mention. This is not necessarily a strength or something that needs attention but just something one of them would like to discuss: for example, discomfort with a particular counselee or reluctance to discuss parenting issues with a parent or guardian.

This Supervision Meeting Outline form not only provides overall structure for the supervision session but also provides numerous opportunities to use creative, nontraditional supervision techniques. Either the supervisor or the supervisee can develop additional figures to facilitate the supervision process.

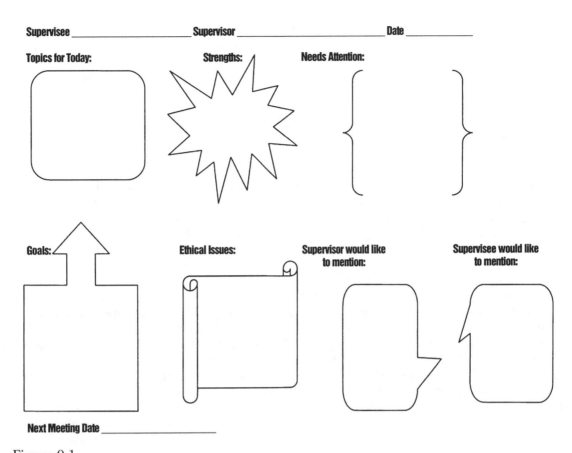

Figure 9.1

Supervision Meeting Outline

ETHICS

Just as informed consent is a very important ethical part of the counseling process, it is also a very ethical and critical part of the supervision relationship. The supervisor needs to be aware that there may be cultural issues that could impede the effective use of nontraditional supervision techniques. Therefore, the supervisor needs to explain to the supervisee the technique and its possible outcomes and to obtain permission to proceed (unless the effectiveness would be compromised). This should be part of the initial informed-consent agreement (e.g., supervision may include nontraditional techniques) that should be included in a signed contract (Studer, 2005) as well as just before the technique is used.

SUMMARY

Roberts (2001) set forth suggested guidelines for site supervisors of professional school counselors. Two of the seven suggested guidelines relate directly to the purpose of this chapter. The first is that the "site supervisors of school counseling interns are the role models for the future of the profession" (p. 212). By practicing creative, nontraditional supervision techniques, the site supervisor gives permission for the counselors-in-training to use creative techniques in their counseling. The second is that "reflection and process time with site supervisors enhances intern professional decision making and skill development" (p. 214). Skovholt and Ronnestad (1992) emphasized the concept of professional reflection that seemed to emanate from high levels of professional interaction, open and supportive work environments, and a "reflective stance" of the counselor, wherein one is given the "time and energy to process alone and with others, significant experiences" (p. 509). The use of creative, nontraditional supervision techniques supports that reflective stance and provides for the time and energy for processing the learning experiences.

Supervision is a key component in the development and practice of professional school counseling. Because of the diversity of experience that each trainee/counselor brings to supervision, it is important that supervisors not rely on a single supervisory approach (Ladany, Marotta, & Muse-Burke, 2001). It is also important to provide opportunities for supervisees to have input into what they need from supervision and how they best can fulfill those needs.

It is hoped that information and ideas in this chapter will be a catalyst for all supervisors to develop their own creative techniques to assist the school counselors-in-training in their development as professionals. Go forth and be creative!

REFERENCES

Britton, P. J., Goodman, J. M., & Rak, C. F. (2002). Presenting workshops on supervision: A didactic–experiential format. *Counselor Education and Supervision, 42,* 31–39.

Jacobs, E. (1992). *Creative counseling techniques: An illustrated guide.* Odessa, FL: Psychological Assessment Resources.

Juhnke, G. A. (1996). Solution-focused supervision: Promoting supervisee skills and confidence through successful solutions. *Counselor Education and Supervision, 36,* 48–58.

Ladany, N., Marotta, S., & Muse-Burke, J. L. (2001). Counselor experience related to complexity of case conceptualization and supervision preference. *Counselor Education and Supervision, 40,* 203–220.

McNamee, C. M., & McWey, L. M. (2004). Using bilateral art to facilitate clinical supervision. *The Arts in Psychotherapy, 31,* 229–245.

Newald-McCalip, R., Sather, J., Strati, J. V., & Dineen, J. (2003). Exploring the process of creative supervision: Initial findings regarding the regenerative model. *Journal of Humanistic Counseling, Education and Development, 43,* 223–237.

Patton, M. J., & Kivlighan, D. M. (1997). Relevance of the supervisory alliance to the counseling alliance and to treatment adherence in counselor training. *Journal of Counseling Psychology, 44,* 108–115.

Perls, F. (1969). *Gestalt therapy verbatim.* Moab, UT: Real People Press.

Roberts, W. B. (2001). Site supervisors of professional school counseling interns: Suggested guidelines. *Professional School Counseling, 4,* 208–216.

Skovholt, T. M., & Ronnestad, M. H. (1992). Themes in therapist and counselor development. *Journal of Counseling & Development, 70,* 505–515.

Studer, J. R. (2005). Supervising school counselors-in-training: A guide for field supervisors. *Professional School Counseling, 8,* 353–359.

Ward, C. C., & House, R. M. (1998). Counseling supervision: A reflective model. *Counselor Education and Supervision, 38,* 23–34.

Williams, A. (1995). *Visual and active supervision: Roles, focus, technique.* New York: Norton.

CHAPTER 10

Ethical and Legal Considerations in Supervision: The Well-Planned Supervision Journey

Marla Peterson

THE PURPOSE of this chapter is to

- discuss ethical behaviors of the supervisor
- provide information on ethical behaviors of supervisees
- identify legal issues in supervision
- present a brief introduction on liability and malpractice
- introduce school policies that influence the supervisee

International travelers know that before they can begin a journey they must obtain a passport. Similarly, experienced school counselors need a passport to supervise students at practicum and internship sites. The minimum requirements for obtaining a school counseling supervision passport are a master's degree in school counseling, a school counseling license or certificate, school counseling experience, and training in supervision.

Once a passport has been acquired, the international traveler must purchase a ticket to a desired destination. The ticket is a contract between the carrier and the passenger that indicates where the traveler is headed, shows when the traveler will leave and return, and lists myriad exemptions if unforeseen events should occur. In the vast majority of cases, travelers who have planned well will return home filled with excitement about their recent trip even though they may have encountered some mishaps along the way. A sprained ankle that resulted from a tumble down the uneven steps of the Parthenon will not deter the traveler from another journey. Trip insurance covered the medical expenses. Goodbye Parthenon! Hello Taj Mahal!

Like the seasoned traveler, many experienced site supervisors have encountered "sprains" and bumps during the supervision of practicum students and interns, but they continue to sign on for more supervisory adventures. These supervisors are deeply committed to helping induct new counselors into the profession of school counseling.

Many licensed or certified professional school counselors already have most of the qualifications needed to acquire a supervision passport. As part of their academic preparation and their experience, they have become familiar with ethical and legal aspects of the school counseling profession. They understand and practice the components of the *ACA Code of Ethics* (American Counseling Association, 2005) that are listed in Appendix C and the *Ethical Standards for School Counselors* of the American School Counselor Association (ASCA; 2004) that are listed in Appendix D. However, supervisors must remind themselves that what has become routine and normalized for them in the area of ethical and legal considerations may need to be made explicit for the supervisee.

The ticket for an international trip or a supervision journey is issued by carriers, and carriers define what responsibilities will and will not be assumed by them. In the language of supervision, the ticket becomes an Affiliation Agreement between the school district and the university. Within that Affiliation Agreement will be language that relates to direct liability, vicarious liability, indemnification, and holding harmless. Both university and school site supervisors need to understand the legal aspects of Affiliation Agreements and convey their content to supervisees.

Selection of a competent carrier is a high priority for most travelers. They want to purchase an airline ticket from a carrier that has state-of-the-art equipment and implements current aviation standards. In the case of supervision sites, the school district is the carrier with whom a ticket (Affiliation Agreement) will be arranged. University training programs have an ethical obligation to establish Affiliation Agreements with school districts where counselors are using today's technology, methods, approaches, and materials to implement school counseling program standards established by ASCA.

Affiliation Agreements should not be confused with Student Contracts. The Student Contract differs from the Affiliation Agreement in that the Student Contract includes goals, activities, and evaluation procedures that will be used to determine if the student has successfully completed work outlined in the contract. A more detailed discussion of Affiliation Agreements can be found later in this chapter.

In any discussion of ethical and legal considerations it becomes apparent that, although they are related, each has a different focus and purpose. According to Bernard and Goodyear (2004),

Ethical codes are conceptually broad in nature, few in number, and open to interpretation by the practitioner (in most cases). Although they are sometimes perceived as safeguards to avoid liability, they are devised for a loftier purpose, that is, a call to excellence. Ethical standards are a statement from a particular profession to the general public regarding what they stand for. (p. 49)

The law enters when it is perceived that a counselor has performed a particular act that has done harm and the aggrieved party brings claims to a regulatory body or civil court. The law is concerned with minimally accepted behavior; ethical codes are concerned with the highest standards of performance. Although there are these distinctions between ethical standards and the law, Meyer, Landis, and Hays (1988) advised that ethical standards can become legally binding because they may be used by the courts to determine professional duty and they guide the thinking of others in the field who may be asked to testify.

Ethical standards and legal issues are discussed separately in this chapter, and each has a separate checklist to guide supervisors in their approach to ethical and legal considerations. However, the symbiotic relationship between ethical behavior and the law is present in both the discussion and the checklists. The section on ethical standards addresses two areas: ethical behavior of supervisors and ethical reminders that supervisors should convey to supervisees. The chapter concludes with legal considerations related to liability and malpractice, affiliation agreements, and school policies.

This chapter is not meant to be an exhaustive examination of all the ethical and legal considerations that affect site supervisors but rather those that seem particularly pertinent. It is important to remember that supervision policies and procedures must be set within the context of school district, university policies, and state and federal laws. Information included in this chapter should be used only in a manner that complies with such regulations, policies, and laws.

Ethical Behavior on the Supervision Journey

The site supervisor needs to consider the following questions: What special ethical guidelines are associated with the role of a supervisor? and What ethical guidelines should be reviewed with the supervisee before the supervisee begins working with students?

An Ethics Check for the Supervisory Role

Experienced as well as new supervisors should periodically review Section F, "Supervision, Training, and Teaching," of the 2005 *ACA Code of Ethics* (see Appendix C) and the Association for Counselor Education and Supervision (ACES; 1993) *Ethical Guidelines for Counseling Supervisors* (see Appendix E). These two documents are essentially in agreement when it comes to ethical behaviors that are expected of supervisors. Because the entire ACES *Ethical Guidelines* document was developed specifically for those who supervise counselors, three specific sections of the *Guidelines* are addressed: (a) Counselee Welfare and Rights, (b) Supervisory Role, and (c) Program Administration Role. An ethics checklist for site supervisors of school counseling students found in Figure 10.1 is organized around these three sections of the *Guidelines* and can be used as a self-check after reviewing the *Guidelines* in their entirety. Although all of the items in the checklist are important, there are some that relate directly to two issues that frequently arise during the supervision process: (a) proper assignment of activities to supervisees and (b) evaluation of performance.

Appropriate Assignment of Activities

Supervisors should not ask trainees to perform activities for which they have no prior preparation. For example, a trainee who has not had training in group processes or group dynamics should not be asked to form and lead a small-group activity for students who have recently experienced a death in the family. The program supervisor, the site supervisor, and the trainee all bear responsibilities for making sure that activities are not conducted "before their time." The time to prevent this from happening occurs when the Student Contract is developed. The contract should clearly delineate goals and activities that are based on the trainee's prior preparation and coursework.

Evaluation of Performance

Processes and good practices for giving evaluative feedback are discussed in chapter 11. Both ethical and legal considerations related to due process enter into assessments of student progress. Supervisees have due process rights in that they should be given academic and performance requirements, be evaluated regularly, receive notice of performance deficiencies, and have an opportunity to be heard if their deficiencies result in removal from a practicum/internship site or dismissal from a program.

Ultimately, the program supervisor, in consultation with the site supervisor, will determine the grade that has been earned or whether satisfactory/unsatisfactory progress has been made. When student performance is questionable, both the program and site supervisors should work together to make sure that students are offered remediation and that due process procedures are followed.

School districts have the right to determine who can provide instruction and services to the students they serve. A supervisee who is doing harm, is excessively absent, may be impaired, develops dual relationships with students, commits other serious ethical violations, or refuses to fulfill Student Contract requirements may be a candidate for dismissal from a school site. It is incumbent on the site supervisor to inform the program supervisor of the circumstances surrounding any dismissal from a school site prior to the action taking place. Together, the site supervisor and program supervisor should take steps to assure that due process measures are accorded the supervisee. It is the responsibility of the program supervisor to follow university due process procedures when making a determination as to whether the supervisee will be

	Yes	No

Counselee Welfare and Rights

1. Have I told supervisees to inform counselees that they are being supervised and that observation and/or recordings of the session may be reviewed by the supervisor? ☐ ☐
2. Have I instructed the supervisee not to communicate or in any way convey to the supervisee's counselees or to other parties that the supervisee is himself/herself licensed? ☐ ☐
3. Have I made the supervisee aware of counselees' rights, including protecting counselees' right to privacy and confidentiality in the counseling relationship and the information resulting from it? ☐ ☐
4. Have I told the supervisee to inform counselees that their right to privacy and confidentiality will not be violated by the supervisory relationship? ☐ ☐
5. Have I informed the supervisee that records of the counseling relationship, including interview notes, test data, correspondence, the electronic storage of these documents, and audio- and videotape recordings, are considered to be confidential professional information and that written consent should be obtained from the counselee (or legal guardian, if a minor) prior to the use of such information for instructional, supervisory, and/or research purposes? ☐ ☐
6. Am I making every effort to monitor both the professional actions and failures to take action of the supervisee? ☐ ☐

Supervisory Role

1. Have I had training in supervision prior to accepting the first supervisee? ☐ ☐
2. Have I participated in professional development activities on supervision? ☐ ☐
3. Have I been assured that the supervisee has read the 2004 edition of the American School Counselor Association's (ASCA) *Ethical Standards for School Counselors?* ☐ ☐
4. Have I informed the supervisee about procedures for contacting the supervisor, or an alternative supervisor, to assist in handling crisis situations? ☐ ☐
5. Am I reviewing actual work samples via audio- and/or videotape or making live observations of the supervisee? ☐ ☐
6. Am I meeting regularly with the supervisee in face-to-face sessions? ☐ ☐
7. Am I providing the supervisee with ongoing formal and informal feedback, in both oral and written form, at the formative and summative stages of the on-site experience? ☐ ☐
8. Am I carefully avoiding any dual relationships with the supervisee that might impair my objectivity and professional judgment? ☐ ☐
9. Am I avoiding the establishment of a psychotherapeutic relationship as a substitute for supervision and addressing personal issues only in terms of the impact of these issues on counselees and on professional functioning? ☐ ☐
10. Am I aware of any personal or professional limitations of the supervisee which are likely to impede future professional performance and, if so, have I recommended (in writing) remedial assistance to the supervisee and shared contents of the recommendation with the program supervisor? ☐ ☐
11. Am I asking the supervisee to perform activities that are commensurate with his or her current level of skills and experiences? ☐ ☐
12. If the supervisee is unable to provide competent professional services following written evaluations, remediation, use of due process procedures, and communication with the program supervisor, am I willing to recommend that the supervisee should be screened from the training program? ☐ ☐
13. If the supervisee is impaired in any way that would interfere with the performance of school counseling duties after having been given feedback and opportunity for remediation, am I willing to recommend to the program supervisor that the supervisee not be licensed/certified as a school counselor? ☐ ☐
14. Do I understand and use principles of informed consent and participation; clarify requirements, expectations, roles, and rules; and follow and make clear to supervisees due process and appeal procedures? ☐ ☐

Figure 10.1

Ethics Checklist for Site Supervisors of School Counseling Students

(Continued)

	Yes	No

Program Administration Role

1. Am I confident that the supervisee is enrolled in a university counselor preparation program that incorporates up-to-date recommendations of ASCA and the American Counseling Association? ☐ ☐

2. Am I providing experiences that integrate theoretical knowledge and practical applications which are built around the ASCA National Model for school counseling programs? ☐ ☐

3. Have I informed the supervisee of the goals, policies, theoretical orientations toward counseling, training, and supervision model or approach on which my supervision is based? ☐ ☐

4. Am I encouraging and assisting the supervisee to define a theoretical orientation toward counseling, to establish supervision goals, and to self-monitor and evaluate progress toward meeting these goals? ☐ ☐

5. Am I limiting the number of supervisees so that each has ample time for supervision and feedback? ☐ ☐

6. Do I clearly understand my role as a site supervisor and the role of the program supervisor in areas such as evaluation, requirements, and confidentiality? ☐ ☐

7. Has the program supervisor communicated with me regarding current professional practices, expectations of students, and preferred models and modalities of supervision? ☐ ☐

8. Have clear lines of communication been established with program supervisors and supervisees relating to specific procedures regarding consultation, performance review, and evaluation of supervisees? ☐ ☐

9. Is evaluation feedback available to supervisees in ways consistent with the Family Rights and Privacy Act and the Buckley Amendment? ☐ ☐

10. If, after determining a supervisee has deficits in the areas of self-understanding and problem resolution which impede professional functioning, I recommend that a supervisee participate in activities such as personal growth groups or personal counseling, I refrain from being the direct provider of these activities for the supervisee? ☐ ☐

11. Do I understand that in resolving conflicts among needs of the counselee, the needs of the supervisee, and the needs of the program that counselee welfare is usually subsumed in federal and state laws and these statues should be the first point of reference? ☐ ☐

12. Do I understand that in resolving conflicts among needs of the counselee, the needs of the supervisee, and the needs of the program (or school), and where laws and ethical standards are not present or are unclear, the good judgment of the supervisor should be guided by the following list?
    a. Relevant legal and ethical standards (e.g., duty to warn, state child abuse laws, etc.) ☐ ☐
    b. Counselee welfare ☐ ☐
    c. Supervisee welfare ☐ ☐
    d. Supervisor welfare ☐ ☐
    e. Program and/or agency service and administrative needs ☐ ☐

Figure 10.1 *(Continued)*

Ethics Checklist for Site Supervisors of School Counseling Students

Note. This figure is based on the *Ethical Guidelines for Counseling Supervisors* (Association for Counselor Education and Supervision, 1993).

assigned to another school site, participate in remediation activities prior to reassignment, or be dismissed from the program.

Site supervisors must not shy away from assessing whether a supervisee has the skills to enter the profession of school counseling. If performance expectations have been communicated and due process procedures have been followed, the fear of litigious actions should not deter professionals from making well-grounded decisions on the performance of supervisees.

Ethical Reminders

Ethical considerations related to the supervisory role must also be accompanied by a review of important ethical issues that may be faced by a supervisee. The site supervisor might well ask, "Hasn't the supervisee discussed ethical issues in coursework, and hasn't the program supervisor reviewed ethical concerns as part of the weekly class meetings of practicum and internship students?" The answer to this question should be a resounding "yes," but the site supervisor should take steps to make sure the supervisee (a) recognizes ethical dilemmas that may occur in a practice setting, (b) understands professional and school procedures for dealing with ethical dilemmas, and (c) has been provided with a copy of ASCA's *Ethical Standards for School Counselors* (see Appendix D). If a supervisee should perform an act that is in violation of these ethical standards, the site supervisor can take comfort in the fact that a review of ethical considerations was conducted prior to the commitment of the violation and that the supervisor provided the supervisee with a copy of the document that contains the ethical standards for the school counseling field.

Certain areas within the ASCA's *Ethical Standards* that should receive particular emphasis include

- confidentiality and informed consent
- dual relationships
- referrals
- danger to self or others
- student records
- technology
- parent rights

Each of the above topics is discussed from the perspective of what supervisees might like to discuss before they begin to work with trainees.

Confidentiality and Informed Consent

The preamble to the ASCA *Ethical Standards for School Counselors* states, "Each person has the right to privacy and thereby the right to expect the counselor–student relationship to comply with all laws, policies, and ethical standards pertaining to confidentiality in the school setting." Supervisors must remind trainees of the trust that is placed in school counselors when counselees share their secrets, fears, and concerns.

Confidentiality in a school setting takes on several added dimensions that may not be present in a community agency or private practice setting because of (a) the age of the students and (b) information expectations that may be held by school staff or a student. Supervisees need to inform students that they

- are attending a university because they are planning to become a counselor
- may tape some of the sessions so they would like both the counselee (if age appropriate) and his or her parent or guardian to sign the "permission to tape" form
- may play the tape for the school counselor site supervisor, the program supervisor, and a school counselor education class but they will use a code number rather than the student's name
- may need to explain to trainees that if counselees reveal information that might be viewed as something to "cause you or someone else to get hurt," then the supervisee might have to tell someone
- will tell counselees that they will seek their permission to share information when the supervisee feels that sharing such information will be helpful

These minimal informed-consent procedures should be presented in language appropriate to the age of the counselee.

Site supervisors should also review school district policies and state laws that apply to the ethical responsibility to provide information to an identified third party who, by his or her relationship with the counselee, is at a high risk of contracting a disease that is commonly known to be communicable and fatal. According to the ASCA *Ethical Standards,* disclosure requires satisfaction of *all* of the following conditions:

- Counselee identifies partner or the partner is highly identifiable.
- Counselor recommends the counselee notify partner and refrain from further high-risk behavior.
- Counselee refuses.
- Counselor informs the counselee of the intent to notify the partner.
- Counselor seeks legal consultation as to the legalities of informing the partner.

Maintaining confidentiality is a hallmark of the counseling profession, and supervisees may need to frequently consult with the site supervisor on issues related to sharing information. Above all, sharing of any information should be done for the primary purpose of aiding the counselee. Further, counselee permission and, under certain circumstances, parental permission should be obtained prior to the release of information.

Dual Relationships

Although the topic of dual relationships may have been discussed multiple times in various counselor preparation courses, supervisees may need assistance in determining when their activities might interfere with their objectivity and, thus, result in harm to a counselee. The following case is illustrative of a dual relationship.

Unbeknown to the program internship coordinator, Evelyn was placed at an internship site in the same district where her spouse was employed in the central Board of Education office. Partway into her internship experience, Evelyn's supervisor determined that Evelyn was not performing satisfactorily and, after consulting numerous times with the program supervisor, determined that Evelyn had to be removed from the internship site. During the process of determining whether Evelyn could continue at the site, pressure was placed on the site supervisor and principal by administrators in the Board office because her spouse had informed his bosses that "Evelyn was getting a raw deal."

In the above case, the dual relationship did not involve the supervisee and counselee. Nevertheless, the case points out the need for supervisees to constantly be on alert to detecting when dual relationships are not productive. If a dual relationship is unavoidable, the ASCA *Ethical Standards* state very clearly that the counselor is responsible for taking action to eliminate or reduce the potential for harm. Safeguards might include referral to another counselor, informed consent, consultation, supervision, and documentation.

Referrals

School district referral policies have the potential for conflicting with the counselor's ethical obligations to counselees who may need assistance. Ethical standards indicate that the professional school counselor makes referrals when necessary or appropriate to outside resources. Appropriate referrals may necessitate informing both parents/guardians and counselees of applicable resources and making proper plans for transitions with minimal interruption of services. However, many school districts have very specific policies that dictate when and how counselors may discuss a referral with parents or guardians. The impetus for such policies is often financial in nature and may place the counselors in a situation whereby they have to weigh what is best for the counselee against the financial implications for the school district.

For example, the policies of the Riverview Gardens School District (1999) in St. Louis County, Missouri, for referrals to outside agencies state:

> The guidance counselor(s) and other professional staff members provide preliminary assessment of student problems and referrals to outside agencies, if necessary. The district will assist and cooperate with other agencies concerning the diagnosis and treatment of a referral student when applicable to his or her educational program in the school district. Except as otherwise required by law, costs for diagnostic and treatment services outside the district are the responsibility of parents or guardians.

Many school districts, like the Riverview Gardens School District, have policy statements on referrals. Site supervisors should inform supervisees of the referral policies that may exist within the school district.

Danger to Self or Others

Section A.7 of the ASCA *Ethical Standards* deals solely with the topic of danger to self or others and indicates that the professional school counselor informs parents/guardians or appropriate authorities when the student's condition indicates a clear and imminent danger to the student or others. This is to be done after careful deliberation and, where possible, after consultation with other counseling professionals. Supervisors need to convey to supervisees that they should take every threat of violence seriously, that the supervisor is to be informed if there is any indication of harm to self or others, and that they will be available to help the supervisee. Together, the supervisor and supervisee will determine the course of action to be taken.

Decisions regarding next steps are complicated by the fact that school counselors are also ethically obligated to consider the welfare of potentially violent students. Language in the ASCA's *Ethical Standards* is permissive in that it indicates a counselor *may* choose to inform the potentially violent student of actions to be taken, *may* involve the student in a three-way communication with parents/guardians when breaching confidentiality, or *may* allow the student to have input as to how and to whom the breach will be made.

School counselors need to stay up-to-date on case law that surrounds the *duty to warn*. Hermann and Finn (2002) noted several cases supervisors can use in discussing the duty to warn:

- In 1999, the U.S. Supreme Court explained that school personnel can be held responsible for failing to protect students from student-on-student violence (*Davis v. Monroe County Board of Education,* 1999).
- In August 2000, a federal court in Kentucky dismissed the claims filed against school personnel in the West Paducah, Kentucky, school shooting (Glaberson, 2000) and found that the perpetrator was the only responsible party for the shootings even though the student assailant had written homicidal and suicidal thoughts in school papers.
- In November 2001, a federal district court in Denver dismissed the lawsuits of families of victims in the Columbine High School shootings that alleged that school officials, including school counselors, failed to recognize warning signs from the student assailants (Kass, 2001). The judge ruled that the warning signs were not enough to predict the impending violence. In this case the warning signs included a violent Web site; the creation of a videotape made for a video production class that portrayed the student assailants, Eric Harris and Dylan Klebold, enacting a scenario in which they shot students with the motive of revenge (McPhee, 2000); and classroom materials presented by Harris and Klebold that expressed their anger, hatred, intent to kill, and possession of firearms.
- School counselors have a duty to use reasonable care to attempt to prevent a student's suicide when they are on notice of a student's suicidal intent and have been held liable for failing to protect students from foreseeable harm (*Eisel v. Board of Education,* 1991).

Student Records

It is important for supervisors to review school policies for entering, accessing, and releasing information contained in student records. Supervisees must understand that student records are confidential. Only authorized school personnel may have access to student information for legitimate educational purposes without the consent of the student (if 18 years of age or older) or parent/guardian (if under 18 years of age).

Technology

Supervisees may have many questions about the appropriate use of technology. The site supervisor should provide the supervisee with a copy of the school district's Internet use policy. If the district's policy statement fails to address issues that commonly occur when technology is used to support school counseling programs, the site supervisor should explain any additional procedures that have been devised to assure safe and effective use of the Internet for counselor-led activities. What are the policies and procedures related to student access and parental permission for the following Internet-based activities?

- Implementing activities that involve use of e-mail (e-mail privileges that may vary with elementary, middle, and high school levels)
- Delivering classroom guidance activities that link to various Internet sites
- Using online career and educational planning sites and assessment sites that include student information and data storage components
- Applying for financial aid online, which involves the provision of family composition and financial data
- Submitting college applications online and providing the data requested by higher education institutions

Parent Rights

For the most part, school counselors' work with minors and parents/guardians of minors is key to a student's maximum development. Diversity among families should be respected. All parents/guardians, custodial and noncustodial, are vested with certain rights and responsibilities for the welfare of their children. In cases of divorce or separation, good-faith effort should be made to keep both parents informed with regard to critical information—unless there is a court order to the contrary.

Reasonable efforts should be made to honor the wishes of parents/guardians concerning information regarding the student. When parents/guardians are provided with accurate, comprehensive, and relevant information in an objective and caring manner, it must be done in ways that are appropriate and consistent with ethical responsibilities to the student. In the process of collaborating with parents, information on family difficulties may be presented. It is important that the supervisee respects the confidentiality of parents and guardians.

THE LAW AND THE SUPERVISION JOURNEY

Consider the following hypothetical situations: The supervisee is injured or harmed at the practicum or internship site; the supervisee has used an inappropriate counseling approach resulting in harm to the counselee; or the supervisee is under consideration for dismissal from the practicum or internship site because impairment is interfering with effective performance. These are situations that site supervisors hope never occur. Program supervisors seek to provide the best possible clinical experiences for students, and they also try to maintain good relationships with school sites. From a site supervisor's perspective, if policies, procedures, and paperwork associated with supervision seem to be unwarranted, they are not! A few extra minutes devoted to preventive steps can help lessen the liability in the event that a supervisee is injured, claims discrimination or defamation, charges educational malpractice, or alleges breach of contract.

At a March 2003 conference on externships, sponsored by the Columbus School of Law, The Catholic University of America, Kathryn Kelly and Kathryn Bender made a presentation titled "Liability Issues for Externships." In their presentation, they cited several court cases that have implications for student clinical sites. Although their presentation focused on legal issues for universities, there are also implications for school districts.

Kelly and Bender (2003) pointed out that if a student is injured at an internship site, the student may allege negligence for the university's failure to provide adequate security or warnings of foreseeable dangers. Such findings against universities have been upheld in the courts. There are recent cases holding universities responsible for a student's sexual assault at a dangerous internship location (*Nova Southeastern University Inc. v. Gross*, 2000). In the *Nova* case, Ms. Gross also sued the community agency where she was completing her internship.

What implications does the *Nova* case have for issues surrounding safety and security at clinical sites? If it is known that a school is located in a high-risk or high-crime area, these facts should be made known to the supervisee prior to placement at the site. After being informed of such conditions, if a supervisee elects to complete a practicum or internship at the high-risk site, the site supervisor should also apprise the trainee of safety and securing precautions that all school personnel are urged to follow. Legal counsel at some universities are now urging that trainees should propose the location where they wish to complete required off-campus experiences. However, trainees are often not in a position to know if the site and site supervisors possess the qualifications deemed necessary by the university counselor preparation program. A compromise that offers more potential for helping reduce liability is to offer supervisees a list of sites from which they can choose.

Another case cited by Kelly and Bender (2003) involved violation of a trainee's privacy when an employee of the university passed along uncorroborated allegations regarding a student in the Education School to the state licensing authorities without a hearing (*Gonzaga University v. Doe*, 2002). Closely related is the situation in which a trainee might allege defamation upon receiving a negative evaluation from a site supervisor. A statement could be defamatory if it unfairly injures the trainee in his or her profession. However, Kelly and Bender also pointed out that if the evaluation is true or if it is not "published" (or made available to a third party), then there is no defamation.

As can be seen from the cases cited by Kelly and Bender (2003), legal actions do happen, and supervisors must (a) understand basic principles of different types of liability and educational malpractice, (b) work with university personnel to make sure that appropriate policies and procedures are included in Affiliation Agreements, (c) apprise supervisees of school district policies, and (d) prepare themselves psychologically for dealing with the stress that is bound to occur when a legal action occurs.

BRIEF PRIMER ON LIABILITY AND EDUCATIONAL MALPRACTICE

Many counselors are so preoccupied with being in a helping mode that they sometimes forget that their good intentions of serving as a site supervisor may become the objects of legal charges and lawsuits. With the supervisory role, two types of liability can emerge: direct liability and vicarious liability. In some cases, the site supervisor could be accused of educational malpractice.

Direct and Vicarious Liability

Direct liability can be charged when the actions of a supervisor were themselves the cause of harm to a supervisee or a counselee. The supervisor does not have to actually carry out the intervention, but if the supervisee follows the suggestion of a supervisor and this results in harm the supervisor may be open to direct liability charges. The following illustrates the concept of direct liability. A supervisor suggested that a supervisee conduct a classroom guidance activity that involved an Internet site that, unbeknown to the supervisor, contained a link to a pornographic site. The supervisee conducted a classroom activity based on the primary content of the Internet site suggested by the supervisor. Several students discovered the porno-graphic link and viewed material at the linked site. The supervisor could be held directly li-able because the supervisee carried out the suggestion offered by the supervisor.

If the supervisee had used the Internet site on his or her own volition without the supervi-sor's suggestion or knowledge, the notion of vicarious liability could apply to the supervisor. Vicarious liability is a legal concept that means that a party may be held responsible for injury or damage, when in reality they were not actively involved in the incident. Individuals who may be charged with vicarious liability are generally in a supervisory role over the person person-ally responsible for the injury/damage.

Educational Malpractice

Most university counselor education faculty understand that if a professional fails to follow ac-ceptable standards of practice that cause harm to the counselee, the professional can be held liable for the harm that was caused. Recently, the concept of *educational malpractice*—students' claims against an institution for failure to provide the process or substance they claim was promised to them as "customers" of the institution—has received significant publicity. In February 2004, Ann D. Springer, associate counsel for the American Association of University Professors, stated:

> As higher education institutions act more like corporations, courts are more willing to see the policies and practices of institutions as "contracts" with the "customers" or "counselees" (stu-dents) regarding the quality of the "product" (education). The more similar institutions are to corporations, the less courts will be willing to defer to the professional judgment of educators and the institutional autonomy of colleges and universities. (Springer, 2004)

Kelly and Bender (2003) indicated that although courts are not inclined to review claims of educational malpractice or breach of contract based on inadequate educational services (*Ross v. Creighton University*, 1992), a student who fails a program may bring an action against the uni-versity claiming malpractice or alleging that the educational promises made in writing or orally were not kept (*Hutchings v. Vanderbilt University*, 2003). Embedded in the notion of educational malpractice is the concept that when practica and internships are part of the student's re-quired educational program, universities should take careful measures when selecting off-campus practice sites. Affiliation Agreements should be in place for each off-campus site.

AFFILIATION AGREEMENTS ARE A NECESSITY

An Affiliation Agreement is between a university and a school district and is developed for the purpose of providing an educational opportunity for students who are preparing to become school counselors. Affiliation Agreements are initiated by the university counselor educator and should be reviewed by university legal counsel prior to presentation to appropriate school personnel for their signature. If an agreement is well written, it will serve as a vehicle for help-ing to prevent legal issues that may emerge. An Affiliation Agreement checklist titled "Legal Policies and Procedures Checklist for Site Supervisors of Counseling Students" is found in Figure 10.2.

Although most of the items on this checklist are self-explanatory, the topic of indemnifica-tion needs elaboration. An indemnity is a specific type of contractual mechanism whereby one party to a contract agrees to hold the other (and presumably innocent) party harmless if a third party brings a claim against the innocent party. Many states have laws that strictly pro-hibit both universities and school districts from signing agreements in which they agree not to hold each other legally responsible for any actions or they agree to reimburse each other for any damages. These are commonly known as "indemnification and hold-harmless clauses." Where such laws exist, variations of the following phrase are often part of the Affiliation Agreement: "Neither of the parties shall assume any liabilities to each other."

	Yes	No
1. Do you understand the principles of direct and vicarious liability?	☐	☐
2. Have you *documented* that you have reviewed the following with each supervisee?		
Confidentiality	☐	☐
Informed consent	☐	☐
Dual relationships	☐	☐
Referral	☐	☐
Duty to warn	☐	☐
Student records	☐	☐
Technology and Internet use policies	☐	☐
Parent/guardian rights	☐	☐
3. Do you have a standard Affiliation Agreement for internship sites that has been reviewed by the university's and school district's legal counsel?	☐	☐
4. At a minimum, does your Affiliation Agreement include statements in the following areas:		
Proper phrasing for indemnification and "hold harmless" clauses	☐	☐
Length and number of hours required	☐	☐
Liability insurance requirements	☐	☐
Compliance with university and school district policies	☐	☐
Orientation to school district policies before working in school	☐	☐
Progress reports and evaluation procedures	☐	☐
Intellectual property rights of materials developed by student during internship	☐	☐
University policies relative to supervisee travel to site	☐	☐
University and agency policies relative to transportation of student counselees	☐	☐
Precautions to safeguard health and safety of supervisee	☐	☐
Right of school site to screen practicum/internship applicants and to refuse applicants	☐	☐
Procedures for removal of supervisee from site prior to completion of internship	☐	☐
5. Have appropriate university and school officials signed the Affiliation Agreement?	☐	☐
6. Has the supervisee received a written statement outlining the responsibilities of the program supervisor, site supervisor, and supervisee?	☐	☐
7. Has the supervisee signed an Ethics Pledge that he or she has received and reviewed materials provided by the university and site supervisor and that he or she will comply with the American School Counselor Association's (2004) *Ethical Standards for School Counselors*?	☐	☐
8. Has the supervisee, faculty supervisor, and site supervisor signed a contract that outlines the objectives, responsibilities, expected outcomes, and methods of evaluation?	☐	☐
9. Are signed copies of all documents stored in a locked file?	☐	☐

Figure 10.2

Legal Policies and Procedures Checklist for Site Supervisors of Counseling Students

SCHOOL DISTRICT POLICIES

It is important for supervisors to review school district policies with the supervisee prior to undertaking tasks outlined in the Student Contract. A list of various school policies or procedures that will have an impact on the trainee are presented in Table 10.1.

THE JOY OF SUPERVISION OUTWEIGHS LEGAL CONSIDERATIONS

Each year hundreds of students successfully complete counseling practica and internship experiences without any legal issues or lawsuits. When lawsuits do arise, they are stressful for all

Table 10.1

School Policies That Inform the Work of a Supervisee

Accidents and Illnesses	Release During School Hours
Acquired Immune Deficiency Syndrome (AIDS)	Rights and Responsibilities
Admission of Suspended or Expelled Students	School Power of Attorney for Care of a Minor Child
Admissions	Student Alcohol and Drug Testing
Alcohol and Drug Use	Student Assignment
Alternative School Programs	Student Clubs and Organizations
Alternative School Services	Student Communicable Diseases
Attendance	Student Conduct
Attendance of Nonresident Students	Student Disciplinary Hearing Authority
Awards and Scholarships	Student Fees and Fines
Bus Conduct	Student Government
Care of School Property	Student Health Services
Child Abuse and Neglect	Student Performances
Child Custody/Parental Access	Student Psychological Services
Code of Behavior and Discipline	Student Publications
Compulsory Attendance Ages	Student Records
Contests for Students	Student Records: Annual Notification of Rights
Detention	Student Records: Inspection, Fees for Copies,
Directory Information Procedure	Disclosure, and Corrections
Discipline Procedures	Student Records: Use of Records
Dress Code	Student Social Events
Food Service	Student Social Services
Fund-Raising Activities	Student Solicitations
Gifts	Student Suspensions
Glucagon Administration Policy	Student Vehicles
Harassment of Students	Supervision of Students
Home Schools	Transfers Within the System
Homeless Students	Unsafe School Choice
Immunizations	Use of Personal Communication Devices in School
Independent Evaluations of Students	Use of Tobacco
Interrogations and Searches	Weapons and Dangerous Instruments
Married and/or Pregnant Students	Withdrawals
Physical Examinations and Medication	Zero Tolerance Expulsions
Procedural Due Process	

parties who may be named in any charges brought forward by a supervisee. The list of parties may be a lengthy one and may include such individuals as the program supervisor, site supervisor, university department head, and so on.

School personnel named in any supervisee lawsuits should immediately consult legal counsel for the school district. Supervisor stress levels will be greatly reduced if the supervisor can supply legal counsel with documentation of professional actions that relate to the lawsuit.

The stress of a lawsuit will be much less, too, if a program supervisor has placed a supervisee with a site supervisor who has the appropriate credentials. The graduate degree, the license, the experience, and the supervisory training offer support if a supervisor's actions are called into question.

SUMMARY

This chapter started with an international traveler analogy, and it is appropriate that it ends in the same manner. Travelers occasionally thumb through their passport and recall pleasant memories represented by each country's passport control stamp. When school counselors graduate from counselor preparation, program supervisors have every right to feel proud that their "stamp" is on the graduate's transcript and diploma. Thoughtful application of ethical and legal principles will enable supervisors to make the supervision journey one that evokes fond recollections of each stamp that was placed on a future school counselor.

REFERENCES

American Counseling Association. (2005). *ACA code of ethics.* Alexandria, VA: Author.

American School Counselor Association. (2004). *Ethical standards for school counselors.* Retrieved from http://www.schoolcounselor.org/content.asp?contentid=173

Association for Counselor Education and Supervision. (1993). *Ethical guidelines for counseling supervisors.* Retrieved from http://www.acesonline.net/ethicalguidelines.htm

Bernard, J. M., & Goodyear, R. K. (2004). *Fundamentals of clinical supervision.* Boston: Allyn & Bacon.

Davis v. Monroe County Board of Education, 119 S. Ct. 1661 (1999).

Eisel v. Board of Education, 597 A.2d 447 (Md. 1991).

Glaberson, W. (2000, August 4). Judges dismiss civil suits in school killings. *The Times-Picayune*, p. A-4.

Gonzaga University v. Doe, 122 S. Ct. 2268 (2002).

Hermann, M. A., & Finn, A. (2002). An ethical and legal perspective on the role of school counselors in preventing violence in schools. *Professional School Counselor, 6,* 46–54.

Hutchings v. Vanderbilt University, 2003 WL 202170 (6th Cir. January 2003).

Kass, J. (2001, November 29). Columbine seeks closure—out of court. *The Christian Science Monitor*, p. 2.

Kelly, K., & Bender, K. (2003). *Liability issues for externships.* Retrieved from http://law.cua.edu/News/conference/externships/friday330d.htm

McPhee, M. (2000, October 3). Lawsuits criticize teachers, DeAngelis, others cited in new papers. *The Denver Post*, p. A-06.

Meyer, R. G., Landis, E. R., & Hays, J. R. (1988). *Law for the psychotherapist.* New York: Norton.

Nova Southeastern University Inc. v. Gross, 758 So.2d 86 (S. Ct. Fla., 2000).

Riverview Gardens School District. (1999). *Riverview Gardens School District policy online* [Student Guidance and Counseling Paragraph 14]. Retrieved March 1, 2005, from http://policy.msbanet.org/riverview/showpolicy.php?file=JHD-C.1C

Ross v. Creighton University, 957 F.2d 410, 414 (7th Cir. 1992).

Springer, A. D. (2004, February). *Legal issues for faculty.* Washington, DC: American Association of University Professors. Retrieved January 4, 2006, from http://www.auup.org/Legal/info%20outlines/04issues.htm

PART IV

Evaluation

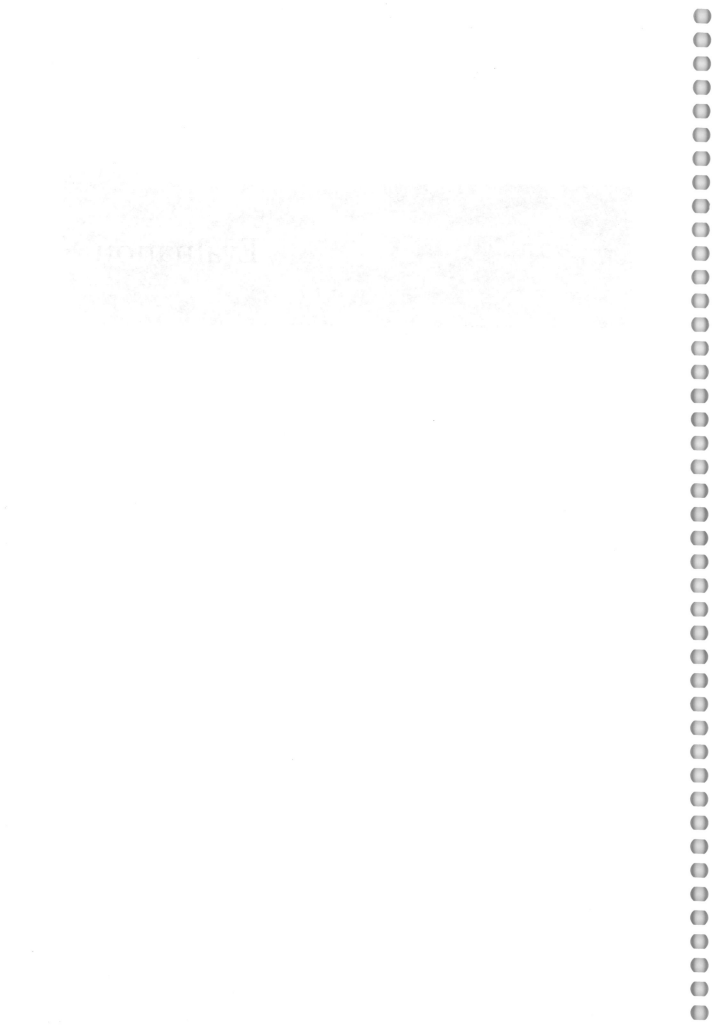

CHAPTER 11

The Evaluation Process and Supervision

THE PURPOSE of this chapter is to

- provide information on the importance of the evaluative process
- define the types of supervisory evaluations
- provide examples of strategies that assist in conducting developmental, clinical, and administrative evaluations

Jessica, a professional secondary school counselor, agreed to supervise Kevin, who was completing his coursework in school counseling and was enrolled in internship, his final class. Throughout the semester the faculty supervisor was in contact with Jessica to check on Kevin's progress, and never once did Jessica express any concern about her intern's development. What Jessica did not admit were her concerns about her trainee's ability to work in a school setting. He did just enough to "get by" and never took the initiative to start any groups or to teach guidance classes other than those specified on his contract. At the end of the semester Kevin was given a high evaluation from his site supervisor.

A few weeks later Jessica met with the program supervisor and confided that Kevin didn't appear to be motivated, he was weak in classroom management, and teachers were unimpressed with his classroom guidance presentations. The program supervisor explained that if this information had been received earlier, they could have had the opportunity to work together to improve these areas so that Kevin would be better prepared as a new professional school counselor. Jessica admitted that she was reluctant to give him negative feedback because she was afraid it would create bad feelings and hostile working conditions since she knew that she would meet him at professional counseling events.

FOR SITE AND PROGRAM SUPERVISORS

Providing evaluative feedback is one of the most important duties of the supervisor (Neufeldt, 1999, as cited in Michaelson, Estrada-Hernandez, & Wadsworth, 2003). This feedback should be based on a series of informal and formal measurements rather than based on a single judgment or situation (Harris, 1994). Too often, supervisees do well academically but lack some of the skills that are needed to perform effectively as a counselor. Trainee evaluation is designed to provide encouragement, to identify problematic areas, and to identify the strategies that would improve and monitor personal and professional growth. Unfortunately, trainees often perceive this process as a threat and are more concerned about their letter grade and credit rather than viewing the evaluation process as an opportunity to develop personally and professionally. If supervisees are aware that assessment will be ongoing with regular feedback and opportunities for improvement, their anxiety may be lessened (Michaelson et al., 2003). This continual observation with feedback is known as *formative* evaluation (Harris, 1994; Nitko, 2004). A judgment that occurs at an end point in time is called *summative* evaluation. In each case, objectives are assessed, and a judgment is provided either in the form of a grade or through a formal scheduled meeting at the end of the clinical experience (Nitko, 2004).

Practices that assist in providing an assessment include the following:

- Emphasizing not only the areas that need to be improved but also the positive attributes of the supervisee (Drapela, 1983). When the supervisor provides positive feedback prior to corrective feedback, the trainee is more likely to listen.
- Communicating concrete, behavioral feedback rather than giving abstract messages. When the evaluation is based on the behavioral objectives specified in the contract, what will be assessed is easier to understand, and the behavior is easier to correct (Gage & Berliner, 1984, as cited in Harris, 1994).
- Recognizing the developmental level of the trainee when giving tasks and feedback. If the supervisor has an expectation for skills that are far beyond the ability level of the supervisee, disappointment will result when the skill is not performed adequately.
- Recognizing that supervising is a multifaceted process. Because both the program supervisor and site supervisor provide an evaluation, it is important that continual communication occurs between each so that enough time is available for improvement, and both are aware of the trainee's strengths as well as areas in which improvement is needed.
- Providing a time for the trainee to self-reflect. High levels of professional reflection are a product of supportive work environments that allow an atmosphere in which cognitive, affective, and behavioral growth can be processed collaboratively (Roberts & Morotti, 2001).
- Discussing concerns and issues in weekly sessions in which ample time is available for addressing problematic areas (Association for Counselor Education and Supervision, 1993). A trusting atmosphere in which all individuals can feel comfortable initiating a conversation about concerns without a fear of repercussions is necessary for learning to occur.

When the trainee is involved in the practicum and internship, an evaluation of his or her performance in the developmental, administrative, and clinical experiences will assist in the development of self-awareness and professional identity. The various types of evaluative assessments within these areas are discussed next.

EVALUATIVE PROCEDURES

Developmental Assessment

Personal growth and insight include gaining greater competence, awareness of affect, respect for individuals from diverse backgrounds, and increased professional identity (Henderson, Newsome, & Veach, 2005). Programs may be of greater value to students if there were a greater emphasis on self-awareness activities. Much has been written about the importance of self-assessment. However, not too many trainees engage in this process because the enormous amount of work that is required in clinical experiences leaves little time for self-reflection. The following creative, self-awareness activities are helpful in individual and group supervision: growth icons, rating scales, critical incidents, journals, and portfolios.

Growth Icons
Exercise 11.1 is a concrete, creative method of visually monitoring growth.

Likert-Type Rating Scales
Growth can be monitored through the use of a Likert-type rating scale that tracks feelings during the clinical experiences. As pointed out in the previous chapters, trainees at the beginning of the experience often feel dependency and excitement mixed with anxiety. Toward

Exercise 11.1

Growth Icons

Objective: To self-reflect on one's role as a professional school counselor.

Materials: Large craft paper, magazines of different genres, paste, and scissors.

Directions: Have trainees cut out pictures from magazines that best represent their feelings about their clinical experiences at the beginning, middle, and end of the experience. After the trainees have selected icons and pasted them on a sheet of paper, collect the representations and repeat the activity at some point mid-semester and again at the end of the semester. Trainees may also be asked to select an icon that represents how they would like to appear at some point in the future.

Following the selection of icons, trainees are invited to share their selections and to clarify anything that seems significant. Group members are encouraged to ask questions about their peers' representations. The supervisor may ask the trainees to identify strategies that will facilitate movement to their desired future image of themselves.

Evaluation: Supervisees will reflect on the progress they have made throughout their clinical experiences.

the terminal supervisory stages, the trainee often feels a sense of pride in accomplishments, is able to identify techniques that work, and is more motivated to try new strategies (Hess, 1986; Stoltenberg & Delworth, 1998; Williams, 1995). Exercise 11.2 describes a strategy called "What's Your Number?" This strategy was adapted from Dr. Joel Diambra, who used this technique at the University of Tennessee in an undergraduate human services class.

Critical Incidents

Each problem we encounter is a learning experience for the next situation. These events are known as *critical incidents* according to Tyson and Pedersen (2000). Trainees can learn from these unique events in that they offer an opportunity to think about, reflect on, and analyze their readiness for the profession. Supervisors can discuss these incidents with their trainees as teaching tools. The following situation is an example of a successful event that was affirming for the trainee.

> I was working with a difficult student. He wanted to talk but never had any direction or goal in mind. One day, our session was completely different because of a new technique I tried with him. I used a solution-focused brief therapy technique known as the "magic wand." I asked him, "If I had a magic wand and waved it so that you would be acting the way you would like to in school, what would you be doing differently?" From that point on he was doing his work, making goals for himself, and coming up with ways to meet his goals. It was satisfying for me to see that this technique helped him.

Another trainee described a negative event that served as a catalyst to think about new ways of thinking and behaving.

> After working with students in a middle school, I thought I was making progress by using appropriate counseling skills. When I met my program supervisor for my supervisory sessions, I was surprised when I was told that listening skills and letting the counselee lead were not enough. I was advised to use more directive skills to focus the session. Although I was upset with this feedback, I do believe that my counseling skills have improved as a result of this information.

Journaling

Keeping a journal is another method for tracking personal and professional growth. The use of journals serves as a tool for critically reflecting growth and learning because of the natural connection between counseling and learning (Burnett & Meacham, 2002). Copeland (1986,

Exercise 11.2

What's Your Number?

Objective: To track and monitor feelings during the clinical experience.

Directions: This activity can be used individually or with a group of student trainees. The trainee selects a number on a Likert scale (ranging from 1 = *worst week* and 10 = *best week ever*) that best represents his or her feelings that week, along with one word that best describes the clinical experiences. Ordinarily, trainees in the initial stages indicate relatively low numbers reflective of the anxiety often felt or high numbers representing the excitement of starting this experience. The ratings fluctuate throughout the term, and at the end of the experience the numbers tend to be on the high end of the scale with oscillation in the middle due to successes or frustrations. Descriptive words at the beginning of the experience range from *eager* to *apprehensive.* Toward the end, the descriptors include such terms as *rethinking* to *optimistic.* A graph that indicates the averages of the trainees' numerical ratings throughout the 15-week practicum experience is presented in Figure 11.1.

as cited in Burnett & Meacham, 2002) stated that journaling progresses through developmental stages from the beginning when the trainee merely records experiences, to the middle stages when there is evidence of thinking about and reflecting on the experiences, and finally to the end stages when the trainee is more critically able to integrate learning that assists in decision making and problem solving.

For trainees who dislike recording, journaling can take the form of video- or audiotapes. Whatever structure the journal takes, organization is vital for identifying and expressing personal feelings, thoughts, and behaviors. The following journaling structure is an example for how the structure can facilitate self-understanding.

- Summarize the activities you performed
- What have you learned from these activities?

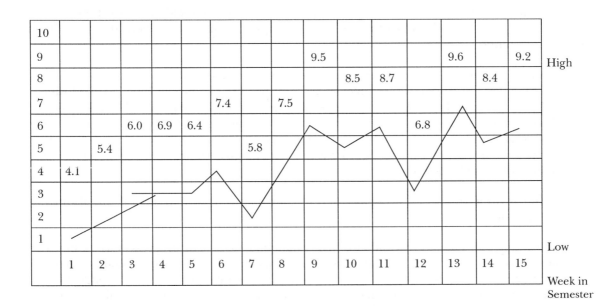

Figure 11.1

Assessment Chart

Note. This self-evaluation graph shows the fluctuating feelings of trainees during the 15-week practicum.

- Observe the professional school counselor
- What are your thoughts/feelings about these activities?
- Evaluate your counseling skills
- What skills did you use to perform the activities?
- Identify your personal feelings
- What were your feelings about these activities?
- Identify your thoughts
- What were your thoughts when you conducted these activities?
- Identify your behaviors
- What did you do to perform these activities?
- Use of ethical/legal guidelines
- What ethical/legal issues did you encounter while performing the activities?
- Other

Discuss any other issues that were part of the experiences that are not mentioned above.

- Learning experiences
- What did you learn about yourself or others from these experiences?
- How will you use this information in the future?

Portfolios

Portfolios also serve as a practical collection of meaningful, professional materials that portray the activities, learning, and growth of the trainee over time. Professional materials, accomplishments, growth over time, and goals with a means to measure objectives are benefits of this type of evaluation (Ametrano, Stickel, & Broughton, 1998; Baltimore, Hickson, George, & Crutchfield, 1996). Electronic portfolios integrate technology with an opportunity to present documents and performance in a format that can be accessed by interested individuals at a convenient time and place. Examples of suggested contents include the following:

- Introduction
  Goals
  Resume
  Reflection process
  Professional disclosure statement
- Examples of "best works"
  Proposals
  Research papers
  Case presentations
  Examples of classroom and counseling activities
- Documentation of knowledge, skills, and competencies learned over time
  Memberships
  Conferences attended
  Recognition and awards
- Academic growth and development
  Evaluation of performance
  Counseling skills
- Evaluation of performance
  Rating forms
  Grades
  Supervisor evaluations
  Demonstration of counseling skills—videotape
  Personal growth scale

Administrative Assessment

Administrative assessment includes an evaluation of such things as work habits, attendance, time management, compliance with ethical and legal issues, ability to communicate effectively, and the ability to follow school rules and policies (Schmidt, 1990). Monitoring the trainee's ability to complete appropriate paperwork and clinical experiences prepares trainees for the school counseling profession and is another type of evaluation. An example of assessment of these responsibilities is found in Figure 11.2.

Clinical Assessment

Clinical assessment includes an evaluation of the skills that are ordinarily associated with the counseling profession, such as consultation, collaboration, counseling dynamics, and assessment of knowledge and application (Schmidt, 1990). An example of a clinical skills assessment checklist is found in Figure 11.3.

Use the following scale to evaluate the trainee in each of the following areas. Circle the number that best describes the characteristic.

1 = minimal effort
2 = satisfactory level
3 = good
4 = excellent

Characteristic	Rating				Comments
	1	2	3	4	
1. **Motivation:** The trainee is self-directed					
2. **Feedback:** The trainee has the ability to accept constructive advice					
3. **Attendance:** The trainee keeps and attends on time to schedule					
4. **Initiative:** The trainee is able to design, implement, and evaluate strategies					
5. **Classroom Management:** The trainee is able to use appropriate discipline strategies					
6. **Consultation:** The trainee is able to work effectively with teachers and parents					
7. **Appointments:** The trainee is on time for his/her appointments					
8. **Organization:** The trainee organizes and completes work on time					
9. **Dress:** The trainee dresses appropriately for the work setting and people with whom he/she works					
10. **Meetings:** The trainee is able to make and keep appointments					
11. **Teaching:** The trainee is able to teach lessons in an interesting manner					
12. **Competence:** The trainee is aware of his/her counseling abilities and does not go beyond training and education.					
13. **Rules:** The trainee understands and is able to follow school rules and procedures.					
14. **Relationships:** The trainee is able to establish appropriate relationships with students, parents, administrators, and teachers.					

Figure 11.2

Assessment of Administrative Skills

Counselor: _____

Throughout the semester, the following skills must be demonstrated. A frequency marking will be indicated each time the skill is used. The following rating scale will be used to determine skill effectiveness. The skills marked by an X should be seen consistently on every tape.

1 = basic understanding and use of skill
2 = mastery of skill
3 = excellent use of skill

Demonstrates the Ability to Maintain a Helpful Counseling Relationship		
Skill	**Date Completed**	**Comments**
1. (X) The counselor explains counseling process		
2. The counselor maintains counseling relationship with at least two counselees for at least two sessions each	Counselee 1 Counselee 1	Counselee 2 Counselee 2
3. (X) The counselor makes statements that reflect counselee's feelings		
4. (X) The counselor makes statements that reflect counselee's content		
5. The counselor provides specific feedback to counselee		
6. (X) The counselor shows empathy/rapport		
7. The counselor uses paraphrase		
8. The counselor uses clarification		
9. (X) The counselor uses open-ended questions		
10. (X) The counselor uses silence		
Action Phase		
Skill	**Date Completed**	**Comments**
1. The counselor uses self-disclosure		
2. The counselor uses confrontation		
3. The counselor explores logical consequences with the counselee		
4. The counselor has counselee identify methods that have been tried to solve previous problems		
Assessment		
Skill	**Date Completed**	**Comments**
1. (X) The counselor and counselee have stated a goal		
2. The counselor and counselee have explored the cognitive aspects of the problem		
3. The counselor and counselee have explored the behavioral aspects of the problem		
4. The counselor and counselee have explored the interpersonal aspects of the problem		
5. The counselor and counselee have explored the frequency and duration of the problem		

Figure 11.3

Clinical Skills Assessment Checklist

(Continued)

Demonstrates the Skill of Helping an Individual Through the Stages of Problem Solving		
Skill	**Date Completed**	**Comments**
1. The counselor explains to the site or university supervisor the rationale and theoretical framework for a counseling strategy used with at least three counselees		
2. The counselor asks counselee what positive skills have been used in the past to solve problems		
Demonstrates That the Outcome of the Counseling Process Is Satisfactory in Terms of a Helpful Relationship and Resolution of the Counselee's Concerns		
Skill	**Date Completed**	**Comments**
1. (X) The counselor or counselee summarizes counseling session		
2. (X) The counselee evaluates session		
3. The counselor demonstrates understanding of legal/ethical issues		

Strengths:

Needs Improvement:

Figure 11.3 *(Continued)*

SUMMARY

It is not enough for the supervisor to simply provide supervisees with experiences as a school counselor; it is also the supervisor's responsibility to provide feedback on performance. Unfortunately, when supervisors only give positive evaluations without identifying areas for improvement, trainees suffer, as may the individuals with whom the trainees will come into contact in the future. Although supervisors often view evaluative aspects of this role as distasteful, it does facilitate trainee growth, and it is a professional obligation. Several evaluative measures that can be used to assess growth in the administrative, developmental, and clinical areas are provided for the supervisor to consider as alternative assessment strategies.

REFERENCES

Ametrano, F. M., Stickel, S., & Broughton, E. (1998, March). *Using portfolios in counselor education programs.* Paper presented at the American Counseling Association Annual Convention, Indianapolis, IN.

Association for Counselor Education and Supervision. (1993). *Ethical guidelines for counseling supervisors.* Alexandria, VA: Author.

Baltimore, M. L., Hickson, J., George, J. D., & Crutchfield, L. B. (1996). Portfolio assessment: A model for counselor education. *Counselor Education and Supervision, 36,* 113–121.

Burnett, P. C., & Meacham, D. (2002). Learning journals as a counseling strategy. *Journal of Counseling & Development, 80,* 410–415.

Drapela, V. J. (1983). *The counselor as consultant and supervisor.* Springfield, IL: Charles C Thomas.

Harris, M. B. (1994). *Supervisory evaluation and feedback.* Greensboro, NC: ERIC Clearinghouse on Counseling and Student Services. (ERIC Document Reproduction Service No. ED372348)

Henderson, D., Newsome, D., & Veach, L. (2005, April). *Using expressive arts in group supervision.* Paper presented at the American Counseling Association Annual Convention, Atlanta, GA.

Hess, A. K. (1986). Growth in supervision stages of supervisee and supervisor development. *Clinical Supervisor, 4,* 51–67.

Michaelson, S. D., Estrada-Hernandez, N., & Wadsworth, J. S. (2003). A competency-based evaluation model for supervising novice counselors-in-training. *Rehabilitation Education, 17,* 215–223.

Nitko, A. J. (2004). *Educational assessment of students* (4th ed.). Upper Saddle River, NJ: Pearson.

Roberts, W. B., & Morotti, A. A. (2001). Site supervisors of professional school counseling interns: Suggested guidelines. *Professional School Counseling, 4,* 208–215.

Schmidt, J. J. (1990). Critical issues for school counselor performance appraisal and supervision. *School Counselor, 38,* 86–94.

Stoltenberg, C. D., & Delworth, U. (1998). *Supervising counselors and therapists: A developmental approach.* San Francisco: Jossey-Bass.

Tyson, L. E., & Pedersen, P. B. (2000). *Critical incidents in school counseling* (2nd ed.). Alexandria, VA: American Counseling Association.

Williams, A. (1995). *Visual and active supervision.* New York: Norton.

CHAPTER 12

Supervision of Practicing School Counselors

THE PURPOSE of this chapter is to

- inform practicing school counselors on methods for receiving supervision on clinical skills. Two strategies include:
- peer supervision or consultation
- self-supervision

Your clinical experiences are over, and you are now employed in an elementary school as a practicing professional school counselor, the job you have dreamed of for a long time. The training you received in your school counseling program was excellent, and you have confidence in your counseling skills. However, within a few months, you realize that you would like more feedback and direction on skills, perspectives, and approaches that could be better suited to working with young school-age youths. The problem is that your supervisor is the building principal who doesn't have a background in counseling. Although the support and suggestions he has given you have been helpful, you really want more feedback on counseling techniques and case conceptualization. Unfortunately, there is no one in the district who has knowledge of school counseling skills with an understanding of supervision for practicing counselors.

FOR SITE SUPERVISORS

Even when a degree is conferred that indicates coursework completion in counseling, it does not mean that counseling skills no longer need to be evaluated or upgraded. In fact, there is evidence that without supervision, counseling skills may actually deteriorate over time (Borders & Usher, 1992). This is not to suggest that school counselors do not receive supervision; the majority do. More likely than not, this supervision is mainly administrative in focus and is typically performed by a building principal who rarely has a background in counseling. Administrative supervision tends to include such areas as attendance, staff relations, parent consultation, meetings, planning, and coordination (Logan, 1997; Roberts & Borders, 1994). It is interesting to note that this type of supervision is often given as a major reason principals assign noncounseling duties (Barrett & Schmidt, 1986, as cited in Page, 1994). For the most part, practicing school counselors do not receive supervision in clinical skills once their academic training has ended (Agnew, Vaught, Getz, & Fortune, 2000; Benshoff & Paisley, 1996), yet school counselors frequently request this type of supervision as a way to sharpen their existing skills (Borders & Usher, 1992) and to learn new techniques. Clinical supervision is defined as a relationship in which one individual facilitates the development of skills, knowledge, and attitude of another (Bernard & Goodyear, 1992, as cited in Sutton & Page, 1994; Loganbill, Hardy, & Delworth, 1982). It also involves discussing difficult cases, staying accountable, debriefing when working with traumatic cases, and providing quality care to counselees (McMahon & Patton, 2000).

Today's students are now struggling with more serious issues than they have in the past (Crutchfield & Borders, 1997; McMahon & Patton, 2000; Roberts & Borders, 1994; Sutton & Page, 1994). In many cases school counselors are the only mental health professionals available to help these students who have increasingly difficult concerns (Sutton & Page, 1994).

Research repeatedly emphasizes that clinical supervision not only is essential to the counselor's personal and professional growth (McMahon & Patton, 2000; Sutton & Page, 1994) but also improves the well-being of the K–12 students with whom the school counselor works. This is a vital implication in our age of accountability. Furthermore, the lack of desirable supervision has been identified as a contributing factor to school counselor stress and burnout (Crutchfield & Borders, 1997). Because clinical supervision is important and desired, why aren't more school counselors receiving this service? Some of the reasons include the following:

- the few number of school counselors within the school setting
- geographical isolation of school counselors from their peers (Crutchfield & Borders, 1997)
- few qualified counselor supervisors who are able to provide the type of clinical supervision that is needed (McMahon & Patton, 2000)
- the unique roles of school counselors in comparison with counselors in other settings (Kahn, 1999)
- financial concerns that restrict available funds for clinical supervision
- administrative concerns about the time school counselors spend in direct service to students (Crutchfield & Borders, 1997)

Despite these drawbacks, school counselors are able to receive clinical supervision in which their skills can be constructively critiqued and subsequently improved. Peer supervision and self-supervision are two viable types of clinical supervision that school counselors report as successful means for enhancing these sought-after skills.

PEER SUPERVISION

A group of professional high school counselors were discouraged because they felt counseling skills that were helpful to them in the past did not seem to get the same results that were needed. Yet, they were uncertain as to how they could become updated and trained in the newest counseling techniques and theories. These counselors decided to form a group with the purpose of helping each other become more effective in their professional relationships. The counselors met for an hour every month to listen and/or view tapes and to provide feedback on the skills represented. Despite these goals, the group broke up after 6 months.

Just as group counseling can be more time effective than individual counseling, group supervision can reach more practicing school counselors at the same time (Crutchfield & Borders, 1997). The question is, how can this type of supervision be implemented in a time- and cost-effective manner?

Supervision by peers is a process in which colleagues work together to provide support, encouragement, feedback, and reassurance with the goal of improving professional skills (Benshoff & Paisley, 1996). These groups can also provide a forum for discussing specific ethical, legal, and professional issues. In addition, peers may assist in identifying a personal bias or a loss of objectivity that could interfere with the counseling process (Greenburg, Lewis, & Johnson, 1985). It makes sense that individuals from the same profession are better qualified to supervise their peers because of their common knowledge of issues and concerns. Peer networks used in a supervisory capacity work best when all participants are considered as equal in status and when there is an emphasis on constructive feedback, with less importance on the evaluation component (Cade, Speed, & Seligman, 1986). This is a format that many prefer to call *peer consultation* as opposed to peer supervision (Bernard, Hackney, & Wilkerson, 2004; Logan, 1997).

Whether this procedure is referred to as peer consultation or peer supervision, individuals who have participated in this type of supervision report a greater understanding of the evaluation process (Remley, Benshoff, & Mowbray, 1987, as cited in Benshoff & Paisley, 1996), a better knowledge of consultation and supervision, and improved self-confidence (Wagner & Smith, 1979, as cited in Benshoff & Paisley, 1996). With these benefits, how is it that the peer supervision group described at the beginning of this section on peer supervision did not meet the needs and expectations of the members? This question is answered through the following studies.

Benshoff and Paisley (1996) conducted a study in which school counselors met in dyads for nine 90-minute sessions, with the purpose of discussing approaches to counseling theories, goal setting, school counseling program concerns, tape critiques, and case presentations. Each participant set specific individual goals in addition to the group goals, and each agreed to tape a counseling session to share with a partner. The partner evaluating the tape was instructed to assess the tape using the following questions as guidelines:

- How did the counselee respond to questions asked by the counselor?
- What strategies worked? What strategies did not work?
- Did the counselor interventions have a purpose?
- Are the interventions consistent with the counselor's philosophical approach to counseling?
- How well did the counselor use basic attending skills?

In addition to making and evaluating tapes, each participant presented a difficult case study at an assigned meeting to the entire group. This 5- to- 7-minute presentation summarized the situation with an explanation of what it was that made this case particularly challenging. The participants gave a positive assessment of this format but requested that the sessions be extended throughout the academic year rather than just one semester. Although participants were satisfied with the level of support provided by peers, some participants believed that more structure and confrontation that focused on specific behaviors were needed.

In another study (Logan, 1997), counselors from various school settings formed a peer consultation group to share materials and resources, to present difficult cases for feedback and suggestions, and to discuss issues for support while maintaining confidentiality. Trust and commitment to developing professional growth were goals of this closed group that met for 6 months. A reevaluation of the program resulted in a peer consultation model that included counselors from various school and grade levels. The revised group met with a consultant once a month to teach and demonstrate supervision practices and to practice supervisory roles as identified by Stoltenberg's integrated developmental model with an emphasis on specific areas (self-awareness and other awareness, motivation, and autonomy). Each month one counselor brought a counseling videotape to the group, and the counselors, trained in Kagan's interpersonal process recall, practiced taking and giving feedback using various roles or perspectives. Additionally, a family sculpting technique was used to metaphorically represent the counselor, the counselee, and the counselee's family.

Metaphors are an indirect form of conceptualizing the counselee in which a picture is formed that is associated with something else (Haley, 1976, as cited in Young & Borders, 1999). For example, one counselor described working with a middle school student who talked about his failure to make and keep friends, his weight problem, and his unsuccessful attempts to contact his noncustodial father. The peer consultant who was listening to the case from a metaphor perspective described "a tire rolling down the road that no one could catch." This picture helped the counselor to understand her counselee as someone who viewed life as "out of control."

In some cases, meeting peers face-to-face for the purpose of consultation is difficult because of geographic isolation or time constraints. However, with the advances in computer technology, new supervisory opportunities are possible. In a 1995 study by Myrick and Sabella (as cited in McMahon, n.d.), supervision was provided to supervisees through e-mail. Using this approach, a counselor would send descriptions of difficult cases electronically to peers. In these communications the counselee was described, the presenting problem was offered, a description of the behaviors or interventions were implemented, and specific areas of counselor concern were explained. After reading and reflecting on the case study, the peers provided feedback, suggestions, and ideas via e-mail communication. The benefit of this form of communication was that it could be accessed at a convenient time and allowed the trainees to think about the comments that were offered without the pressure of an immediate response.

A similar study was conducted with school counselors in Australia (McMahon, n.d.). Supervision was provided over a period of 12 weeks through e-mail. Participants were divided into four groups, and each week a participant from each group presented a case. At the end of the study most participants indicated that they highly valued the connection with their colleagues, the feedback, and the ideas that were given, even though some believed that immediate feedback was preferable to waiting for the opinions of others. Some of the disadvantages mentioned included confusion as to the meaning behind the written feedback and some participants' tendency to place a greater emphasis on feedback from individuals who were more highly educated and credentialed to the exclusion of the opinions expressed by others.

Although supervision using technology may be more cost-effective and scheduling concerns may be alleviated, there are many considerations in the use of this type of supervision. For one, confidentiality cannot be guaranteed, despite precautions that may be taken. In addition, the differences in supervisory laws and regulations among states may limit the amount and type of supervision. Finally, not everyone will have equal access to the Internet (McMahon, n.d.).

Peer supervision is effective particularly when there is a range of experiences and counseling skill levels among group members. Benefits include greater independence, with less reliance on expert supervisors (Fraleigh & Buchheimer, 1969, as cited in Benshoff & Paisley, 1996), greater self-confidence and self-direction (Wagner & Smith, 1979, as cited in Benshoff & Paisley, 1996), and the opportunity to use peers as role models (Houts, 1980, as cited in Benshoff & Paisley, 1996). Some disadvantages to this method include time constraints, scheduling concerns (Agnew et al., 2000), the risk of not staying on-task when working with peers, and an overemphasis on encouragement with a reluctance to provide negative feedback (Rinkel & Hackney, 1982, as cited in Benshoff & Paisley, 1996). Furthermore, for this type of supervision to be effective, the goals and purpose of peer supervision are to be clearly understood and administrative support secured (Agnew et al., 2000).

Although each school system has its own personality, climate, and structure that work for that particular district, several guidelines and a checklist are provided to help in developing a peer consultation model. Each of these factors are considerations to ensure that the peer supervision model does not fail as in the example at the beginning of this section.

- All participants should be trained in the supervision process.
- In triads, dyads, or groups of three to six counselors, the structure should be determined and goals identified. The process works best when the structure is written down and copies are provided to each participant (Bernard et al., 2004).
- Once a process has been decided, peers need to be chosen carefully, to be assigned roles, and to practice with a pilot model. When viewing a counseling tape, participants may be assigned roles and asked to provide feedback from that particular role. For example, a peer may choose to take on the role of the counselee's mother and provide feedback from

the mother's perspective. Or, the participant will critique the tape from a predetermined theory or create a metaphor for the counselor, counselee, or counseling session.

- Concrete feedback is preferable to abstract information, particularly when discussing counseling skills, approaches, and case conceptualization (Crutchfield & Borders, 1997).
- Support is to be centered on providing professional input rather than discussing such things as institutional politics, programs, or personnel (Bernard et al., 2004).
- Each peer supervision participant provides feedback based on his or her assumed role. The feedback focuses on the counselor's skills rather than his or her personality characteristics (Bernard et al., 2004).
- A trained supervisor who is teaching peer supervisory concepts serves as a role model and teaches supervisory techniques to all participants.
- Equal, adequate time is allotted to all participants to present direct samples of their professional work (Agnew et al., 2000).
- Group members are rotated so that more experienced members can work with less experienced members.
- Administrative support is sought and time set aside for training and practice (Agnew et al., 2000; Crutchfield & Borders, 1997)
- Adequate funding is provided for training counselors in supervision (Agnew et al., 2000; Page, 1994).
- All members share a basic philosophy regarding the benefits of the consultation process.
- Each member commits to participation at a determined time using an identified role.
- The peer supervision model has specific objectives that determine goal attainment and assessment (Crutchfield & Borders, 1997).
- There is an identified assessment process with specific measurable objectives in place and adequate time to renegotiate procedures (Bernard et al., 2004).
- Participants have knowledge and support of the school counseling profession.
- Ethical standards that parallel the counseling or consultation process are established (Bernard et al., 2004).
- An encouraging, supportive atmosphere is present in which support or challenge can be addressed when it occurs.

School counselors work in intense, emotional situations that are often so stressful that support is needed to minimize the effects of stress and burnout (McMahon & Patton, 2000). Peer consultation is an ideal model for practitioners to share concerns, solicit feedback, and ease personal stress. A checklist for forming a peer consultation group is provided in Figure 12.1. The same principles that guide peer supervision can be applied to the development of one's own skills through another type of supervision: self-supervision.

SELF-SUPERVISION

Self-supervision is a process in which professionals independently monitor, guide, and evaluate their own professional growth (Bernard & Goodyear, 1998, as cited in Monk & Sinclair, 2002), with the end result of more quality services. Self-supervision techniques have been shown to increase nondirective responses, empathy, open-ended questions, and the use of metaphor (Dennin & Ellis, 2003). This process is challenging and can be difficult because the counselor is forced to investigate and reflect on personal thoughts, feelings, and behaviors that may negatively affect his or her performance. Monk and Sinclair (2002) proposed the use of a social constructionist model for self-supervision. This approach to supervision emphasizes learning as the foundation for counseling. Individuals make meaning through their view of self, others, and the situations they encounter. Self-supervision assists in examining personal discourse, power, and temporary essentialism (Burnett & Meacham, 2002). Each of these is discussed below.

The following steps are recommended for creating a peer supervision/consultation group.

_____ Plan for peer supervision
       Determine funding
       Obtain administrative support
_____ Recruit participants
_____ Number in group?
       Districtwide with counselors from different levels, or school counselors working in similar settings?
_____ Identify a mentor to teach supervision skills
_____ Establish goals
_____ Establish objectives (to be used for evaluation)
       Case studies
       Legal/ethical issues
       Counseling skill refinement
_____ Decide on a peer consultation process.
       Dyadic?   Triadic?   Small group?
_____ Structure development
       How often to meet?
       When?
       Where?
       Discussion of ethical and legal concerns
       Plan for format (length of time to present/length of time to provide feedback)
_____ Personal goals established with strategies for meeting the goals
_____ Evaluation process to determine goal/objective attainment
_____ Assign roles
_____ Assess the process and revise structure
_____ Educate employers/supervisors of results

Figure 12.1

Checklist for Beginning a Peer Consultation Group

Personal Discourse

A personal discourse refers to the beliefs, thoughts, and feelings that give meaning to one's life and influence one's behaviors (Monk & Sinclair, 2002). Examining a personal discourse provides an opportunity to evaluate whether personal biases, rigid beliefs, and narrow-mindedness are negatively affecting the counseling session. Personal discourses can be examined through the questions in Exercise 12.1.

Power

A counseling relationship is sometimes viewed as an authority differential in which the counselor holds more power over the counselee. This unequal relationship may impede productive counseling. Self-supervision using social constructivism invites the counselor to think about the ways in which he or she exerts power over others. For example, a counselor may mistakenly make phone calls, research information, complete materials, make appointments, and so on rather than empowering the counselee to do these tasks for himself or herself. Power influences may be examined by asking the following questions in Exercise 12.2.

Temporary Essentialism

A guiding principle in social constructivism is that each counselee sees his or her world differently (Monk & Sinclair, 2002), and it is critical that the counselor understands his or her counselee's world. This ability to put oneself in another's shoes is known as temporary essentialism. The following questions in Exercise 12.3 can help in gaining a glimpse of the counselee's world.

Self-supervision is economical in that other professionals are not required in supervising oneself, but the counselor does need to be willing to take the risks involved with self-examination and be prepared to adapt to the insight gained (Monk & Sinclair, 2002). A dif-

Exercise 12.1

Examining Personal Discourse

- How are my cultural beliefs negatively affecting my relationship with my counselee?

- What are some of my thoughts regarding gender, race, or ethnicity that are limiting my counseling effectiveness?

- What am I doing that is preventing my counselee from changing?

- What is preventing me from changing?

- What strengths do I bring to the counseling arena?

- What areas do I need to improve?

- What strategies are needed to improve these areas?

- What evaluative data is needed to indicate growth?

- What do I need to be a more effective counselor?

ficult task! Unfortunately, studies documenting the effectiveness of this method are few. School counselors can study this process more thoroughly by engaging in tasks and documenting results while evaluating themselves.

SUMMARY

Although practicing school counselors often receive administrative supervision from their school principals, they often express more need for clinical supervision. Clinical supervision provides counselors with the opportunity to obtain knowledge and practice in different counseling theories and techniques. Although there are many benefits to counselors when they receive feedback on skills, it can be costly, particularly when there is not an individual in the school system with expertise in school counseling and supervision. Despite these barriers, peer supervision and self-supervision are two methods in which practicing counselors can receive the clinical supervision that is needed.

Exercise 12.2

Examining Power Influences

- How have the power differences in a counseling relationship negatively influenced the counselee?

- How have power differences made my role as a counselor less effective?

- What do I believe about the counseling process and my counselee's ability to change?

Exercise 12.3

Understanding the Counselee's World

- How can I better understand the counselee's experiences and the meaning attributed to these experiences?

- What guides the counselee's view of self and the world?

- What are the counselee's strengths that can assist with problem solving?

- In what way did I hinder my ability to see the situation from the counselee's view?

REFERENCES

Agnew, T., Vaught, C. C., Getz, H. G., & Fortune, J. (2000). Peer group clinical supervision program fosters confidence and professionalism. *Professional School Counseling, 4,* 6–12.

Benshoff, J. M., & Paisley, P. O. (1996). The structured peer consultation model for school counselors. *Journal of Counseling & Development, 74,* 314–318.

Bernard, J. M., Hackney, H. & Wilkerson, K. (2004, April). *Requisite skills for engaging in peer supervision.* Paper presented at the American Counseling Association Annual Convention, Kansas City, KS.

Borders, L. D., & Usher, C. H. (1992). Post-degree supervision: Existing and preferred practices. *Journal of Counseling & Development, 70,* 594–599.

Burnett, P. C., & Meacham, D. (2002). Learning journals as a counseling strategy. *Journal of Counseling & Development, 80,* 410–415.

Cade, B. W., Speed, B., & Seligman, P. (1986). Working in teams: The pros and cons. *Clinical Supervision, 4,* 105–117.

Crutchfield, L. B., & Borders, L. D. (1997). Impact of two clinical peer supervision models on practicing school counselors. *Journal of Counseling & Development, 75,* 219–230.

Dennin, M. K., & Ellis, M. V. (2003). Effects of self-supervision for counselor trainees. *Journal of Counseling Psychology, 50,* 69–83.

Greenburg, S. L., Lewis, G. J., & Johnson, M. (1985). Peer consultation groups for private practitioners. *Professional Psychology: Research and Practice, 16,* 437–447.

Kahn, B. B. (1999). Priorities and practices in field supervision of school counseling students. *Professional School Counseling, 3,* 128–136.

Logan, W. L. (1997). Peer consultation group: Doing what works for counselors. *Professional School Counseling, 1,* 4–6.

Loganbill, C., Hardy, E., & Delworth, U. (1982). Supervision: A conceptual model. *Counseling Psychologist, 10,* 3–42.

McMahon, M. (n.d.). *Structured peer group supervision by e-mail: An option for school guidance and counselling personnel.* Unpublished manuscript, Queensland University of Technology, Brisbane, Australia.

McMahon, M., & Patton, W. (2000). Conversations on clinical supervision: Benefits perceived by school counselors. *British Journal of Guidance & Counselling, 28,* 339–348.

Monk, G., & Sinclair, S. L. (2002). Toward discursive presence: Advancing a social constructionist approach to self-supervision. *The Clinical Supervisor, 21,* 109–128.

Page, B. J. (1994). Post-degree supervision of school counselors. *Professional School Counselor, 42,* 32–39.

Roberts, E. B., & Borders, L. D. (1994). Supervision of school counselors: Administrative, program, and counseling. *The School Counselor, 41,* 149–157.

Sutton, J. M., & Page, B. J. (1994). Post-degree clinical supervision of school counselors. *School Counselor, 42,* 32–39.

Young, J. S., & Borders, L. D. (1999). The intentional use of metaphor in counseling supervision. *The Clinical Supervisor, 18,* 137–149.

Appendixes

Multicultural Competencies and Objectives

I. Counselor Awareness of Own Cultural Values and Biases

A. *Attitudes and Beliefs*

1. Culturally skilled counselors have moved from being culturally unaware to being aware of and sensitive to their own cultural heritage and to valuing and respecting differences.
2. Culturally skilled counselors are aware of how their own cultural backgrounds and experiences and attitudes, values, and biases influence psychological processes.
3. Culturally skilled counselors are able to recognize the limits of their competencies and expertise.
4. Culturally skilled counselors are comfortable with differences that exist between themselves and clients in terms of race, ethnicity, culture, and beliefs.

B. *Knowledge*

1. Culturally skilled counselors have specific knowledge about their own racial and cultural heritage and how it personally and professionally affects their definitions of normality–abnormality and the process of counseling.
2. Culturally skilled counselors possess knowledge and understanding about how oppression, racism, discrimination, and stereotyping affect them personally and in their work. This allows them to acknowledge their own racist attitudes, beliefs, and feelings. Although this standard applies to all groups, for White counselors it may mean that they understand how they may have directly or indirectly benefited from individual, institutional, and cultural racism (White identity development models).
3. Culturally skilled counselors possess knowledge about their social impact on others. They are knowledgeable about communication style differences, how their style may clash or foster the counseling process with minority clients, and how to anticipate the impact it may have on others.

C. *Skills*

1. Culturally skilled counselors seek out educational, consultative, and training experience to improve their understanding and effectiveness in working with culturally different populations. Being able to recognize the limits of their competencies, they (a) seek consultation, (b) seek further training or education, (c) refer out to more qualified individuals or resources, or (d) engage in a combination of these.

2. Culturally skilled counselors are constantly seeking to understand themselves as racial and cultural beings and are actively seeking a nonracist identity.

II. Counselor Awareness of Client's Worldview

A. *Attitudes and Beliefs*
1. Culturally skilled counselors are aware of their negative emotional reactions toward other racial and ethnic groups that may prove detrimental to their clients in counseling. They are willing to contrast their own beliefs and attitudes with those of their culturally different clients in a nonjudgmental fashion.
2. Culturally skilled counselors are aware of their stereotypes and preconceived notions that they may hold toward other racial and ethnic minority groups.

B. *Knowledge*
1. Culturally skilled counselors possess specific knowledge and information about the particular group they are working with. They are aware of the life experiences, cultural heritage, and historical background of their culturally different clients. This particular competency is strongly linked to the "minority identity development models" available in the literature.
2. Culturally skilled counselors understand how race, culture, ethnicity, and so forth may affect personality formation, vocational choices, manifestation of psychological disorders, help-seeking behavior, and the appropriateness or inappropriateness of counseling approaches.
3. Culturally skilled counselors understand and have knowledge about sociopolitical influences that impinge upon the life of racial and ethnic minorities. Immigration issues, poverty, racism, stereotyping, and powerlessness all leave major scars that may influence the counseling process.

C. *Skills*
1. Culturally skilled counselors should familiarize themselves with relevant research and the latest findings regarding mental health and mental disorders of various ethnic and racial groups. They should actively seek out educational experiences that foster their knowledge, understanding, and cross-cultural skills.
2. Culturally skilled counselors become actively involved with minority individuals outside of the counseling setting (community events, social and political functions, celebrations, friendships, neighborhood groups, and so forth) so that their perspective of minorities is more than an academic or helping exercise.

III. Culturally Appropriate Intervention Strategies

A. *Attitudes and Beliefs*
1. Culturally skilled counselors respect clients' religious and/or spiritual beliefs and values, including attributions and taboos, because they affect worldview, psychosocial functioning, and expressions of distress.
2. Culturally skilled counselors respect indigenous helping practices and respect minority community intrinsic help-giving networks.
3. Culturally skilled counselors value bilingualism and do not view another language as an impediment to counseling (monolingualism may be the culprit).

B. *Knowledge*
1. Culturally skilled counselors have a clear and explicit knowledge and understanding of the generic characteristics of counseling and therapy (culture bound, class bound, and monolingual) and how they may clash with the cultural values of various minority groups.

2. Culturally skilled counselors are aware of institutional barriers that prevent minorities from using mental health services.
3. Culturally skilled counselors have knowledge of the potential bias in assessment instruments and use procedures and interpret findings keeping in mind the cultural and linguistic characteristics of the clients.
4. Culturally skilled counselors have knowledge of minority family structures, hierarchies, values, and beliefs. They are knowledgeable about the community characteristics and the resources in the community as well as the family.
5. Culturally skilled counselors should be aware of relevant discriminatory practices at the social and community level that may be affecting the psychological welfare of the population being served.

C. *Skills*
1. Culturally skilled counselors are able to engage in a variety of verbal and nonverbal helping responses. They are able to *send* and *receive* both *verbal* and *nonverbal* messages *accurately* and *appropriately*. They are not tied down to only one method or approach to helping but recognize that helping styles and approaches may be culture bound. When they sense that their helping style is limited and potentially inappropriate, they can anticipate and ameliorate its negative impact.
2. Culturally skilled counselors are able to exercise institutional intervention skills on behalf of their clients. They can help clients determine whether a "problem" stems from racism or bias in others (the concept of health paranoia) so that clients do not inappropriately personalize problems.
3. Culturally skilled counselors are not averse to seeking consultation with traditional healers and religious and spiritual leaders and practitioners in the treatment of culturally different clients when appropriate.
4. Culturally skilled counselors take responsibility for interacting in the language requested by the client and, if not feasible, make appropriate referral. A serious problem arises when the linguistic skills of a counselor do not match the language of the client. This being the case, counselors should (a) seek a translator with cultural knowledge and appropriate professional background and (b) refer to a knowledgeable and competent bilingual counselor.
5. Culturally skilled counselors have training and expertise in the use of traditional assessment and testing instruments. They not only understand the technical aspects of the instruments but are also aware of the cultural limitations. This allows them to use test instruments for the welfare of the diverse clients.
6. Culturally skilled counselors should attend to as well as work to eliminate biases, prejudices, and discriminatory practices. They should be cognizant of sociopolitical contexts in conducting evaluation and providing interventions and should develop sensitivity to issues of oppression, sexism, elitism, and racism.
7. Culturally skilled counselors take responsibility in educating their clients to the processes of psychological intervention, such as goals, expectations, legal rights, and the counselor's orientation.

Additional Resources for Supervision and Training

Online Resources

- American Counseling Association (ACA)
  http://www.counseling.org
    This organization is dedicated to the growth of individuals in the counseling profession and those with whom they work. The *Journal of Counseling & Development* and *Counseling Today* are published by this organization.
- Association for Counselor Education and Supervision (ACES)
  http://www.acesonline.net/
    ACES has as its mission to improve education, credentialing, and supervision of counselors to improve guidance, counseling, and student development services throughout all settings. *Counselor Education and Supervision* is the official journal of this association.
- American School Counselor Association (ASCA)
  http://www.schoolcounselor.org
    This organization is dedicated to the professional development of school counselors and supports the academic, personal/social, and career development of K–12 students. The *Professional School Counseling Journal* and *ASCA School Counselor* magazine are published by this organization.
- Supervision video
  http://digitalmedia.utk.edu:8080/ramgen/10942.rm
    This is a video to help teach supervisors about the art of supervision. You can get this site by downloading Real Player. It is a free download. After you have installed this on your computer, then put in the addresses on the menu provided by Real Player.

Books

- Baird, B. N. (2005). *The internship, practicum, and field placement handbook: A guide for the helping professions* (4th ed.). Upper Saddle River, NJ: Pearson.
    All individuals in the helping profession can benefit from the information in this book. A short summary of the supervision process is included with chapters that discuss issues of diversity, stress and self-care, and assault. Numerous forms that can be adapted for specific settings are included in this book.
- Borders, L. D., & Brown, L. L. (2005). *The new handbook of counseling supervision.* Mahwah, NJ: Erlbaum/Lahaska Press.
    This book is a revision of the original counseling supervision book by Borders and Leddick titled *Handbook of Counseling Supervision.* There are numerous exercises, vignettes, materials, and information regarding supervision of counselors.

- Boylan, J. C., Malley, P. B., & Reilly, E. P. (2001). *Practicum and internship: Textbook and resource guide for counseling and psychotherapy.* New York: Brunner-Routledge.

  Counselor supervisors and supervisees in all areas of counseling can benefit from the chapters in this book that range from an overview of supervision to issues and guidelines for working with special populations. A variety of materials and forms are available in this book for adaptation to a specific setting.
- Bradley, L., & Ladany, N. (Eds.). (2001). *Counselor supervision: Principles, process and practice* (3rd ed.). Philadelphia: Brunner-Routledge.

  This book provides a definition of supervision and supervisory activities. In addition, a description of a supervisory relationship, multicultural factors, theoretical approaches to counselor supervision, group supervision models, and supervision in specialized counseling fields are included. The final section of the book includes issues regarding supervision, such as evaluation, research, advocacy, ethical issues, and a supervisory model.
- Morrissette, P. J. (2001). *Self-supervision: A primer for counselors and human service professionals.* New York: Brunner-Routledge.

  The history of counselor self-supervision and the counselor–client relationship is discussed in this book. Additional topics include counselor self-care and issues that must be examined when reflecting on one's work.
- Neufeldt, S. A. (in press). *Supervision strategies for the first practicum* (3rd ed.). Alexandria, VA: American Counseling Association.

  This book provides information about the supervision process for all counselors, regardless of specialty area. In addition, supervisors can structure their sessions using the week-by-week course outline with learning objectives that are included.
- Posner, G. J. (2005). *Field experience: A guide to reflective teaching* (6th ed.). Boston: Pearson.

  Although this book is based on supervising students in the teaching profession, the materials are common to all types of supervision regardless of the profession. Reflective learning, personal self-exploration, and a working portfolio are discussed. Several sample logs and instruments are included in this book.
- Russell-Chapin, L. A., & Ivey, A. E. (2004). *Your supervised practicum and internship: Field resources for turning theory into action.* Belmont, CA: Thomson.

  Supervisory models and suggestions for becoming an effective supervisee and becoming culturally competent are included in this text. Additional chapters include information on research outcomes, staying professionally healthy, and becoming an advocate. This book pertains to individuals in all areas of counseling.
- Stoltenberg, C. D., McNeill, B., & Delworth, U. (1997). *IDM supervision: An integrated developmental model for supervising counselors and therapists.* New York: Wiley.

  The Integrated Developmental Model (IDM) is discussed as well as guidelines for applying this model to the supervision process. This model can be applied to all counseling areas and includes strategies for the supervisor to use as the supervisee develops and grows.

Videos, DVDs, and CD-ROMs

- *Affect Simulation: The Process and Stimulus Vignettes* (38 minutes)

  Several vignettes are shown with counselees presenting difficult issues. Supervisees have an opportunity to view these scenarios and to process their feelings and thoughts regarding these issues. Available from Microtraining and Multicultural Development.
- *Clinical Supervisor Training* (CD-ROM) (no time specified)

  Numerous vignettes are presented to illustrate supervision methods. Available from Insight Media.
- *Five Approaches to Supervision: Developmental, Integrated, IPR, Psychodynamic, and Microskills* (approximately 90 minutes)

Supervision is shown from five supervision models. Feedback is given based on the various models to show how the counseling session can be viewed from each of these models. Available from Microtraining and Multicultural Development.

- *Interpersonal Process Recall: Theory and Introduction* (59 minutes)
  Interpersonal process recall (IPR) is demonstrated by Dr. Norman Kagan. A wealth of information is provided in this video. Dr. Kagan demonstrates the IPR process. Available from Microtraining and Multicultural Development.
- *Learning to Think Like a Supervisor* (35 minutes)
  This video by L. DiAnne Borders and James Benshoff describes the discrimination model. The vignettes demonstrate different supervisory roles and foci. Available from ACA.
- *Legal Liability in Clinical Supervision* (25 minutes)
  Dr. Ted Remley, counselor educator and attorney, addresses legal issues that affect the clinical supervision process. Specific recommendations are offered to minimize liability. Available from ACA.
- *Microcounseling Supervision: Helping Students Classify and Rate Interview Behavior* (45 minutes)
  This video assists students in analyzing and classifying interview behaviors, and the Counseling Interview Rating Form is also available to assist students in identifying behaviors. Available from Microtraining and Multicultural Development.
- *Role Induction in Counseling Supervision: Clarifying Duties and Responsibilities* (40 minutes)
  This video is a training tool for supervisors and supervisees. The supervisory process is introduced and the responsibilities of the supervisor are discussed, including the role of the evaluator of supervisees' performance. Available from ACA.
- *The Written Supervision Contract: Documenting Ethics in Action* (45 minutes)
  Writing a supervision contract fulfills the need for accountability, legal, and ethical responsibilities and provides clear and consistent documentation. This video demonstrates how a written contract is introduced and applied through supervision vignettes. Available from ACA.

ACA Code of Ethics

ACA CODE OF ETHICS

ACA Code of Ethics Preamble

The American Counseling Association is an educational, scientific, and professional organization whose members work in a variety of settings and serve in multiple capacities. ACA members are dedicated to the enhancement of human development throughout the life span. Association members recognize diversity and embrace a cross-cultural approach in support of the worth, dignity, potential, and uniqueness of people within their social and cultural contexts.

Professional values are an important way of living out an ethical commitment. Values inform principles. Inherently held values that guide our behaviors or exceed prescribed behaviors are deeply ingrained in the counselor and developed out of personal dedication, rather than the mandatory requirement of an external organization.

ACA Code of Ethics Purpose

The *ACA Code of Ethics* serves five main purposes:

1. The *Code* enables the association to clarify to current and future members, and to those served by members, the nature of the ethical responsibilities held in common by its members.
2. The *Code* helps support the mission of the association.
3. The *Code* establishes principles that define ethical behavior and best practices of association members.
4. The *Code* serves as an ethical guide designed to assist members in constructing a professional course of action that best serves those utilizing counseling services and best promotes the values of the counseling profession.
5. The *Code* serves as the basis for processing of ethical complaints and inquiries initiated against members of the association.

The *ACA Code of Ethics* contains eight main sections that address the following areas:

Section A: The Counseling Relationship
Section B: Confidentiality, Privileged Communication, and Privacy
Section C: Professional Responsibility
Section D: Relationships With Other Professionals
Section E: Evaluation, Assessment, and Interpretation
Section F: Supervision, Training, and Teaching
Section G: Research and Publication
Section H: Resolving Ethical Issues

Each section of the *ACA Code of Ethics* begins with an Introduction. The introductions to each section discuss what counselors should aspire to with regard to ethical behavior and responsibility. The Introduction helps set the tone for that particular section and provides a starting point that invites reflection on the ethical mandates contained in each part of the *ACA Code of Ethics.*

When counselors are faced with ethical dilemmas that are difficult to resolve, they are expected to engage in a carefully considered ethical decision-making process. Reasonable differences of opinion can and do exist among counselors with respect to the ways in which values, ethical principles, and ethical standards would be applied when they conflict. While there is no specific ethical decision-making model that is most effective, counselors are expected to be familiar with a credible model of decision making that can bear public scrutiny and its application.

Through a chosen ethical decision-making process and evaluation of the context of the situation, counselors are empowered to make decisions that help expand the capacity of people to grow and develop.

A brief glossary is given to provide readers with a concise description of some of the terms used in the *ACA Code of Ethics.*

SECTION A:
THE COUNSELING RELATIONSHIP

Introduction

Counselors encourage client growth and development in ways that foster the interest and welfare of clients and promote formation of healthy relationships. Counselors actively attempt to understand the diverse cultural backgrounds of the clients they serve.

Counselors also explore their own cultural identities and how these affect their values and beliefs about the counseling process.

Counselors are encouraged to contribute to society by devoting a portion of their professional activity to services for which there is little or no financial return (*pro bono publico*).

A.1. Welfare of Those Served by Counselors

A.1.a. Primary Responsibility
The primary responsibility of counselors is to respect the dignity and to promote the welfare of clients.

A.1.b. Records
Counselors maintain records necessary for rendering professional services to their clients and as required by laws, regulations, or agency or institution procedures. Counselors include sufficient and timely documentation in their client records to facilitate the delivery and continuity of needed services. Counselors take reasonable steps to ensure that documentation in records accurately reflects client progress and services provided. If errors are made in client records, counselors take steps to properly note the correction of such errors according to agency or institutional policies. (*See A.12.g.7., B.6., B.6.g., G.2.j.*)

A.1.c. Counseling Plans
Counselors and their clients work jointly in devising integrated counseling plans that offer reasonable promise of success and are consistent with abilities and circumstances of clients. Counselors and clients regularly review counseling plans to assess their continued viability and effectiveness, respecting the freedom of choice of clients. (*See A.2.a., A.2.d., A.12.g.*)

A.1.d. Support Network Involvement
Counselors recognize that support networks hold various meanings in the lives of clients and consider enlisting the support, understanding, and involvement of others (e.g., religious/spiritual/community leaders, family members, friends) as positive resources, when appropriate, with client consent.

A.1.e. Employment Needs
Counselors work with their clients considering employment in jobs that are consistent with the overall abilities, vocational limitations, physical restrictions, general temperament, interest and aptitude patterns, social skills, education, general qualifications, and other

relevant characteristics and needs of clients. When appropriate, counselors appropriately trained in career development will assist in the placement of clients in positions that are consistent with the interest, culture, and the welfare of clients, employers, and/or the public.

A.2. Informed Consent in the Counseling Relationship

(See A.12.g., B.5., B.6.b., E.3., E.13.b., F.1.c., G.2.a.)

A.2.a. Informed Consent

Clients have the freedom to choose whether to enter into or remain in a counseling relationship and need adequate information about the counseling process and the counselor. Counselors have an obligation to review in writing and verbally with clients the rights and responsibilities of both the counselor and the client. Informed consent is an ongoing part of the counseling process, and counselors appropriately document discussions of informed consent throughout the counseling relationship.

A.2.b. Types of Information Needed

Counselors explicitly explain to clients the nature of all services provided. They inform clients about issues such as, but not limited to, the following: the purposes, goals, techniques, procedures, limitations, potential risks, and benefits of services; the counselor's qualifications, credentials, and relevant experience; continuation of services upon the incapacitation or death of a counselor; and other pertinent information. Counselors take steps to ensure that clients understand the implications of diagnosis, the intended use of tests and reports, fees, and billing arrangements. Clients have the right to confidentiality and to be provided with an explanation of its limitations (including how supervisors and/or treatment team professionals are involved); to obtain clear information about their records; to participate in the ongoing counseling plans; and to refuse any services or modality change and to be advised of the consequences of such refusal.

A.2.c. Developmental and Cultural Sensitivity

Counselors communicate information in ways that are both developmentally and culturally appropriate. Counselors use clear and understandable language when discussing issues related to informed consent. When clients have difficulty understanding the language used by counselors, they provide necessary services (e.g., arranging for a qualified interpreter or translator) to ensure comprehension by clients. In collaboration with clients, counselors consider cultural implications of informed consent procedures and, where possible, counselors adjust their practices accordingly.

A.2.d. Inability to Give Consent

When counseling minors or persons unable to give voluntary consent, counselors seek the assent of clients to services, and include them in decision making as appropriate. Counselors recognize the need to balance the ethical rights of clients to make choices, their capacity to give consent or assent to receive services, and parental or familial legal rights and responsibilities to protect these clients and make decisions on their behalf.

A.3. Clients Served by Others

When counselors learn that their clients are in a professional relationship with another mental health professional, they request release from clients to inform the other professionals and strive to establish positive and collaborative professional relationships.

A.4. Avoiding Harm and Imposing Values

A.4.a. Avoiding Harm

Counselors act to avoid harming their clients, trainees, and research participants and to minimize or to remedy unavoidable or unanticipated harm.

A.4.b. Personal Values

Counselors are aware of their own values, attitudes, beliefs, and behaviors and avoid imposing values that are inconsistent with counseling goals. Counselors respect the diversity of clients, trainees, and research participants.

A.5. Roles and Relationships With Clients

(See F.3., F.10., G.3.)

A.5.a. Current Clients

Sexual or romantic counselor–client interactions or relationships with current clients, their romantic partners, or their family members are prohibited.

A.5.b. Former Clients

Sexual or romantic counselor–client interactions or relationships with former clients, their romantic partners, or their family members are prohibited for a period of 5 years following the last professional contact. Counselors, before engaging in sexual or romantic interactions or relationships with clients, their romantic partners, or client family members after 5 years following the last professional contact, demonstrate forethought and document (in written form) whether the interactions or relationship can be viewed as exploitive in some way and/or whether there is still potential to harm the former client; in cases of potential exploitation and/or harm, the counselor avoids entering such an interaction or relationship.

A.5.c. Nonprofessional Interactions or Relationships (Other Than Sexual or Romantic Interactions or Relationships)

Counselor–client nonprofessional relationships with clients, former clients, their romantic partners, or their family members should be avoided, except when the interaction is potentially beneficial to the client. (See A.5.d.)

A.5.d. Potentially Beneficial Interactions

When a counselor–client nonprofessional interaction with a client or former client may be potentially beneficial to the client or former client, the counselor must document in case records, prior to the interaction (when feasible), the rationale for such an interaction, the potential benefit, and anticipated consequences for the client or former client and other individuals significantly involved with the client or former client. Such interactions should be initiated with appropriate client consent. Where unintentional harm occurs to the client or former client, or to an individual significantly involved with the client or former client, due to the nonprofessional interaction, the counselor must show evidence of an attempt to remedy such harm. Examples of potentially beneficial interactions include, but are not limited to, attending a formal ceremony (e.g., a wedding/commitment ceremony or graduation); purchasing a service or product provided by a client or former client (excepting unrestricted bartering); hospital visits to an ill family member; mutual membership in a professional association, organization, or community. (See A.5.c.)

A.5.e. Role Changes in the Professional Relationship

When a counselor changes a role from the original or most recent contracted relationship, he or she obtains informed consent from the client and explains the right of the client to refuse services related to the change. Examples of role changes include

1. changing from individual to relationship or family counseling, or vice versa;
2. changing from a nonforensic evaluative role to a therapeutic role, or vice versa;
3. changing from a counselor to a researcher role (i.e., enlisting clients as research participants), or vice versa; and
4. changing from a counselor to a mediator role, or vice versa.

Clients must be fully informed of any anticipated consequences (e.g., financial, legal, personal, or therapeutic) of counselor role changes.

A.6. Roles and Relationships at Individual, Group, Institutional, and Societal Levels

A.6.a. Advocacy

When appropriate, counselors advocate at individual, group, institutional, and societal levels to examine potential barriers and obstacles that inhibit access and/or the growth and development of clients.

A.6.b. Confidentiality and Advocacy

Counselors obtain client consent prior to engaging in advocacy efforts on behalf of an identifiable client to improve the provision of services and to work toward removal of systemic barriers or obstacles that inhibit client access, growth, and development.

A.7. Multiple Clients

When a counselor agrees to provide counseling services to two or more persons who have a relationship, the counselor clarifies at the outset which person or persons are clients and the nature of the relationships the counselor will have with each involved person. If it becomes apparent that the counselor may be called upon to perform potentially conflicting roles, the counselor will clarify, adjust, or withdraw from roles appropriately. *(See A.8.a., B.4.)*

A.8. Group Work

(See B.4.a.)

A.8.a. Screening

Counselors screen prospective group counseling/therapy participants. To the extent possible, counselors select members whose needs and goals are compatible with goals of the group, who will not impede the group process, and whose well-being will not be jeopardized by the group experience.

A.8.b. Protecting Clients

In a group setting, counselors take reasonable precautions to protect clients from physical, emotional, or psychological trauma.

A.9. End-of-Life Care for Terminally Ill Clients

A.9.a. Quality of Care

Counselors strive to take measures that enable clients

1. to obtain high-quality end-of-life care for their physical, emotional, social, and spiritual needs;
2. to exercise the highest degree of self-determination possible;
3. to be given every opportunity possible to engage in informed decision making regarding their end-of-life care; and
4. to receive complete and adequate assessment regarding their ability to make competent, rational decisions on their own behalf from a mental health professional who is experienced in end-of-life care practice.

A.9.b. Counselor Competence, Choice, and Referral

Recognizing the personal, moral, and competence issues related to end-of-life decisions, counselors may choose to work or not work with terminally ill clients who wish to explore their end-of-life options. Counselors provide appropriate referral information to ensure that clients receive the necessary help.

A.9.c. Confidentiality

Counselors who provide services to terminally ill individuals who are considering hastening their own deaths have the option of breaking or not breaking confidentiality, depending on applicable laws and the specific circumstances of the situation and after seeking consultation or supervision from appropriate professional and legal parties. *(See B.5.c., B.7.c.)*

A.10. Fees and Bartering

A.10.a. Accepting Fees From Agency Clients

Counselors refuse a private fee or other remuneration for rendering services to persons who are entitled to such services through the counselor's employing agency or institution. The policies of a particular agency may make explicit provisions for agency clients to receive counseling services from members of its staff in private practice. In such instances, the clients must be informed of other options open to them should they seek private counseling services.

A.10.b. Establishing Fees

In establishing fees for professional counseling services, counselors consider the financial status of clients and locality. In the event that the established fee structure is inappropriate for a client, counselors assist clients in attempting to find comparable services of acceptable cost.

A.10.c. Nonpayment of Fees

If counselors intend to use collection agencies or take legal measures to collect fees from clients who do not pay for services as agreed upon, they first inform clients of intended actions and offer clients the opportunity to make payment.

A.10.d. Bartering

Counselors may barter only if the relationship is not exploitive or harmful and does not place the counselor in an unfair advantage, if the client requests it, and if such arrangements are an accepted practice among professionals in the community. Counselors consider the cultural implications of bartering and discuss relevant concerns with clients and document such agreements in a clear written contract.

A.10.e. Receiving Gifts

Counselors understand the challenges of accepting gifts from clients and recognize that in some cultures, small gifts are a token of respect and showing gratitude. When determining whether or not to accept a gift from clients, counselors take into account the therapeutic relationship, the monetary value of the gift, a client's motivation for giving the gift, and the counselor's motivation for wanting or declining the gift.

A.11. Termination and Referral

A.11.a. Abandonment Prohibited

Counselors do not abandon or neglect clients in counseling. Counselors assist in making appropriate arrangements for the continuation of treatment, when necessary, during interruptions such as vacations, illness, and following termination.

A.11.b. Inability to Assist Clients

If counselors determine an inability to be of professional assistance to clients, they avoid entering or continuing counseling relationships. Counselors are knowledgeable about culturally and clinically appropriate referral resources and suggest these alternatives. If clients decline the suggested referrals, counselors should discontinue the relationship.

A.11.c. Appropriate Termination

Counselors terminate a counseling relationship when it becomes reasonably apparent that the client no longer needs assistance, is not likely to benefit, or is being harmed by continued counseling. Counselors may terminate counseling when in jeopardy of harm by the client, or another person with whom the client has a relationship, or when clients do not pay fees as agreed upon. Counselors provide pretermination counseling and recommend other service providers when necessary.

A.11.d. Appropriate Transfer of Services

When counselors transfer or refer clients to other practitioners, they ensure that appropriate clinical and administrative processes are completed and open communication is maintained with both clients and practitioners.

A.12. Technology Applications

A.12.a. Benefits and Limitations

Counselors inform clients of the benefits and limitations of using information technology applications in the counseling process and in business/billing procedures. Such technologies include but are not limited to computer hardware and software, telephones, the World Wide Web, the Internet, online assessment instruments, and other communication devices.

A.12.b. Technology-Assisted Services

When providing technology-assisted distance counseling services, counselors determine that clients are intellectually, emotionally, and physically capable of using the application and that the application is appropriate for the needs of clients.

A.12.c. Inappropriate Services

When technology-assisted distance counseling services are deemed inappropriate by the counselor or client, counselors consider delivering services face to face.

A.12.d. Access

Counselors provide reasonable access to computer applications when providing technology-assisted distance counseling services.

A.12.e. Laws and Statutes

Counselors ensure that the use of technology does not violate the laws of any local, state, national, or international entity and observe all relevant statutes.

A.12.f. Assistance

Counselors seek business, legal, and technical assistance when using technology applications, particularly when the use of such applications crosses state or national boundaries.

A.12.g. Technology and Informed Consent

As part of the process of establishing informed consent, counselors do the following:

1. Address issues related to the difficulty of maintaining the confidentiality of electronically transmitted communications.

2. Inform clients of all colleagues, supervisors, and employees, such as Informational Technology (IT) administrators, who might have authorized or unauthorized access to electronic transmissions.
3. Urge clients to be aware of all authorized or unauthorized users including family members and fellow employees who have access to any technology clients may use in the counseling process.
4. Inform clients of pertinent legal rights and limitations governing the practice of a profession over state lines or international boundaries.
5. Use encrypted Web sites and e-mail communications to help ensure confidentiality when possible.
6. When the use of encryption is not possible, counselors notify clients of this fact and limit electronic transmissions to general communications that are not client specific.
7. Inform clients if and for how long archival storage of transaction records are maintained.
8. Discuss the possibility of technology failure and alternate methods of service delivery.
9. Inform clients of emergency procedures, such as calling 911 or a local crisis hotline, when the counselor is not available.
10. Discuss time zone differences, local customs, and cultural or language differences that might impact service delivery.
11. Inform clients when technology-assisted distance counseling services are not covered by insurance. *(See A.2.)*

A.12.h. Sites on the World Wide Web
Counselors maintaining sites on the World Wide Web (the Internet) do the following:

1. Regularly check that electronic links are working and professionally appropriate.
2. Establish ways clients can contact the counselor in case of technology failure.
3. Provide electronic links to relevant state licensure and professional certification boards to protect consumer rights and facilitate addressing ethical concerns.
4. Establish a method for verifying client identity.

5. Obtain the written consent of the legal guardian or other authorized legal representative prior to rendering services in the event the client is a minor child, an adult who is legally incompetent, or an adult incapable of giving informed consent.
6. Strive to provide a site that is accessible to persons with disabilities.
7. Strive to provide translation capabilities for clients who have a different primary language while also addressing the imperfect nature of such translations.
8. Assist clients in determining the validity and reliability of information found on the World Wide Web and other technology applications.

SECTION B: CONFIDENTIALITY, PRIVILEGED COMMUNICATION, AND PRIVACY

Introduction

Counselors recognize that trust is a cornerstone of the counseling relationship. Counselors aspire to earn the trust of clients by creating an ongoing partnership, establishing and upholding appropriate boundaries, and maintaining confidentiality. Counselors communicate the parameters of confidentiality in a culturally competent manner.

B.1. Respecting Client Rights

B.1.a. Multicultural/Diversity Considerations
Counselors maintain awareness and sensitivity regarding cultural meanings of confidentiality and privacy. Counselors respect differing views toward disclosure of information. Counselors hold ongoing discussions with clients as to how, when, and with whom information is to be shared.

B.1.b. Respect for Privacy
Counselors respect client rights to privacy. Counselors solicit private information from clients only when it is beneficial to the counseling process.

B.1.c. Respect for Confidentiality
Counselors do not share confidential information without client consent or without sound legal or ethical justification.

B.1.d. Explanation of Limitations

At initiation and throughout the counseling process, counselors inform clients of the limitations of confidentiality and seek to identify foreseeable situations in which confidentiality must be breached. *(See A.2.b.)*

B.2. Exceptions

B.2.a. Danger and Legal Requirements

The general requirement that counselors keep information confidential does not apply when disclosure is required to protect clients or identified others from serious and foreseeable harm or when legal requirements demand that confidential information must be revealed. Counselors consult with other professionals when in doubt as to the validity of an exception. Additional considerations apply when addressing end-of-life issues. *(See A.9.c.)*

B.2.b. Contagious, Life-Threatening Diseases

When clients disclose that they have a disease commonly known to be both communicable and life threatening, counselors may be justified in disclosing information to identifiable third parties, if they are known to be at demonstrable and high risk of contracting the disease. Prior to making a disclosure, counselors confirm that there is such a diagnosis and assess the intent of clients to inform the third parties about their disease or to engage in any behaviors that may be harmful to an identifiable third party.

B.2.c. Court-Ordered Disclosure

When subpoenaed to release confidential or privileged information without a client's permission, counselors obtain written, informed consent from the client or take steps to prohibit the disclosure or have it limited as narrowly as possible due to potential harm to the client or counseling relationship.

B.2.d. Minimal Disclosure

To the extent possible, clients are informed before confidential information is disclosed and are involved in the disclosure decision-making process. When circumstances require the disclosure of confidential information, only essential information is revealed.

B.3. Information Shared With Others

B.3.a. Subordinates

Counselors make every effort to ensure that privacy and confidentiality of clients are maintained by subordinates, including employees, supervisees, students, clerical assistants, and volunteers. *(See F.1.c.)*

B.3.b. Treatment Teams

When client treatment involves a continued review or participation by a treatment team, the client will be informed of the team's existence and composition, information being shared, and the purposes of sharing such information.

B.3.c. Confidential Settings

Counselors discuss confidential information only in settings in which they can reasonably ensure client privacy.

B.3.d. Third-Party Payers

Counselors disclose information to third-party payers only when clients have authorized such disclosure.

B.3.e. Transmitting Confidential Information

Counselors take precautions to ensure the confidentiality of information transmitted through the use of computers, electronic mail, facsimile machines, telephones, voicemail, answering machines, and other electronic or computer technology. *(See A.12.g.)*

B.3.f. Deceased Clients

Counselors protect the confidentiality of deceased clients, consistent with legal requirements and agency or setting policies.

B.4. Groups and Families

B.4.a. Group Work

In group work, counselors clearly explain the importance and parameters of confidentiality for the specific group being entered.

B.4.b. Couples and Family Counseling

In couples and family counseling, counselors clearly define who is considered "the client" and discuss expectations and limitations of confidentiality. Counselors seek agreement and document in writing such agreement among all involved parties having capacity to give consent concerning each individual's right to confidentiality and any obligation to preserve the confidentiality of information known.

B.5. Clients Lacking Capacity to Give Informed Consent

B.5.a. Responsibility to Clients
When counseling minor clients or adult clients who lack the capacity to give voluntary, informed consent, counselors protect the confidentiality of information received in the counseling relationship as specified by federal and state laws, written policies, and applicable ethical standards.

B.5.b. Responsibility to Parents and Legal Guardians
Counselors inform parents and legal guardians about the role of counselors and the confidential nature of the counseling relationship. Counselors are sensitive to the cultural diversity of families and respect the inherent rights and responsibilities of parents/guardians over the welfare of their children/charges according to law. Counselors work to establish, as appropriate, collaborative relationships with parents/guardians to best serve clients.

B.5.c. Release of Confidential Information
When counseling minor clients or adult clients who lack the capacity to give voluntary consent to release confidential information, counselors seek permission from an appropriate third party to disclose information. In such instances, counselors inform clients consistent with their level of understanding and take culturally appropriate measures to safeguard client confidentiality.

B.6. Records

B.6.a. Confidentiality of Records
Counselors ensure that records are kept in a secure location and that only authorized persons have access to records.

B.6.b. Permission to Record
Counselors obtain permission from clients prior to recording sessions through electronic or other means.

B.6.c. Permission to Observe
Counselors obtain permission from clients prior to observing counseling sessions, reviewing session transcripts, or viewing recordings of sessions with supervisors, faculty, peers, or others within the training environment.

B.6.d. Client Access
Counselors provide reasonable access to records and copies of records when requested by competent clients. Counselors limit the access of clients to their records, or portions of their records, only when there is compelling evidence that such access would cause harm to the client. Counselors document the request of clients and the rationale for withholding some or all of the record in the files of clients. In situations involving multiple clients, counselors provide individual clients with only those parts of records that relate directly to them and do not include confidential information related to any other client.

B.6.e. Assistance With Records
When clients request access to their records, counselors provide assistance and consultation in interpreting counseling records.

B.6.f. Disclosure or Transfer
Unless exceptions to confidentiality exist, counselors obtain written permission from clients to disclose or transfer records to legitimate third parties. Steps are taken to ensure that receivers of counseling records are sensitive to their confidential nature. (See A.3., E.4.)

B.6.g. Storage and Disposal After Termination
Counselors store records following termination of services to ensure reasonable future access, maintain records in accordance with state and federal statutes governing records, and dispose of client records and other sensitive materials in a manner that protects client confidentiality. When records are of an artistic nature, counselors obtain client (or guardian) consent with regard to handling of such records or documents. (See A.1.b.)

B.6.h. Reasonable Precautions
Counselors take reasonable precautions to protect client confidentiality in the event of the counselor's termination of practice, incapacity, or death. (See C.2.h.)

B.7. Research and Training

B.7.a. Institutional Approval
When institutional approval is required, counselors provide accurate information about their research proposals and obtain approval prior to conducting their research. They conduct research in accordance with the approved research protocol.

B.7.b. Adherence to Guidelines
Counselors are responsible for understanding and adhering to state, federal, agency, or institutional policies or applicable guidelines regarding confidentiality in their research practices.

B.7.c. Confidentiality of Information Obtained in Research
Violations of participant privacy and confidentiality are risks of participation in research involving human participants. Investigators maintain all research records in a secure manner. They explain to participants the risks of violations of privacy and confidentiality and disclose to participants any limits of confidentiality that reasonably can be expected. Regardless of the degree to which confidentiality will be maintained, investigators must disclose to participants any limits of confidentiality that reasonably can be expected. *(See G.2.e.)*

B.7.d. Disclosure of Research Information
Counselors do not disclose confidential information that reasonably could lead to the identification of a research participant unless they have obtained the prior consent of the person. Use of data derived from counseling relationships for purposes of training, research, or publication is confined to content that is disguised to ensure the anonymity of the individuals involved. *(See G.2.a., G.2.d.)*

B.7.e. Agreement for Identification
Identification of clients, students, or supervisees in a presentation or publication is permissible only when they have reviewed the material and agreed to its presentation or publication. *(See G.4.d.)*

B.8. Consultation

B.8.a. Agreements
When acting as consultants, counselors seek agreements among all parties involved concerning each individual's rights to confidentiality, the obligation of each individual to preserve confidential information, and the limits of confidentiality of information shared by others.

B.8.b. Respect for Privacy
Information obtained in a consulting relationship is discussed for professional purposes only with persons directly involved with the case. Written and oral reports present only data germane to the purposes of the consultation, and every effort is made to protect client identity and to avoid undue invasion of privacy.

B.8.c. Disclosure of Confidential Information
When consulting with colleagues, counselors do not disclose confidential information that reasonably could lead to the identification of a client or other person or organization with whom they have a confidential relationship unless they have obtained the prior consent of the person or organization or the disclosure cannot be avoided. They disclose information only to the extent necessary to achieve the purposes of the consultation. *(See D.2.d.)*

SECTION C:
PROFESSIONAL RESPONSIBILITY

Introduction

Counselors aspire to open, honest, and accurate communication in dealing with the public and other professionals. They practice in a nondiscriminatory manner within the boundaries of professional and personal competence and have a responsibility to abide by the *ACA Code of Ethics*. Counselors actively participate in local, state, and national associations that foster the development and improvement of counseling. Counselors advocate to promote change at the individual, group, institutional, and societal levels that improves the quality of life for individuals and groups and removes potential barriers to the provision or access of appropriate services being offered. Counselors have a responsibility to the public to engage in counseling practices that are based on rigorous research methodologies. In addition, counselors engage in self-care activities to maintain and promote their emotional, physical, mental, and spiritual well-being to best meet their professional responsibilities.

C.1. Knowledge of Standards

Counselors have a responsibility to read, understand, and follow the *ACA Code of Ethics* and adhere to applicable laws and regulations.

C.2. Professional Competence

C.2.a. Boundaries of Competence

Counselors practice only within the boundaries of their competence, based on their education, training, supervised experience, state and national professional credentials, and appropriate professional experience. Counselors gain knowledge, personal awareness, sensitivity, and skills pertinent to working with a diverse client population. *(See A.9.b., C.4.e., E.2., F.2., F.11.b.)*

C.2.b. New Specialty Areas of Practice

Counselors practice in specialty areas new to them only after appropriate education, training, and supervised experience. While developing skills in new specialty areas, counselors take steps to ensure the competence of their work and to protect others from possible harm. *(See F.6.f.)*

C.2.c. Qualified for Employment

Counselors accept employment only for positions for which they are qualified by education, training, supervised experience, state and national professional credentials, and appropriate professional experience. Counselors hire for professional counseling positions only individuals who are qualified and competent for those positions.

C.2.d. Monitor Effectiveness

Counselors continually monitor their effectiveness as professionals and take steps to improve when necessary. Counselors in private practice take reasonable steps to seek peer supervision as needed to evaluate their efficacy as counselors.

C.2.e. Consultation on Ethical Obligations

Counselors take reasonable steps to consult with other counselors or related professionals when they have questions regarding their ethical obligations or professional practice.

C.2.f. Continuing Education

Counselors recognize the need for continuing education to acquire and maintain a reasonable level of awareness of current scientific and professional information in their fields of activity. They take steps to maintain competence in the skills they use, are open to new procedures, and keep current with the diverse populations and specific populations with whom they work.

C.2.g. Impairment

Counselors are alert to the signs of impairment from their own physical, mental, or emotional problems and refrain from offering or providing professional services when such impairment is likely to harm a client or others. They seek assistance for problems that reach the level of professional impairment, and, if necessary, they limit, suspend, or terminate their professional responsibilities until such time it is determined that they may safely resume their work. Counselors assist colleagues or supervisors in recognizing their own professional impairment and provide consultation and assistance when warranted with colleagues or supervisors showing signs of impairment and intervene as appropriate to prevent imminent harm to clients. *(See A.11.b., F.8.b.)*

C.2.h. Counselor Incapacitation or Termination of Practice

When counselors leave a practice, they follow a prepared plan for transfer of clients and files. Counselors prepare and disseminate to an identified colleague or "records custodian" a plan for the transfer of clients and files in the case of their incapacitation, death, or termination of practice.

C.3. Advertising and Soliciting Clients

C.3.a. Accurate Advertising

When advertising or otherwise representing their services to the public, counselors identify their credentials in an accurate manner that is not false, misleading, deceptive, or fraudulent.

C.3.b. Testimonials

Counselors who use testimonials do not solicit them from current clients nor former clients nor any other persons who may be vulnerable to undue influence.

C.3.c. Statements by Others

Counselors make reasonable efforts to ensure that statements made by others about them or the profession of counseling are accurate.

C.3.d. Recruiting Through Employment
Counselors do not use their places of employment or institutional affiliation to recruit or gain clients, supervisees, or consultees for their private practices.

C.3.e. Products and Training Advertisements
Counselors who develop products related to their profession or conduct workshops or training events ensure that the advertisements concerning these products or events are accurate and disclose adequate information for consumers to make informed choices. *(See C.6.d.)*

C.3.f. Promoting to Those Served
Counselors do not use counseling, teaching, training, or supervisory relationships to promote their products or training events in a manner that is deceptive or would exert undue influence on individuals who may be vulnerable. However, counselor educators may adopt textbooks they have authored for instructional purposes.

C.4. Professional Qualifications

C.4.a. Accurate Representation
Counselors claim or imply only professional qualifications actually completed and correct any known misrepresentations of their qualifications by others. Counselors truthfully represent the qualifications of their professional colleagues. Counselors clearly distinguish between paid and volunteer work experience and accurately describe their continuing education and specialized training. *(See C.2.a.)*

C.4.b. Credentials
Counselors claim only licenses or certifications that are current and in good standing.

C.4.c. Educational Degrees
Counselors clearly differentiate between earned and honorary degrees.

C.4.d. Implying Doctoral-Level Competence
Counselors clearly state their highest earned degree in counseling or closely related field. Counselors do not imply doctoral-level competence when only possessing a master's degree in counseling or a related field by referring to themselves as "Dr." in a counseling context when their doctorate is not in counseling or a related field.

C.4.e. Program Accreditation Status
Counselors clearly state the accreditation status of their degree programs at the time the degree was earned.

C.4.f. Professional Membership
Counselors clearly differentiate between current, active memberships and former memberships in associations. Members of the American Counseling Association must clearly differentiate between professional membership, which implies the possession of at least a master's degree in counseling, and regular membership, which is open to individuals whose interests and activities are consistent with those of ACA but are not qualified for professional membership.

C.5. Nondiscrimination

Counselors do not condone or engage in discrimination based on age, culture, disability, ethnicity, race, religion/spirituality, gender, gender identity, sexual orientation, marital status/partnership, language preference, socioeconomic status, or any basis proscribed by law. Counselors do not discriminate against clients, students, employees, supervisees, or research participants in a manner that has a negative impact on these persons.

C.6. Public Responsibility

C.6.a. Sexual Harassment
Counselors do not engage in or condone sexual harassment. Sexual harassment is defined as sexual solicitation, physical advances, or verbal or nonverbal conduct that is sexual in nature, that occurs in connection with professional activities or roles, and that either

1. is unwelcome, is offensive, or creates a hostile workplace or learning environment, and counselors know or are told this; or
2. is sufficiently severe or intense to be perceived as harassment to a reasonable person in the context in which the behavior occurred.

Sexual harassment can consist of a single intense or severe act or multiple persistent or pervasive acts.

C.6.b. Reports to Third Parties

Counselors are accurate, honest, and objective in reporting their professional activities and judgments to appropriate third parties, including courts, health insurance companies, those who are the recipients of evaluation reports, and others. *(See B.3., E.4.)*

C.6.c. Media Presentations

When counselors provide advice or comment by means of public lectures, demonstrations, radio or television programs, prerecorded tapes, technology-based applications, printed articles, mailed material, or other media, they take reasonable precautions to ensure that

1. the statements are based on appropriate professional counseling literature and practice,
2. the statements are otherwise consistent with the *ACA Code of Ethics,* and
3. the recipients of the information are not encouraged to infer that a professional counseling relationship has been established.

C.6.d. Exploitation of Others

Counselors do not exploit others in their professional relationships. *(See C.3.e.)*

C.6.e. Scientific Bases for Treatment Modalities

Counselors use techniques/procedures/modalities that are grounded in theory and/or have an empirical or scientific foundation. Counselors who do not must define the techniques/procedures as "unproven" or "developing" and explain the potential risks and ethical considerations of using such techniques/procedures and take steps to protect clients from possible harm. *(See A.4.a., E.5.c., E.5.d.)*

C.7. Responsibility to Other Professionals

C.7.a. Personal Public Statements

When making personal statements in a public context, counselors clarify that they are speaking from their personal perspectives and that they are not speaking on behalf of all counselors or the profession.

SECTION D: RELATIONSHIPS WITH OTHER PROFESSIONALS

Introduction

Professional counselors recognize that the quality of their interactions with colleagues can influence the quality of services provided to clients. They work to become knowledgeable about colleagues within and outside the field of counseling. Counselors develop positive working relationships and systems of communication with colleagues to enhance services to clients.

D.1. Relationships With Colleagues, Employers, and Employees

D.1.a. Different Approaches

Counselors are respectful of approaches to counseling services that differ from their own. Counselors are respectful of traditions and practices of other professional groups with which they work.

D.1.b. Forming Relationships

Counselors work to develop and strengthen interdisciplinary relations with colleagues from other disciplines to best serve clients.

D.1.c. Interdisciplinary Teamwork

Counselors who are members of interdisciplinary teams delivering multifaceted services to clients keep the focus on how to best serve the clients. They participate in and contribute to decisions that affect the well-being of clients by drawing on the perspectives, values, and experiences of the counseling profession and those of colleagues from other disciplines. *(See A.1.a.)*

D.1.d. Confidentiality

When counselors are required by law, institutional policy, or extraordinary circumstances to serve in more than one role in judicial or administrative proceedings, they clarify role expectations and the parameters of confidentiality with their colleagues. *(See B.1.c., B.1.d., B.2.c., B.2.d., B.3.b.)*

D.1.e. Establishing Professional and Ethical Obligations

Counselors who are members of interdisciplinary teams clarify professional and ethical obligations of the team as a whole and of its individual members. When a team decision raises ethical concerns, counselors first attempt to resolve the concern within the team. If they cannot reach resolution among team members, counselors pursue other avenues to address their concerns consistent with client well-being.

D.1.f. Personnel Selection and Assignment
Counselors select competent staff and assign responsibilities compatible with their skills and experiences.

D.1.g. Employer Policies
The acceptance of employment in an agency or institution implies that counselors are in agreement with its general policies and principles. Counselors strive to reach agreement with employers as to acceptable standards of conduct that allow for changes in institutional policy conducive to the growth and development of clients.

D.1.h. Negative Conditions
Counselors alert their employers of inappropriate policies and practices. They attempt to effect changes in such policies or procedures through constructive action within the organization. When such policies are potentially disruptive or damaging to clients or may limit the effectiveness of services provided and change cannot be effected, counselors take appropriate further action. Such action may include referral to appropriate certification, accreditation, or state licensure organizations, or voluntary termination of employment.

D.1.i. Protection From Punitive Action
Counselors take care not to harass or dismiss an employee who has acted in a responsible and ethical manner to expose inappropriate employer policies or practices.

D.2. Consultation

D.2.a. Consultant Competency
Counselors take reasonable steps to ensure that they have the appropriate resources and competencies when providing consultation services. Counselors provide appropriate referral resources when requested or needed. (See C.2.a.)

D.2.b. Understanding Consultees
When providing consultation, counselors attempt to develop with their consultees a clear understanding of problem definition, goals for change, and predicted consequences of interventions selected.

D.2.c. Consultant Goals
The consulting relationship is one in which consultee adaptability and growth toward self-direction are consistently encouraged and cultivated.

D.2.d. Informed Consent in Consultation
When providing consultation, counselors have an obligation to review, in writing and verbally, the rights and responsibilities of both counselors and consultees. Counselors use clear and understandable language to inform all parties involved about the purpose of the services to be provided, relevant costs, potential risks and benefits, and the limits of confidentiality. Working in conjunction with the consultee, counselors attempt to develop a clear definition of the problem, goals for change, and predicted consequences of interventions that are culturally responsive and appropriate to the needs of consultees. (See A.2.a., A.2.b.)

SECTION E:
EVALUATION, ASSESSMENT, AND INTERPRETATION

Introduction

Counselors use assessment instruments as one component of the counseling process, taking into account the client personal and cultural context. Counselors promote the well-being of individual clients or groups of clients by developing and using appropriate educational, psychological, and career assessment instruments.

E.1. General

E.1.a. Assessment
The primary purpose of educational, psychological, and career assessment is to provide measurements that are valid and reliable in either comparative or absolute terms. These include, but are not limited to, measurements of ability, personality, interest, intelligence, achievement, and performance. Counselors

recognize the need to interpret the statements in this section as applying to both quantitative and qualitative assessments.

E.1.b. Client Welfare

Counselors do not misuse assessment results and interpretations, and they take reasonable steps to prevent others from misusing the information these techniques provide. They respect the client's right to know the results, the interpretations made, and the bases for counselors' conclusions and recommendations.

E.2. Competence to Use and Interpret Assessment Instruments

E.2.a. Limits of Competence

Counselors utilize only those testing and assessment services for which they have been trained and are competent. Counselors using technology-assisted test interpretations are trained in the construct being measured and the specific instrument being used prior to using its technology-based application. Counselors take reasonable measures to ensure the proper use of psychological and career assessment techniques by persons under their supervision. *(See A.12.)*

E.2.b. Appropriate Use

Counselors are responsible for the appropriate application, scoring, interpretation, and use of assessment instruments relevant to the needs of the client, whether they score and interpret such assessments themselves or use technology or other services.

E.2.c. Decisions Based on Results

Counselors responsible for decisions involving individuals or policies that are based on assessment results have a thorough understanding of educational, psychological, and career measurement, including validation criteria, assessment research, and guidelines for assessment development and use.

E.3. Informed Consent in Assessment

E.3.a. Explanation to Clients

Prior to assessment, counselors explain the nature and purposes of assessment and the specific use of results by potential recipients. The explanation will be given in the language of the client (or other legally authorized person on behalf of the client), unless an explicit exception has been agreed upon in advance. Counselors consider the client's personal or cultural context, the level of the client's understanding of the results, and the impact of the results on the client. *(See A.2., A.12.g., F.1.c.)*

E.3.b. Recipients of Results

Counselors consider the examinee's welfare, explicit understandings, and prior agreements in determining who receives the assessment results. Counselors include accurate and appropriate interpretations with any release of individual or group assessment results. *(See B.2.c., B.5.)*

E.4. Release of Data to Qualified Professionals

Counselors release assessment data in which the client is identified only with the consent of the client or the client's legal representative. Such data are released only to persons recognized by counselors as qualified to interpret the data. *(See B.1., B.3., B.6.b.)*

E.5. Diagnosis of Mental Disorders

E.5.a. Proper Diagnosis

Counselors take special care to provide proper diagnosis of mental disorders. Assessment techniques (including personal interview) used to determine client care (e.g., locus of treatment, type of treatment, or recommended follow-up) are carefully selected and appropriately used.

E.5.b. Cultural Sensitivity

Counselors recognize that culture affects the manner in which clients' problems are defined. Clients' socioeconomic and cultural experiences are considered when diagnosing mental disorders. *(See A.2.c.)*

E.5.c. Historical and Social Prejudices in the Diagnosis of Pathology

Counselors recognize historical and social prejudices in the misdiagnosis and pathologizing of certain individuals and groups and the role of mental health professionals in perpetuating these prejudices through diagnosis and treatment.

E.5.d. Refraining From Diagnosis

Counselors may refrain from making and/or reporting a diagnosis if they believe it would cause harm to the client or others.

E.6. Instrument Selection

E.6.a. Appropriateness of Instruments

Counselors carefully consider the validity, reliability, psychometric limitations, and appropriateness of instruments when selecting assessments.

E.6.b. Referral Information

If a client is referred to a third party for assessment, the counselor provides specific referral questions and sufficient objective data about the client to ensure that appropriate assessment instruments are utilized. *(See A.9.b., B.3.)*

E.6.c. Culturally Diverse Populations

Counselors are cautious when selecting assessments for culturally diverse populations to avoid the use of instruments that lack appropriate psychometric properties for the client population. *(See A.2.c., E.5.b.)*

E.7. Conditions of Assessment Administration

(See A.12.b, A.12.d.)

E.7.a. Administration Conditions

Counselors administer assessments under the same conditions that were established in their standardization. When assessments are not administered under standard conditions, as may be necessary to accommodate clients with disabilities, or when unusual behavior or irregularities occur during the administration, those conditions are noted in interpretation, and the results may be designated as invalid or of questionable validity.

E.7.b. Technological Administration

Counselors ensure that administration programs function properly and provide clients with accurate results when technological or other electronic methods are used for assessment administration.

E.7.c. Unsupervised Assessments

Unless the assessment instrument is designed, intended, and validated for self-administration and/or scoring, counselors do not permit inadequately supervised use.

E.7.d. Disclosure of Favorable Conditions

Prior to administration of assessments, conditions that produce most favorable assessment results are made known to the examinee.

E.8. Multicultural Issues/ Diversity in Assessment

Counselors use with caution assessment techniques that were normed on populations other than that of the client. Counselors recognize the effects of age, color, culture, disability, ethnic group, gender, race, language preference, religion, spirituality, sexual orientation, and socioeconomic status on test administration and interpretation, and place test results in proper perspective with other relevant factors. *(See A.2.c., E.5.b.)*

E.9. Scoring and Interpretation of Assessments

E.9.a. Reporting

In reporting assessment results, counselors indicate reservations that exist regarding validity or reliability due to circumstances of the assessment or the inappropriateness of the norms for the person tested.

E.9.b. Research Instruments

Counselors exercise caution when interpreting the results of research instruments not having sufficient technical data to support respondent results. The specific purposes for the use of such instruments are stated explicitly to the examinee.

E.9.c. Assessment Services

Counselors who provide assessment scoring and interpretation services to support the assessment process confirm the validity of such interpretations. They accurately describe the purpose, norms, validity, reliability, and applications of the procedures and any special qualifications applicable to their use. The public offering of an automated test interpretations service is considered a professional-to-professional consultation. The formal responsibility of the consultant is to the consultee, but the ultimate and overriding responsibility is to the client. *(See D.2.)*

E.10. Assessment Security

Counselors maintain the integrity and security of tests and other assessment techniques consistent with legal and contractual obligations. Counselors do not appropriate, reproduce, or modify published assessments or parts thereof without acknowledgment and permission from the publisher.

E.11. Obsolete Assessments and Outdated Results

Counselors do not use data or results from assessments that are obsolete or outdated for the current purpose. Counselors make every effort to prevent the misuse of obsolete measures and assessment data by others.

E.12. Assessment Construction

Counselors use established scientific procedures, relevant standards, and current professional knowledge for assessment design in the development, publication, and utilization of educational and psychological assessment techniques.

E.13. Forensic Evaluation: Evaluation for Legal Proceedings

E.13.a. Primary Obligations

When providing forensic evaluations, the primary obligation of counselors is to produce objective findings that can be substantiated based on information and techniques appropriate to the evaluation, which may include examination of the individual and/or review of records. Counselors are entitled to form professional opinions based on their professional knowledge and expertise that can be supported by the data gathered in evaluations. Counselors will define the limits of their reports or testimony, especially when an examination of the individual has not been conducted.

E.13.b. Consent for Evaluation

Individuals being evaluated are informed in writing that the relationship is for the purposes of an evaluation and is not counseling in nature, and entities or individuals who will receive the evaluation report are identified. Written consent to be evaluated is obtained from those being evaluated unless a court orders evaluations to be conducted without the written consent of individuals being evaluated. When children or vulnerable adults are being evaluated, informed written consent is obtained from a parent or guardian.

E.13.c. Client Evaluation Prohibited

Counselors do not evaluate individuals for forensic purposes they currently counsel or individuals they have counseled in the past. Counselors do not accept as counseling clients individuals they are evaluating or individuals they have evaluated in the past for forensic purposes.

E.13.d. Avoid Potentially Harmful Relationships

Counselors who provide forensic evaluations avoid potentially harmful professional or personal relationships with family members, romantic partners, and close friends of individuals they are evaluating or have evaluated in the past.

SECTION F: SUPERVISION, TRAINING, AND TEACHING

Introduction

Counselors aspire to foster meaningful and respectful professional relationships and to maintain appropriate boundaries with supervisees and students. Counselors have theoretical and pedagogical foundations for their work and aim to be fair, accurate, and honest in their assessments of counselors-in-training.

F.1. Counselor Supervision and Client Welfare

F.1.a. Client Welfare

A primary obligation of counseling supervisors is to monitor the services provided by other counselors or counselors-in-training. Counseling supervisors monitor client welfare and supervisee clinical performance and professional development. To fulfill these obligations, supervisors meet regularly with supervisees to review case notes, samples of clinical work, or live observations. Supervisees have a responsibility to understand and follow the *ACA Code of Ethics.*

F.1.b. Counselor Credentials
Counseling supervisors work to ensure that clients are aware of the qualifications of the supervisees who render services to the clients. *(See A.2.b.)*

F.1.c. Informed Consent and Client Rights
Supervisors make supervisees aware of client rights including the protection of client privacy and confidentiality in the counseling relationship. Supervisees provide clients with professional disclosure information and inform them of how the supervision process influences the limits of confidentiality. Supervisees make clients aware of who will have access to records of the counseling relationship and how these records will be used. *(See A.2.b., B.1.d.)*

F.2. Counselor Supervision Competence

F.2.a. Supervisor Preparation
Prior to offering clinical supervision services, counselors are trained in supervision methods and techniques. Counselors who offer clinical supervision services regularly pursue continuing education activities including both counseling and supervision topics and skills. *(See C.2.a., C.2.f.)*

F.2.b. Multicultural Issues/ Diversity in Supervision
Counseling supervisors are aware of and address the role of multiculturalism/diversity in the supervisory relationship.

F.3. Supervisory Relationships

F.3.a. Relationship Boundaries With Supervisees
Counseling supervisors clearly define and maintain ethical professional, personal, and social relationships with their supervisees. Counseling supervisors avoid nonprofessional relationships with current supervisees. If supervisors must assume other professional roles (e.g., clinical and administrative supervisor, instructor) with supervisees, they work to minimize potential conflicts and explain to supervisees the expectations and responsibilities associated with each role. They do not engage in any form of nonprofessional inter-

action that may compromise the supervisory relationship.

F.3.b. Sexual Relationships
Sexual or romantic interactions or relationships with current supervisees are prohibited.

F.3.c. Sexual Harassment
Counseling supervisors do not condone or subject supervisees to sexual harassment. *(See C.6.a.)*

F.3.d. Close Relatives and Friends
Counseling supervisors avoid accepting close relatives, romantic partners, or friends as supervisees.

F.3.e. Potentially Beneficial Relationships
Counseling supervisors are aware of the power differential in their relationships with supervisees. If they believe nonprofessional relationships with a supervisee may be potentially beneficial to the supervisee, they take precautions similar to those taken by counselors when working with clients. Examples of potentially beneficial interactions or relationships include attending a formal ceremony; hospital visits; providing support during a stressful event; or mutual membership in a professional association, organization, or community. Counseling supervisors engage in open discussions with supervisees when they consider entering into relationships with them outside of their roles as clinical and/or administrative supervisors. Before engaging in nonprofessional relationships, supervisors discuss with supervisees and document the rationale for such interactions, potential benefits or drawbacks, and anticipated consequences for the supervisee. Supervisors clarify the specific nature and limitations of the additional role(s) they will have with the supervisee.

F.4. Supervisor Responsibilities

F.4.a. Informed Consent for Supervision
Supervisors are responsible for incorporating into their supervision the principles of informed consent and participation. Supervisors inform supervisees of the policies and procedures to which they are to adhere and the mechanisms for due process appeal of individual supervisory actions.

F.4.b. Emergencies and Absences
Supervisors establish and communicate to supervisees procedures for contacting them or,

in their absence, alternative on-call supervisors to assist in handling crises.

F.4.c. Standards for Supervisees

Supervisors make their supervisees aware of professional and ethical standards and legal responsibilities. Supervisors of postdegree counselors encourage these counselors to adhere to professional standards of practice. *(See C.1.)*

F.4.d. Termination of the Supervisory Relationship

Supervisors or supervisees have the right to terminate the supervisory relationship with adequate notice. Reasons for withdrawal are provided to the other party. When cultural, clinical, or professional issues are crucial to the viability of the supervisory relationship, both parties make efforts to resolve differences. When termination is warranted, supervisors make appropriate referrals to possible alternative supervisors.

F.5. Counseling Supervision Evaluation, Remediation, and Endorsement

F.5.a. Evaluation

Supervisors document and provide supervisees with ongoing performance appraisal and evaluation feedback and schedule periodic formal evaluative sessions throughout the supervisory relationship.

F.5.b. Limitations

Through ongoing evaluation and appraisal, supervisors are aware of the limitations of supervisees that might impede performance. Supervisors assist supervisees in securing remedial assistance when needed. They recommend dismissal from training programs, applied counseling settings, or state or voluntary professional credentialing processes when those supervisees are unable to provide competent professional services. Supervisors seek consultation and document their decisions to dismiss or refer supervisees for assistance. They ensure that supervisees are aware of options available to them to address such decisions. *(See C.2.g.)*

F.5.c. Counseling for Supervisees

If supervisees request counseling, supervisors provide them with acceptable referrals. Counselors do not provide counseling services to supervisees. Supervisors address interpersonal competencies in terms of the impact of these issues on clients, the supervisory relationship, and professional functioning. *(See F.3.a.)*

F.5.d. Endorsement

Supervisors endorse supervisees for certification, licensure, employment, or completion of an academic or training program only when they believe supervisees are qualified for the endorsement. Regardless of qualifications, supervisors do not endorse supervisees whom they believe to be impaired in any way that would interfere with the performance of the duties associated with the endorsement.

F.6. Responsibilities of Counselor Educators

F.6.a. Counselor Educators

Counselor educators who are responsible for developing, implementing, and supervising educational programs are skilled as teachers and practitioners. They are knowledgeable regarding the ethical, legal, and regulatory aspects of the profession, are skilled in applying that knowledge, and make students and supervisees aware of their responsibilities. Counselor educators conduct counselor education and training programs in an ethical manner and serve as role models for professional behavior. *(See C.1., C.2.a., C.2.c.)*

F.6.b. Infusing Multicultural Issues/Diversity

Counselor educators infuse material related to multiculturalism/diversity into all courses and workshops for the development of professional counselors.

F.6.c. Integration of Study and Practice

Counselor educators establish education and training programs that integrate academic study and supervised practice.

F.6.d. Teaching Ethics

Counselor educators make students and supervisees aware of the ethical responsibilities and standards of the profession and the ethical responsibilities of students to the profession. Counselor educators infuse ethical considerations throughout the curriculum. *(See C.1.)*

F.6.e. Peer Relationships

Counselor educators make every effort to ensure that the rights of peers are not compromised when students or supervisees lead counseling groups or provide clinical supervision. Counselor educators take steps to ensure that students and supervisees understand they have the same ethical obligations as counselor educators, trainers, and supervisors.

F.6.f. Innovative Theories and Techniques

When counselor educators teach counseling techniques/procedures that are innovative, without an empirical foundation, or without a well-grounded theoretical foundation, they define the counseling techniques/procedures as "unproven" or "developing" and explain to students the potential risks and ethical considerations of using such techniques/procedures.

F.6.g. Field Placements

Counselor educators develop clear policies within their training programs regarding field placement and other clinical experiences. Counselor educators provide clearly stated roles and responsibilities for the student or supervisee, the site supervisor, and the program supervisor. They confirm that site supervisors are qualified to provide supervision and inform site supervisors of their professional and ethical responsibilities in this role.

F.6.h. Professional Disclosure

Before initiating counseling services, counselors-in-training disclose their status as students and explain how this status affects the limits of confidentiality. Counselor educators ensure that the clients at field placements are aware of the services rendered and the qualifications of the students and supervisees rendering those services. Students and supervisees obtain client permission before they use any information concerning the counseling relationship in the training process. *(See A.2.b.)*

F.7. Student Welfare

F.7.a. Orientation

Counselor educators recognize that orientation is a developmental process that continues throughout the educational and clinical training of students. Counseling faculty provide prospec-tive students with information about the counselor education program's expectations:

1. the type and level of skill and knowledge acquisition required for successful completion of the training;
2. program training goals, objectives, and mission, and subject matter to be covered;
3. bases for evaluation;
4. training components that encourage self-growth or self-disclosure as part of the training process;
5. the type of supervision settings and requirements of the sites for required clinical field experiences;
6. student and supervisee evaluation and dismissal policies and procedures; and
7. up-to-date employment prospects for graduates.

F.7.b. Self-Growth Experiences

Counselor education programs delineate requirements for self-disclosure or self-growth experiences in their admission and program materials. Counselor educators use professional judgment when designing training experiences they conduct that require student and supervisee self-growth or self-disclosure. Students and supervisees are made aware of the ramifications their self-disclosure may have when counselors whose primary role as teacher, trainer, or supervisor requires acting on ethical obligations to the profession. Evaluative components of experiential training experiences explicitly delineate predetermined academic standards that are separate and do not depend on the student's level of self-disclosure. Counselor educators may require trainees to seek professional help to address any personal concerns that may be affecting their competency.

F.8. Student Responsibilities

F.8.a. Standards for Students

Counselors-in-training have a responsibility to understand and follow the *ACA Code of Ethics* and adhere to applicable laws, regulatory policies, and rules and policies governing professional staff behavior at the agency or placement setting. Students have the same obligation to clients as those required of professional counselors. *(See C.1., H.1.)*

F.8.b. Impairment

Counselors-in-training refrain from offering or providing counseling services when their physical, mental, or emotional problems are likely to harm a client or others. They are alert to the signs of impairment, seek assistance for problems, and notify their program supervisors when they are aware that they are unable to effectively provide services. In addition, they seek appropriate professional services for themselves to remediate the problems that are interfering with their ability to provide services to others. *(See A.1., C.2.d., C.2.g.)*

F.9. Evaluation and Remediation of Students

F.9.a. Evaluation

Counselors clearly state to students, prior to and throughout the training program, the levels of competency expected, appraisal methods, and timing of evaluations for both didactic and clinical competencies. Counselor educators provide students with ongoing performance appraisal and evaluation feedback throughout the training program.

F.9.b. Limitations

Counselor educators, throughout ongoing evaluation and appraisal, are aware of and address the inability of some students to achieve counseling competencies that might impede performance. Counselor educators

1. assist students in securing remedial assistance when needed,
2. seek professional consultation and document their decision to dismiss or refer students for assistance, and
3. ensure that students have recourse in a timely manner to address decisions to require them to seek assistance or to dismiss them and provide students with due process according to institutional policies and procedures. *(See C.2.g.)*

F.9.c. Counseling for Students

If students request counseling or if counseling services are required as part of a remediation process, counselor educators provide acceptable referrals.

F.10. Roles and Relationships Between Counselor Educators and Students

F.10.a. Sexual or Romantic Relationships

Sexual or romantic interactions or relationships with current students are prohibited.

F.10.b. Sexual Harassment

Counselor educators do not condone or subject students to sexual harassment. *(See C.6.a.)*

F.10.c. Relationships With Former Students

Counselor educators are aware of the power differential in the relationship between faculty and students. Faculty members foster open discussions with former students when considering engaging in a social, sexual, or other intimate relationship. Faculty members discuss with the former student how their former relationship may affect the change in relationship.

F.10.d. Nonprofessional Relationships

Counselor educators avoid nonprofessional or ongoing professional relationships with students in which there is a risk of potential harm to the student or that may compromise the training experience or grades assigned. In addition, counselor educators do not accept any form of professional services, fees, commissions, reimbursement, or remuneration from a site for student or supervisee placement.

F.10.e. Counseling Services

Counselor educators do not serve as counselors to current students unless this is a brief role associated with a training experience.

F.10.f. Potentially Beneficial Relationships

Counselor educators are aware of the power differential in the relationship between faculty and students. If they believe a nonprofessional relationship with a student may be potentially beneficial to the student, they take precautions similar to those taken by counselors when working with clients. Examples of potentially beneficial interactions or relationships include, but are not limited to, attending a formal ceremony; hospital visits; providing support during a stressful event; or mutual membership in a professional association, organization, or community. Counselor educators engage in open discussions with students when they consider entering into relationships with students outside of their roles as teachers and supervisors. They discuss with students the rationale for such interactions, the potential benefits and drawbacks, and the anticipated consequences for the student. Educators clarify the specific nature and limitations of the additional role(s) they will have with the student prior to engaging in a nonprofessional relationship. Nonprofessional relationships with students should be time-limited and initiated with student consent.

F.11. Multicultural/Diversity Competence in Counselor Education and Training Programs

F.11.a. Faculty Diversity
Counselor educators are committed to recruiting and retaining a diverse faculty.

F.11.b. Student Diversity
Counselor educators actively attempt to recruit and retain a diverse student body. Counselor educators demonstrate commitment to multicultural/diversity competence by recognizing and valuing diverse cultures and types of abilities students bring to the training experience. Counselor educators provide appropriate accommodations that enhance and support diverse student well-being and academic performance.

F.11.c. Multicultural/Diversity Competence
Counselor educators actively infuse multicultural/diversity competency in their training and supervision practices. They actively train students to gain awareness, knowledge, and skills in the competencies of multicultural practice. Counselor educators include case examples, role-plays, discussion questions, and other classroom activities that promote and represent various cultural perspectives.

SECTION G: RESEARCH AND PUBLICATION

Introduction
Counselors who conduct research are encouraged to contribute to the knowledge base of the profession and promote a clearer understanding of the conditions that lead to a healthy and more just society. Counselors support efforts of researchers by participating fully and willingly whenever possible. Counselors minimize bias and respect diversity in designing and implementing research programs.

G.1. Research Responsibilities

G.1.a. Use of Human Research Participants
Counselors plan, design, conduct, and report research in a manner that is consistent with pertinent ethical principles, federal and state laws, host institutional regulations, and scientific standards governing research with human research participants.

G.1.b. Deviation From Standard Practice
Counselors seek consultation and observe stringent safeguards to protect the rights of research participants when a research problem suggests a deviation from standard or acceptable practices.

G.1.c. Independent Researchers
When independent researchers do not have access to an Institutional Review Board (IRB), they should consult with researchers who are familiar with IRB procedures to provide appropriate safeguards.

G.1.d. Precautions to Avoid Injury
Counselors who conduct research with human participants are responsible for the welfare of participants throughout the research process and should take reasonable precautions to avoid causing injurious psychological, emotional, physical, or social effects to participants.

G.1.e. Principal Researcher Responsibility
The ultimate responsibility for ethical research practice lies with the principal researcher. All others involved in the research activities share ethical obligations and responsibility for their own actions.

G.1.f. Minimal Interference
Counselors take reasonable precautions to avoid causing disruptions in the lives of research participants that could be caused by their involvement in research.

G.1.g. Multicultural/Diversity Considerations in Research

When appropriate to research goals, counselors are sensitive to incorporating research procedures that take into account cultural considerations. They seek consultation when appropriate.

G.2. Rights of Research Participants

(See A.2., A.7.)

G.2.a. Informed Consent in Research

Individuals have the right to consent to become research participants. In seeking consent, counselors use language that

1. accurately explains the purpose and procedures to be followed,
2. identifies any procedures that are experimental or relatively untried,
3. describes any attendant discomforts and risks,
4. describes any benefits or changes in individuals or organizations that might be reasonably expected,
5. discloses appropriate alternative procedures that would be advantageous for participants,
6. offers to answer any inquiries concerning the procedures,
7. describes any limitations on confidentiality,
8. describes the format and potential target audiences for the dissemination of research findings, and
9. instructs participants that they are free to withdraw their consent and to discontinue participation in the project at any time without penalty.

G.2.b. Deception

Counselors do not conduct research involving deception unless alternative procedures are not feasible and the prospective value of the research justifies the deception. If such deception has the potential to cause physical or emotional harm to research participants, the research is not conducted, regardless of prospective value. When the methodological requirements of a study necessitate concealment or deception, the investigator explains the reasons for this action as soon as possible during the debriefing.

G.2.c. Student/Supervisee Participation

Researchers who involve students or supervisees in research make clear to them that the decision regarding whether or not to participate in research activities does not affect one's academic standing or supervisory relationship. Students or supervisees who choose not to participate in educational research are provided with an appropriate alternative to fulfill their academic or clinical requirements.

G.2.d. Client Participation

Counselors conducting research involving clients make clear in the informed consent process that clients are free to choose whether or not to participate in research activities. Counselors take necessary precautions to protect clients from adverse consequences of declining or withdrawing from participation.

G.2.e. Confidentiality of Information

Information obtained about research participants during the course of an investigation is confidential. When the possibility exists that others may obtain access to such information, ethical research practice requires that the possibility, together with the plans for protecting confidentiality, be explained to participants as a part of the procedure for obtaining informed consent.

G.2.f. Persons Not Capable of Giving Informed Consent

When a person is not capable of giving informed consent, counselors provide an appropriate explanation to, obtain agreement for participation from, and obtain the appropriate consent of a legally authorized person.

G.2.g. Commitments to Participants

Counselors take reasonable measures to honor all commitments to research participants. *(See A.2.c.)*

G.2.h. Explanations After Data Collection

After data are collected, counselors provide participants with full clarification of the nature of the study to remove any misconceptions participants might have regarding the research. Where scientific or human values justify delaying or withholding information, counselors take reasonable measures to avoid causing harm.

G.2.i. Informing Sponsors

Counselors inform sponsors, institutions, and publication channels regarding research procedures and outcomes. Counselors ensure that appropriate bodies and authorities are given pertinent information and acknowledgment.

G.2.j. Disposal of Research Documents and Records

Within a reasonable period of time following the completion of a research project or study, counselors take steps to destroy records or documents (audio, video, digital, and written) containing confidential data or information that identifies research participants. When records are of an artistic nature, researchers obtain participant consent with regard to handling of such records or documents. *(See B.4.a., B.4.g.)*

G.3. Relationships With Research Participants (When Research Involves Intensive or Extended Interactions)

G.3.a. Nonprofessional Relationships

Nonprofessional relationships with research participants should be avoided.

G.3.b. Relationships With Research Participants

Sexual or romantic counselor–research participant interactions or relationships with current research participants are prohibited.

G.3.c. Sexual Harassment and Research Participants

Researchers do not condone or subject research participants to sexual harassment.

G.3.d. Potentially Beneficial Interactions

When a nonprofessional interaction between the researcher and the research participant may be potentially beneficial, the researcher must document, prior to the interaction (when feasible), the rationale for such an interaction, the potential benefit, and anticipated consequences for the research participant. Such interactions should be initiated with appropriate consent of the research participant. Where unintentional harm occurs to the research participant due to the nonprofessional interaction, the researcher must show evidence of an attempt to remedy such harm.

G.4. Reporting Results

G.4.a. Accurate Results

Counselors plan, conduct, and report research accurately. They provide thorough discussions of the limitations of their data and alternative hypotheses. Counselors do not engage in misleading or fraudulent research, distort data, misrepresent data, or deliberately bias their results. They explicitly mention all variables and conditions known to the investigator that may have affected the outcome of a study or the interpretation of data. They describe the extent to which results are applicable for diverse populations.

G.4.b. Obligation to Report Unfavorable Results

Counselors report the results of any research of professional value. Results that reflect unfavorably on institutions, programs, services, prevailing opinions, or vested interests are not withheld.

G.4.c. Reporting Errors

If counselors discover significant errors in their published research, they take reasonable steps to correct such errors in a correction erratum, or through other appropriate publication means.

G.4.d. Identity of Participants

Counselors who supply data, aid in the research of another person, report research results, or make original data available take due care to disguise the identity of respective participants in the absence of specific authorization from the participants to do otherwise. In situations where participants self-identify their involvement in research studies, researchers take active steps to ensure that data are adapted/changed to protect the identity and welfare of all parties and that discussion of results does not cause harm to participants.

G.4.e. Replication Studies

Counselors are obligated to make available sufficient original research data to qualified professionals who may wish to replicate the study.

G.5. Publication

G.5.a. Recognizing Contributions

When conducting and reporting research, counselors are familiar with and give recognition to previous work on the topic, observe copyright laws, and give full credit to those to whom credit is due.

G.5.b. Plagiarism

Counselors do not plagiarize; that is, they do not present another person's work as their own work.

G.5.c. Review/Republication of Data or Ideas

Counselors fully acknowledge and make editorial reviewers aware of prior publication of ideas or data when such ideas or data are submitted for review or publication.

G.5.d. Contributors

Counselors give credit through joint authorship, acknowledgment, footnote statements, or other appropriate means to those who have contributed significantly to research or concept development in accordance with such contributions. The principal contributor is listed first, and minor technical or professional contributions are acknowledged in notes or introductory statements.

G.5.e. Agreement of Contributors

Counselors who conduct joint research with colleagues or students/supervisees establish agreements in advance regarding allocation of tasks, publication credit, and types of acknowledgment that will be received.

G.5.f. Student Research

For articles that are substantially based on students' course papers, projects, dissertations, or theses, and on which students have been the primary contributors, they are listed as principal authors.

G.5.g. Duplicate Submission

Counselors submit manuscripts for consideration to only one journal at a time. Manuscripts that are published in whole or in substantial part in another journal or published work are not submitted for publication without acknowledgment and permission from the previous publication.

G.5.h. Professional Review

Counselors who review material submitted for publication, research, or other scholarly purposes respect the confidentiality and propri-

etary rights of those who submitted it. Counselors use care to make publication decisions based on valid and defensible standards. Counselors review article submissions in a timely manner and based on their scope and competency in research methodologies. Counselors who serve as reviewers at the request of editors or publishers make every effort to only review materials that are within their scope of competency and use care to avoid personal biases.

SECTION H: RESOLVING ETHICAL ISSUES

Introduction

Counselors behave in a legal, ethical, and moral manner in the conduct of their professional work. They are aware that client protection and trust in the profession depend on a high level of professional conduct. They hold other counselors to the same standards and are willing to take appropriate action to ensure that these standards are upheld.

Counselors strive to resolve ethical dilemmas with direct and open communication among all parties involved and seek consultation with colleagues and supervisors when necessary. Counselors incorporate ethical practice into their daily professional work. They engage in ongoing professional development regarding current topics in ethical and legal issues in counseling.

H.1. Standards and the Law

(See F.9.a.)

H.1.a. Knowledge

Counselors understand the *ACA Code of Ethics* and other applicable ethics codes from other professional organizations or from certification and licensure bodies of which they are members. Lack of knowledge or misunderstanding of an ethical responsibility is not a defense against a charge of unethical conduct.

H.1.b. Conflicts Between Ethics and Laws

If ethical responsibilities conflict with law, regulations, or other governing legal authority, counselors make known their commitment to the *ACA Code of Ethics* and take steps to resolve the conflict. If the conflict cannot be resolved by such means, counselors may adhere to the requirements of law, regulations, or other governing legal authority.

H.2. Suspected Violations

H.2.a. Ethical Behavior Expected
Counselors expect colleagues to adhere to the *ACA Code of Ethics.* When counselors possess knowledge that raises doubts as to whether another counselor is acting in an ethical manner, they take appropriate action. *(See H.2.b., H.2.c.)*

H.2.b. Informal Resolution
When counselors have reason to believe that another counselor is violating or has violated an ethical standard, they attempt first to resolve the issue informally with the other counselor if feasible, provided such action does not violate confidentiality rights that may be involved.

H.2.c. Reporting Ethical Violations
If an apparent violation has substantially harmed or is likely to substantially harm a person or organization and is not appropriate for informal resolution or is not resolved properly, counselors take further action appropriate to the situation. Such action might include referral to state or national committees on professional ethics, voluntary national certification bodies, state licensing boards, or to the appropriate institutional authorities. This standard does not apply when an intervention would violate confidentiality rights or when counselors have been retained to review the work of another counselor whose professional conduct is in question.

H.2.d. Consultation
When uncertain as to whether a particular situation or course of action may be in violation of the *ACA Code of Ethics,* counselors consult with other counselors who are knowledgeable about ethics and the *ACA Code of Ethics,* with colleagues, or with appropriate authorities.

H.2.e. Organizational Conflicts
If the demands of an organization with which counselors are affiliated pose a conflict with the *ACA Code of Ethics,* counselors specify the nature of such conflicts and express to their supervisors or other responsible officials their commitment to the *ACA Code of Ethics.* When possible, counselors work toward change within the organization to allow full adherence to the *ACA Code of Ethics.* In doing so, they address any confidentiality issues.

H.2.f. Unwarranted Complaints
Counselors do not initiate, participate in, or encourage the filing of ethics complaints that are made with reckless disregard or willful ignorance of facts that would disprove the allegation.

H.2.g. Unfair Discrimination Against Complainants and Respondents
Counselors do not deny persons employment, advancement, admission to academic or other programs, tenure, or promotion based solely upon their having made or their being the subject of an ethics complaint. This does not preclude taking action based upon the outcome of such proceedings or considering other appropriate information.

H.3. Cooperation With Ethics Committees

Counselors assist in the process of enforcing the *ACA Code of Ethics.* Counselors cooperate with investigations, proceedings, and requirements of the ACA Ethics Committee or ethics committees of other duly constituted associations or boards having jurisdiction over those charged with a violation. Counselors are familiar with the *ACA Policies and Procedures for Processing Complaints of Ethical Violations* and use it as a reference for assisting in the enforcement of the *ACA Code of Ethics.*

GLOSSARY OF TERMS

Advocacy – promotion of the well-being of individuals and groups, and the counseling profession within systems and organizations. Advocacy seeks to remove barriers and obstacles that inhibit access, growth, and development.

Assent – to demonstrate agreement, when a person is otherwise not capable or competent to give formal consent (e.g., informed consent) to a counseling service or plan.

Client – an individual seeking or referred to the professional services of a counselor for help with problem resolution or decision making.

Counselor – a professional (or a student who is a counselor-in-training) engaged in a counseling practice or other counseling-related services. Counselors fulfill many roles and responsibilities such as counselor educators, researchers, supervisors, practitioners, and consultants.

Counselor Educator – a professional counselor engaged primarily in developing, implementing, and supervising the educational preparation of counselors-in-training.

Counselor Supervisor – a professional counselor who engages in a formal relationship with a practicing counselor or counselor-in-training for the purpose of overseeing that individual's counseling work or clinical skill development.

Culture – membership in a socially constructed way of living, which incorporates collective values, beliefs, norms, boundaries, and lifestyles that are cocreated with others who share similar worldviews comprising biological, psychosocial, historical, psychological, and other factors.

Diversity – the similarities and differences that occur within and across cultures, and the intersection of cultural and social identities.

Documents – any written, digital, audio, visual, or artistic recording of the work within the counseling relationship between counselor and client.

Examinee – a recipient of any professional counseling service that includes educational, psychological, and career appraisal utilizing qualitative or quantitative techniques.

Forensic Evaluation – any formal assessment conducted for court or other legal proceedings.

Multicultural/Diversity Competence – a capacity whereby counselors possess cultural and diversity awareness and knowledge about self and others, and how this awareness and knowledge is applied effectively in practice with clients and client groups.

Multicultural/Diversity Counseling – counseling that recognizes diversity and embraces approaches that support the worth, dignity, potential, and uniqueness of individuals within their historical, cultural, economic, political, and psychosocial contexts.

Student – an individual engaged in formal educational preparation as a counselor-in-training.

Supervisee – a professional counselor or counselor-in-training whose counseling work or clinical skill development is being overseen in a formal supervisory relationship by a qualified trained professional.

Supervisor – counselors who are trained to oversee the professional clinical work of counselors and counselors-in-training.

Teaching – all activities engaged in as part of a formal educational program designed to lead to a graduate degree in counseling.

Training – the instruction and practice of skills related to the counseling profession. Training contributes to the ongoing proficiency of students and professional counselors.

American School Counselor Association *Ethical Standards for School Counselors*

The American School Counselor Association's (ASCA) *Ethical Standards for School Counselors* were adopted by the ASCA Delegate Assembly, March 19, 1984; revised March 27, 1992; June 25, 1998; and June 26, 2004.

Preamble

The American School Counselor Association (ASCA) is a professional organization whose members are certified/licensed in school counseling with unique qualifications and skills to address the academic, personal/social, and career development needs of all students. Professional school counselors are advocates, leaders, collaborators, and consultants who create opportunities for equity in access and success in educational opportunities by connecting their programs to the mission of schools and subscribing to the following tenets of professional responsibility:

- Each person has the right to be respected, be treated with dignity, and have access to a comprehensive school counseling program that advocates for and affirms all students from diverse populations regardless of ethnic/racial status, age, economic status, special needs, English as a second language or other language group, immigration status, sexual orientation, gender, gender identity/expression, family type, religious/spiritual identity, and appearance.
- Each person has the right to receive the information and support needed to move toward self-direction and self-development and affirmation within one's group identities, with special care being given to students who have historically not received adequate educational services: students of color, low socioeconomic students, students with disabilities, and students with nondominant language backgrounds.
- Each person has the right to understand the full magnitude and meaning of his/her educational choices and how those choices will affect future opportunities.
- Each person has the right to privacy and thereby the right to expect the counselor–student relationship to comply with all laws, policies, and ethical standards pertaining to confidentiality in the school setting.

In this document, ASCA specifies the principles of ethical behavior necessary to maintain the high standards of integrity, leadership, and professionalism among its members. The *Ethical Standards for School Counselors* were developed to clarify the nature of ethical responsibilities held in common by school counseling professionals. The purposes of this document are to:

- Serve as a guide for the ethical practices of all professional school counselors regardless of level, area, population served, or membership in this professional association;
- Provide self-appraisal and peer evaluations regarding counselor responsibilities to students, parents/guardians, colleagues and professional associates, schools, communities, and the counseling profession; and
- Inform those served by the school counselor of acceptable counselor practices and expected professional behavior.

A.1. Responsibilities to Students
The professional school counselor:

a. Has a primary obligation to the student, who is to be treated with respect as a unique individual.
b. Is concerned with the educational, academic, career, personal, and social needs and encourages the maximum development of every student.
c. Respects the student's values and beliefs and does not impose the counselor's personal values.
d. Is knowledgeable of laws, regulations, and policies relating to students and strives to protect and inform students regarding their rights.

A.2. Confidentiality
The professional school counselor:

a. Informs students of the purposes, goals, techniques, and rules of procedure under which they may receive counseling at or before the time when the counseling relationship is entered. Disclosure notice includes the limits of confidentiality such as the possible necessity for consulting with other professionals, privileged communication, and legal or authoritative restraints. The meaning and limits of confidentiality are defined in developmentally appropriate terms to students.
b. Keeps information confidential unless disclosure is required to prevent clear and imminent danger to the student or others or when legal requirements demand that confidential information be revealed. Counselors will consult with appropriate professionals when in doubt as to the validity of an exception.
c. In absence of state legislation expressly forbidding disclosure, considers the ethical responsibility to provide information to an identified third party who, by his/her relationship with the student, is at a high risk of contracting a disease that is commonly known to be communicable and fatal. Disclosure requires satisfaction of all of the following conditions:
   - Student identifies partner or the partner is highly identifiable
   - Counselor recommends the student notify partner and refrain from further high-risk behavior
   - Student refuses
   - Counselor informs the student of the intent to notify the partner
   - Counselor seeks legal consultation as to the legalities of informing the partner
d. Requests of the court that disclosure not be required when the release of confidential information may potentially harm a student or the counseling relationship.
e. Protects the confidentiality of students' records and releases personal data in accordance with prescribed laws and school policies. Student information stored and transmitted electronically is treated with the same care as traditional student records.
f. Protects the confidentiality of information received in the counseling relationship as specified by federal and state laws, written policies, and applicable ethical standards. Such information is only to be revealed to others with the informed consent of the student, consistent with the counselor's ethical obligation.

g. Recognizes his/her primary obligation for confidentiality is to the student but balances that obligation with an understanding of the legal and inherent rights of parents/guardians to be the guiding voice in their children's lives.

A.3. Counseling Plans
The professional school counselor:

a. Provides students with a comprehensive school counseling program that includes a strong emphasis on working jointly with all students to develop academic and career goals.
b. Advocates for counseling plans supporting students' right to choose from the wide array of options when they leave secondary education. Such plans will be regularly reviewed to update students regarding critical information they need to make informed decisions.

A.4. Dual Relationships
The professional school counselor:

a. Avoids dual relationships that might impair his/her objectivity and increase the risk of harm to the student (e.g., counseling one's family members, close friends, or associates). If a dual relationship is unavoidable, the counselor is responsible for taking action to eliminate or reduce the potential for harm. Such safeguards might include informed consent, consultation, supervision, and documentation.
b. Avoids dual relationships with school personnel that might infringe on the integrity of the counselor–student relationship.

A.5. Appropriate Referrals
The professional school counselor:

a. Makes referrals when necessary or appropriate to outside resources. Appropriate referrals may necessitate informing both parents/guardians and students of applicable resources and making proper plans for transitions with minimal interruption of services. Students retain the right to discontinue the counseling relationship at any time.

A.6. Group Work
The professional school counselor:

a. Screens prospective group members and maintains an awareness of participants' needs and goals in relation to the goals of the group. The counselor takes reasonable precautions to protect members from physical and psychological harm resulting from interaction within the group.
b. Notifies parents/guardians and staff of group participation if the counselor deems it appropriate and if consistent with school board policy or practice.
c. Establishes clear expectations in the group setting and clearly states that confidentiality in group counseling cannot be guaranteed. Given the developmental and chronological nature of minors in schools, the counselor recognizes the tenuous nature of confidentiality for minors renders some topics inappropriate for group work in a school setting.
d. Follows up with group members and documents proceedings as appropriate.

A.7. Danger to Self or Others
The professional school counselor:

a. Informs parents/guardians or appropriate authorities when the student's condition indicates a clear and imminent danger to the student or others. This is to be done after careful deliberation and, where possible, after consultation with other counseling professionals.

b. Will attempt to minimize threat to a student and may choose to (1) inform the student of actions to be taken, (2) involve the student in a three-way communication with parents/guardians when breaching confidentiality, or (3) allow the student to have input as to how and to whom the breach will be made.

A.8. Student Records
The professional school counselor:

a. Maintains and secures records necessary for rendering professional services to the student as required by laws, regulations, institutional procedures, and confidentiality guidelines.
b. Keeps sole-possession records separate from students' educational records in keeping with state laws.
c. Recognizes the limits of sole-possession records and understands these records are a memory aid for the creator and in absence of privileged communication may be subpoenaed and may become educational records when they (1) are shared with others in verbal or written form, (2) include information other than professional opinion or personal observations, and/or (3) are made accessible to others.
d. Establishes a reasonable timeline for purging sole-possession records or case notes. Suggested guidelines include shredding sole-possession records when the student transitions to the next level, transfers to another school, or graduates. Careful discretion and deliberation should be applied before destroying sole-possession records that may be needed by a court of law such as notes on child abuse, suicide, sexual harassment, or violence.

A.9. Evaluation, Assessment, and Interpretation
The professional school counselor:

a. Adheres to all professional standards regarding selecting, administering, and interpreting assessment measures and only utilizes assessment measures that are within the scope of practice for school counselors.
b. Seeks specialized training regarding the use of electronically based testing programs in administering, scoring, and interpreting that may differ from that required in more traditional assessments.
c. Considers confidentiality issues when utilizing evaluative or assessment instruments and electronically based programs.
d. Provides interpretation of the nature, purposes, results, and potential impact of assessment/evaluation measures in language the student(s) can understand.
e. Monitors the use of assessment results and interpretations, and takes reasonable steps to prevent others from misusing the information.
f. Uses caution when utilizing assessment techniques, making evaluations, and interpreting the performance of populations not represented in the norm group on which an instrument is standardized.
g. Assesses the effectiveness of his/her program in having an impact on students' academic, career, and personal/social development through accountability measures, especially examining efforts to close achievement, opportunity, and attainment gaps.

A.10. Technology
The professional school counselor:

a. Promotes the benefits of and clarifies the limitations of various appropriate technological applications. The counselor promotes technological applications (1) that are appropriate for the student's individual needs, (2) that the student understands how to use, and (3) for which follow-up counseling assistance is provided.

   b. Advocates for equal access to technology for all students, especially those historically underserved.

   c. Takes appropriate and reasonable measures for maintaining confidentiality of student information and educational records stored or transmitted over electronic media including although not limited to fax, electronic mail, and instant messaging.

   d. While working with students on a computer or similar technology, takes reasonable and appropriate measures to protect students from objectionable and/or harmful online material.

   e. Who is engaged in the delivery of services involving technologies such as the telephone, videoconferencing, and the Internet takes responsible steps to protect students and others from harm.

A.11. Student Peer Support Program
The professional school counselor:

Has unique responsibilities when working with student-assistance programs. The school counselor is responsible for the welfare of students participating in peer-to-peer programs under his/her direction.

B. Responsibilities to Parents/Guardians

B.1. Parent Rights and Responsibilities
The professional school counselor:

   a. Respects the rights and responsibilities of parents/guardians for their children and endeavors to establish, as appropriate, a collaborative relationship with parents/guardians to facilitate the student's maximum development.

   b. Adheres to laws, local guidelines, and ethical standards of practice when assisting parents/guardians experiencing family difficulties that interfere with the student's effectiveness and welfare.

   c. Respects the confidentiality of parents/guardians.

   d. Is sensitive to diversity among families and recognizes that all parents/guardians, custodial and noncustodial, are vested with certain rights and responsibilities for the welfare of their children by virtue of their role and according to law.

B.2. Parents/Guardians and Confidentiality
The professional school counselor:

   a. Informs parents/guardians of the counselor's role with emphasis on the confidential nature of the counseling relationship between the counselor and student.

   b. Recognizes that working with minors in a school setting may require counselors to collaborate with students' parents/guardians.

   c. Provides parents/guardians with accurate, comprehensive, and relevant information in an objective and caring manner, as is appropriate and consistent with ethical responsibilities to the student.

   d. Makes reasonable efforts to honor the wishes of parents/guardians concerning information regarding the student, and in cases of divorce or separation exercises a good-faith effort to keep both parents informed with regard to critical information with the exception of a court order.

C. Responsibilities to Colleagues and Professional Associates

C.1. Professional Relationships
The professional school counselor:

a. Establishes and maintains professional relationships with faculty, staff, and administration to facilitate an optimum counseling program.
b. Treats colleagues with professional respect, courtesy, and fairness. The qualifications, views, and findings of colleagues are represented to accurately reflect the image of competent professionals.
c. Is aware of and utilizes related professionals, organizations, and other resources to whom the student may be referred.

C.2. Sharing Information With Other Professionals
The professional school counselor:

a. Promotes awareness and adherence to appropriate guidelines regarding confidentiality, the distinction between public and private information, and staff consultation.
b. Provides professional personnel with accurate, objective, concise, and meaningful data necessary to adequately evaluate, counsel, and assist the student.
c. If a student is receiving services from another counselor or other mental health professional, the counselor, with student and/or parent/guardian consent, will inform the other professional and develop clear agreements to avoid confusion and conflict for the student.
d. Is knowledgeable about release of information and parental rights in sharing information.

D. Responsibilities to the School and Community

D.1. Responsibilities to the School
The professional school counselor:

a. Supports and protects the educational program against any infringement not in students' best interest.
b. Informs appropriate officials in accordance with school policy of conditions that may be potentially disruptive or damaging to the school's mission, personnel, and property while honoring the confidentiality between the student and counselor.
c. Is knowledgeable and supportive of the school's mission and connects his/her program to the school's mission.
d. Delineates and promotes the counselor's role and function in meeting the needs of those served. Counselors will notify appropriate officials of conditions that may limit or curtail their effectiveness in providing programs and services.
e. Accepts employment only for positions for which he/she is qualified by education, training, supervised experience, state and national professional credentials, and appropriate professional experience.
f. Advocates that administrators hire only qualified and competent individuals for professional counseling positions.
g. Assists in developing (1) curricular and environmental conditions appropriate for the school and community, (2) educational procedures and programs to meet students' developmental needs, and (3) a systematic evaluation process for comprehensive, developmental, standards-based school counseling programs, services, and personnel. The counselor is guided by the findings of the evaluation data in planning programs and services.

D.2. Responsibilities to the Community
The professional school counselor:

a. Collaborates with agencies, organizations, and individuals in the community in the best interest of students and without regard to personal reward or remuneration.
b. Extends his/her influence and opportunity to deliver a comprehensive school counseling program to all students by collaborating with community resources for student success.

E. Responsibilities to Self

E.1. Professional Competence
The professional school counselor:

a. Functions within the boundaries of individual professional competence and accepts responsibility for the consequences of his/her actions.

b. Monitors personal well-being and effectiveness and does not participate in any activity that may lead to inadequate professional services or harm to a student.

c. Strives through personal initiative to maintain professional competence including technological literacy and to keep abreast of professional information. Professional and personal growth are ongoing throughout the counselor's career.

E.2. Diversity
The professional school counselor:

a. Affirms the diversity of students, staff, and families.

b. Expands and develops awareness of his/her own attitudes and beliefs affecting cultural values and biases and strives to attain cultural competence.

c. Possesses knowledge and understanding about how oppression, racism, discrimination, and stereotyping affects her/him personally and professionally.

d. Acquires educational, consultation, and training experiences to improve awareness, knowledge, skills, and effectiveness in working with diverse populations: ethnic/racial status, age, economic status, special needs, ESL or ELL, immigration status, sexual orientation, gender, gender identity/expression, family type, religious/spiritual identity, and appearance.

F. Responsibilities to the Profession

F.1. Professionalism
The professional school counselor:

a. Accepts the policies and procedures for handling ethical violations as a result of maintaining membership in the American School Counselor Association.

b. Conducts herself/himself in such a manner as to advance individual ethical practice and the profession.

c. Conducts appropriate research and reports findings in a manner consistent with acceptable educational and psychological research practices. The counselor advocates for the protection of the individual student's identity when using data for research or program planning.

d. Adheres to ethical standards of the profession, other official policy statements, such as ASCA's position statements, role statement, and the ASCA National Model, and relevant statutes established by federal, state, and local governments, and when these are in conflict works responsibly for change.

e. Clearly distinguishes between statements and actions made as a private individual and those made as a representative of the school counseling profession.

f. Does not use his/her professional position to recruit or gain clients, consultees for his/her private practice or to seek and receive unjustified personal gains, unfair advantage, inappropriate relationships, or unearned goods or services.

F.2. Contribution to the Profession
The professional school counselor:

a. Actively participates in local, state, and national associations fostering the development and improvement of school counseling.

b. Contributes to the development of the profession through the sharing of skills, ideas, and expertise with colleagues.

c. Provides support and mentoring to novice professionals.

G. Maintenance of Standards

Ethical behavior among professional school counselors, association members, and nonmembers is expected at all times. When there exists serious doubt as to the ethical behavior of colleagues or if counselors are forced to work in situations or abide by policies that do not reflect the standards as outlined in these *Ethical Standards for School Counselors*, the counselor is obligated to take appropriate action to rectify the condition. The following procedures may serve as a guide:

1. The counselor should consult confidentially with a professional colleague to discuss the nature of a complaint to see if the professional colleague views the situation as an ethical violation.
2. When feasible, the counselor should directly approach the colleague whose behavior is in question to discuss the complaint and seek resolution.
3. If resolution is not forthcoming at the personal level, the counselor shall utilize the channels established within the school, school district, the state school counseling association, and ASCA's Ethics Committee.
4. If the matter still remains unresolved, referral for review and appropriate action should be made to the Ethics Committee in the following sequence:
   * state school counselor association
   * American School Counselor Association
5. The ASCA Ethics Committee is responsible for:
   * educating and consulting with the membership regarding ethical standards
   * periodically reviewing and recommending changes in code
   * receiving and processing questions to clarify the application of such standards; questions must be submitted in writing to the ASCA Ethics chair.
   * handling complaints of alleged violations of the ethical standards. At the national level, complaints should be submitted in writing to the ASCA Ethics Committee, c/o the Executive Director, American School Counselor Association, 1101 King St., Suite 625, Alexandria, VA 22314.

Association for Counselor Education and Supervision *Ethical Guidelines for Counseling Supervisors*

*Adopted by ACES Executive Council and
Delegate Assembly, March 1993*

Preamble

The Association for Counselor Education and Supervision (ACES) is composed of people engaged in the professional preparation of counselors and people responsible for the ongoing supervision of counselors. ACES is a founding division of the American Counseling Association (ACA) and as such adheres to ACA's current ethical standards and to general codes of competence adopted throughout the mental health community.

ACES believes that counselor educators and counseling supervisors in universities and in applied counseling settings, including the range of education and mental health delivery systems, carry responsibilities unique to their job roles. Such responsibilities may include administrative supervision, clinical supervision, or both. Administrative supervision refers to those supervisory activities which increase the efficiency of the delivery of counseling services, whereas clinical supervision includes the supportive and educative activities of the supervisor designed to improve the application of counseling theory and technique directly to clients.

Counselor educators and counseling supervisors encounter situations which challenge the help given by general ethical standards of the profession at large. These situations require more specific guidelines that provide appropriate guidance in everyday practice.

The *Ethical Guidelines for Counseling Supervisors* are intended to assist professionals by helping them:

1. Observe ethical and legal protection of clients' and supervisee's rights;
2. Meet the training and professional development needs of supervisees in ways consistent with clients' welfare and programmatic requirements; and
3. Establish policies, procedures, and standards for implementing programs.

The specification of ethical guidelines enables ACES members to focus on and to clarify the ethical nature of responsibilities held in common. Such guidelines should be reviewed formally every five years, or more often if needed, to meet the needs of ACES members for guidance.

The *Ethical Guidelines for Counseling Supervisors* are meant to help ACES members in conducting supervision. ACES is not currently in a position to hear complaints about alleged noncompliance with these guidelines. Any complaints about the ethical behavior of any ACA member should be measured against the ACA *Ethical Standards* and a complaint lodged with ACA in accordance with its procedures for doing so.

One overriding assumption underlying this document is that supervision should be ongoing throughout a counselor's career and not stop when a particular level of education, certification, or membership in a professional organization is attained.

<u>Definitions of Terms</u>

Applied Counseling Settings – Public or private organizations of counselors such as community mental health centers, hospitals, schools, and group or individual private practice settings.

Supervisees – Counselors-in-training in university programs at any level who work with clients in applied settings as part of their university training program, and counselors who have completed their formal education and are employed in an applied counseling setting.

Supervisors – Counselors who have been designated within their university or agency to directly oversee the professional clinical work of counselors. Supervisors also may be persons who offer supervision to counselors seeking state licensure and so provide supervision outside of the administrative aegis of an applied counseling setting.

1. Client Welfare and Rights

1.01. The primary obligation of supervisors is to train counselors so that they respect the integrity and promote the welfare of their clients. Supervisors should have supervisees inform clients that they are being supervised and that observation and/or recordings of the session may be reviewed by the supervisor.

1.02. Supervisors who are licensed counselors and are conducting supervision to aid a supervisee to become licensed should instruct the supervisee not to communicate or in any way convey to the supervisee's clients or to other parties that the supervisee is himself/herself licensed.

1.03. Supervisors should make supervisees aware of clients' rights, including protecting clients' right to privacy and confidentiality in the counseling relationship and the information resulting from it. Clients also should be informed that their right to privacy and confidentiality will not be violated by the supervisory relationship.

1.04. Records of the counseling relationship, including interview notes, test data, correspondence, the electronic storage of these documents, and audio- and videotape recordings, are considered to be confidential professional information. Supervisors should see that these materials are used in counseling, research, and training and supervision of counselors with the full knowledge of the clients and that permission to use these materials is granted by the applied counseling setting offering service to the client. This professional information is to be used for full protection of the client. Written consent from the client (or legal guardian, if a minor) should be secured prior to the use of such information for instructional, supervisory, and/or research purposes. Policies of the applied counseling setting regarding client records also should be followed.

1.05. Supervisors shall adhere to current professional and legal guidelines when conducting research with human participants such as Section D-1 of the ACA *Ethical Standards*.

1.06. Counseling supervisors are responsible for making every effort to monitor both the professional actions, and failures to take action, of their supervisees.

2. Supervisory Role

Inherent and integral to the role of supervisor are responsibilities for:

    a. monitoring client welfare:

    b. encouraging compliance with relevant legal, ethical, and professional standards for clinical practice;

    c. monitoring clinical performance and professional development of supervisees; and

    d. evaluating and certifying current performance and potential of supervisees for academic, screening, selection, placement, employment, and credentialing purposes.

2.01. Supervisors should have had training in supervision prior to initiating their role as supervisors.

2.02. Supervisors should pursue professional and personal continuing education activities such as advanced courses, seminars, and professional conferences on a regular and ongoing basis. These activities should include both counseling and supervision topics and skills.

2.03. Supervisors should make their supervisees aware of professional and ethical standards and legal responsibilities of the counseling profession.

2.04. Supervisors of postdegree counselors who are seeking state licensure should encourage these counselors to adhere to the standards for practice established by the state licensure board of the state in which they practice.

2.05. Procedures for contacting the supervisor, or an alternative supervisor, to assist in handling crisis situations should be established and communicated to supervisees.

2.06. Actual work samples via audio- and/or videotape or live observation in addition to case notes should be reviewed by the supervisor as a regular part of the ongoing supervisory process.

2.07. Supervisors of counselors should meeting regularly in face-to-face sessions with their supervisees.

2.08. Supervisors should provide supervisees with ongoing feedback on their performance. This feedback should take a variety of forms, both formal and informal, and should include verbal and written evaluations. It should be formative during the supervisory experience and summative at the conclusion of the experience.

2.09. Supervisors who have multiple roles (e.g., teacher, clinical supervisor, administrative supervisor, etc.) with supervisees should minimize potential conflicts. Where possible, the roles should be divided among several supervisors. Where this is not possible, careful explanation should be conveyed to the supervisee as to the expectations and responsibilities associated with each supervisory role.

2.10. Supervisors should not participate in any form of sexual contact with supervisees. Supervisors should not engage in any form of social contact or interaction which would compromise the supervisor–supervisee relationship. Dual relationships with supervisees that might impair the supervisor's objectivity and professional judgment should be avoided and/or the supervisory relationship terminated.

2.11. Supervisors should not establish a psychotherapeutic relationship as a substitute for supervision. Personal issues should be addressed in supervision only in terms of the impact of these issues on clients and on professional functioning.

2.12. Supervisors, through ongoing supervisee assessment and evaluation, should be aware of any personal or professional limitations of supervisees which are likely to impede future professional performance. Supervisors have the responsibility of recommending remedial assistance to the supervisee and of screening from the training program, applied counseling setting, or state licensure those supervisees who are unable to provide competent professional services. These recommendations should be clearly and professionally explained in writing to the supervisees who are so evaluated.

2.13. Supervisors should not endorse a supervisee for certification, licensure, completion of an academic training program, or continued employment if the supervisor believes the supervisee is impaired in any way that would interfere with the performance of counseling duties. The presence of any such impairment should begin a process of feedback and remediation wherever possible so that the supervisee understands the nature of the impairment and has the opportunity to remedy the problem and continue with his/her professional development.

2.14. Supervisors should incorporate the principles of informed consent and participation; clarity of requirements, expectations, roles and rules; and due process and appeal into the establishment of policies and procedures of their institutions, program, courses, and individual supervisory relationships. Mechanisms for due process appeal of individual supervisory actions should be established and made available to all supervisees.

3. Program Administration Role

3.01. Supervisors should ensure that the programs conducted and experiences provided are in keeping with current guidelines and standards of ACA and its divisions.

3.02. Supervisors should teach courses and/or supervise clinical work only in areas where they are fully competent and experienced.

3.03. To achieve the highest quality of training and supervision, supervisors should be active participants in peer review and peer supervision procedures.

3.04. Supervisors should provide experiences that integrate theoretical knowledge and practical application. Supervisors also should provide opportunities in which supervisees are able to apply the knowledge they have learned and understand the rationale for the skills they have acquired. The knowledge and skills conveyed should reflect current practice, research findings, and available resources.

3.05. Professional competencies, specific courses, and/or required experiences expected of supervisees should be communicated to them in writing prior to admission to the training program or placement/employment by the applied counseling setting, and, in case of continued employment, in a timely manner.

3.06. Supervisors should accept only those persons as supervisees who meet identified entry level requirements for admission to a program of counselor training or for placement in an applied counseling setting. In the case of private supervision in search of state licensure, supervisees should have completed all necessary prerequisites as determined by the state licensure board.

3.07. Supervisors should inform supervisees of the goals, policies, theoretical orientations toward counseling, training, and supervision model or approach on which the supervision is based.

3.08. Supervisees should be encouraged and assisted to define their own theoretical orientation toward counseling, to establish supervision goals for themselves, and to monitor and evaluate their progress toward meeting these goals.

3.09. Supervisors should assess supervisees' skills and experience in order to establish standards for competent professional behavior. Supervisors should restrict supervisees' activities to those that are commensurate with their current level of skills and experiences.

3.10. Supervisors should obtain practicum and fieldwork sites that meet minimum standards for preparing students to become effective counselors. No practicum or fieldwork setting should be approved unless it truly replicates a counseling work setting.

3.11. Practicum and fieldwork classes would be limited in size according to established professional standards to ensure that each student has ample opportunity for individual supervision and feedback. Supervisors in applied counseling settings should have a limited number of supervisees.

3.12. Supervisors in university settings should establish and communicate specific policies and procedures regarding field placement of students. The respective roles of the student counselor, the university supervisor, and the field supervisor should be clearly differentiated in areas such as evaluation, requirements, and confidentiality.

3.13. Supervisors in training programs should communicate regularly with supervisors in agencies used as practicum and/or fieldwork sites regarding current professional practices, expectations of students, and preferred models and modalities of supervision.

3.14. Supervisors at the university should establish clear lines of communication among themselves, the field supervisors, and the students/supervisees.

3.15. Supervisors should establish and communicate to supervisees and to field supervisors specific procedures regarding consultation, performance review, and evaluation of supervisees.

3.16. Evaluations of supervisee performance in universities and in applied counseling settings should be available to supervisees in ways consistent with the Family Rights and Privacy Act and the Buckley Amendment.

3.17. Forms of training that focus primarily on self-understanding and problem resolution (e.g., personal growth groups or individual counseling) should be voluntary. Those who conduct these forms of training should not serve simultaneously as supervisors of the supervisees involved in the training.

3.18. A supervisor may recommend participation in activities such as personal growth groups or personal counseling when it has been determined that a supervisee has deficits in the areas of self-understanding and problem resolution which impede his/her professional functioning. The supervisors should not be the direct provider of these activities for the supervisee.

3.19. When a training program conducts a personal growth or counseling experience involving relatively intimate self-disclosure, care should be taken to eliminate or minimize potential role conflicts for faculty and/or agency supervisors who may conduct these experiences and who also serve as teachers, group leaders, and clinical directors.

3.20. Supervisors should use the following prioritized sequence in resolving conflicts among the needs of the client, the needs of the supervisee, and the needs of the program or agency. Insofar as the client must be protected, it should be understood that client welfare is usually subsumed in federal and state laws such that these statutes should be the first point of reference. Where laws and ethical standards are not present or are unclear, the good judgment of the supervisor should be guided by the following list:

    a. Relevant legal and ethical standards (e.g., duty to warn, state child abuse laws, etc.);

    b. Client welfare;

    c. Supervisee welfare;

    d. Supervisor welfare; and

    e. Program and/or agency service and administrative needs.

Index

Index